SG24-5518-00

IBM

International Technical Support Organization

Best Practices for Tivoli Logical Design

March 2000

Take Note!

Before using this information and the product it supports, be sure to read the general information in Appendix C, "Special notices" on page 269.

First Edition (March 2000)

This edition applies to Tivoli Management Framework Version 3.6.2 and Tivoli core applications Versions 3.6.1 and 3.6.2.

This document created or updated on March 3, 2000.

Comments may be addressed to:
IBM Corporation, International Technical Support Organization
Dept. OSJB Building 003 Internal Zip 2834
11400 Burnet Road
Austin, Texas 78758-3493

Contents

Preface . . . ix
The team that wrote this redbook . . . ix
Comments welcome . . . xi

Part 1. Tivoli Logical Design fundamentals . . . 1

Chapter 1. Introduction . . . 3
1.1 Architecture and solution design fundamentals . . . 3
1.1.1 Gathering and understanding the requirements and drivers . . . 4
1.1.2 Creating different solutions . . . 5
1.1.3 Evaluating the solutions . . . 6
1.1.4 The complete flow . . . 6
1.2 Tivoli architecture and design considerations . . . 7
1.2.1 Physical issues . . . 8
1.2.2 Logical issues . . . 10
1.3 What is a Logical Design . . . 11
1.3.1 Developing a Logical Design . . . 12
1.3.2 Gather and consolidate detailed requirements . . . 13
1.3.3 Decide on a naming convention . . . 15
1.3.4 Construct a Policy Region schema . . . 15
1.3.5 Construct a Profile Manager schema . . . 16
1.3.6 Set the Tivoli Administrators . . . 16
1.3.7 Bringing it all together . . . 17
1.3.8 Review and evaluate the design . . . 17
1.4 Best practices . . . 18

Chapter 2. Naming convention . . . 19
2.1 Naming convention for Tivoli Enterprise Software objects . . . 19
2.2 Best practices . . . 21
2.3 Sample naming convention . . . 23

Chapter 3. Policy region design . . . 27
3.1 What are policy regions? . . . 27
3.2 Why create policy regions? . . . 27
3.3 Policy region hierarchy . . . 29
3.4 Best practices and design considerations . . . 31
3.5 Nodes, applications, and subscribers policy region design . . . 33
3.5.1 Nodes policy region . . . 34
3.5.2 Application policy region . . . 36
3.5.3 Subscribers or List policy region . . . 37

Chapter 4. Profile Manager design 41
4.1 Overview 41
4.2 Profiles and profile-based applications 41
4.3 Profile managers 43
4.3.1 Subscribers 44
4.3.2 Database profile manager 44
4.3.3 Dataless profile manager 45
4.3.4 Profile manager hierarchy. 46
4.4 Profile managers and profile distribution. 48
4.5 Designing the profile managers' schema 50
4.5.1 The goals 50
4.5.2 Best practices. 51
4.6 Subscribers' and applications' profile manager design 53
4.6.1 Subscribers' profile manager design. 53
4.6.2 Applications' profile manager design 60
4.7 Profile manager policies. 66

Chapter 5. Administrators' considerations. 67
5.1 Input requirements 67
5.1.1 Single administrator 68
5.1.2 Organization. 72
5.1.3 Summary of input requirements 77
5.2 Critical considerations 77
5.2.1 Interview the workers 78
5.2.2 Number of administrators and system performance 79
5.2.3 TMR roles versus resource roles 79
5.2.4 Avoid giving remote access 81
5.2.5 Unique current login name in an TMR. 81
5.2.6 Avoid using default root user 82
5.2.7 Specify NT domain name in setting administrator login name . . . 83
5.2.8 Effective resource roles assignment 83
5.2.9 Access resources without appropriate OS authority 84
5.2.10 User login name auditing 84
5.2.11 Mapping administrators' user name 85
5.2.12 Single administrator for multiple users performing similar jobs . 85
5.2.13 Tivoli desktop limit 86
5.2.14 Accountability. 86
5.2.15 Administrators in collections 89
5.2.16 Desktops icons: What to place on an administrator's desktop. . 90
5.2.17 Inter-region administration 91
5.3 Administrators' desktop design. 91
5.3.1 Administrator role requirements for Tivoli desktop 92
5.3.2 Administrators' visibility 92

5.4 How administrators work 97
5.4.1 ID mapping. 97
5.4.2 Checking security and executing 100

Chapter 6. Interconnected TMRs considerations 105
6.1 The Hub-Spoke model architecture 105
6.2 Tivoli base components in a Hub-Spoke model 107
6.3 Organizing the managed resources 108
6.3.1 Nodes, applications, and subscribers model. 108
6.3.2 Subscription hierarchies 111
6.3.3 Subscribing X exchanging resources 111
6.3.4 Authorization roles across TMR boundaries 113
6.3.5 RIM considerations. 114

Chapter 7. Policies 117
7.1 What are policies? 117
7.1.1 Policy objects and policy methods 117
7.1.2 Default policies. 117
7.1.3 Validation policies. 118
7.2 Profile policies 118
7.3 Profile manager policies 119
7.4 Using policies. 120
7.4.1 Changing Tivoli supplied default. 120
7.4.2 Policies and policy regions 121
7.4.3 Using default policies 122
7.4.4 Using validation policies. 122
7.5 Working with policies 123
7.5.1 How policies are written 123
7.5.2 Tivoli commands for policies. 125
7.5.3 How to use the commands 125

Chapter 8. Bringing it all together. 131
8.1 Policy regions, profile manager, and administrators together 131
8.1.1 Policy regions, policies, and resource roles 131
8.1.2 Policy regions and profile managers. 132
8.1.3 Distributing profiles. 134
8.1.4 Roles, distribution, and subscription 136
8.2 Major design options 140
8.2.1 Centralized or distributed administration. 140
8.2.2 Grouping resources 141

Chapter 9. Creating a logical design. 143
9.1 Gathering information and requirements. 144
9.1.1 Information sources 145

9.1.2 Consolidating the information . . . 148
9.2 Designing process . . . 154
9.2.1 General design flow . . . 154
9.2.2 Policy region schema . . . 158
9.2.3 Profile manager schema . . . 159
9.2.4 Tivoli administrators schema . . . 160
9.3 Checking the result . . . 161

Part 2. Case studies . . . 163

Chapter 10. First scenario . . . 165
10.1 BWET Corporation overview . . . 165
10.2 Gathering and consolidating requirements . . . 166
10.2.1 Physical issues . . . 167
10.2.2 Logical issues . . . 167
10.3 Logical design . . . 171
10.3.1 Naming convention . . . 172
10.3.2 Policy region design . . . 172
10.3.3 Profile manager design . . . 178

Chapter 11. Second scenario . . . 185
11.1 BWET Corporation overview . . . 185
11.2 Gathering and consolidating requirements . . . 191
11.2.1 Physical issues . . . 191
11.2.2 Logical issues . . . 195
11.2.3 Consolidating information . . . 204
11.3 Logical design . . . 208
11.3.1 Initial and base policy region schema . . . 208
11.3.2 Profile manager schema . . . 216
11.3.3 Administrators' schema and administrators, desktop design . . 222

Part 3. Appendices . . . 237

Appendix A. Tivoli administrators roles . . . 239
A.1 Tivoli Framework . . . 240
A.2 Tivoli Remote Control . . . 244
A.3 Tivoli Software Distribution . . . 245
A.4 Tivoli Enterprise Console . . . 248
A.5 Tivoli Distributed Monitoring . . . 251
A.6 Tivoli Inventory . . . 253
A.7 Tivoli Security Management . . . 255
A.8 Tivoli User Administration . . . 256

Appendix B. Desktop design files . . . 259
B.1 Original desktop dialog file . . . 259
B.2 Modified desktop dialog file. . . . 266

Appendix C. Special notices . . . 269

Appendix D. Related publications . . . 273
D.1 IBM Redbooks . . . 273
D.2 IBM Redbooks collections . . . 273
D.3 Other resources . . . 274
D.4 Referenced Web sites . . . 275

How to get IBM Redbooks . . . 277
IBM Redbooks fax order form . . . 278

Glossary . . . 279

Index . . . 281

IBM Redbooks review . . . 289

Preface

Designing a Tivoli Management solution requires careful planning and includes numerous details.

The primary objective of this redbook is to describe and define a set of guidelines and specify the design elements involved in the logical design of a Tivoli implementation.

This redbook is targeted at both architects and implementers responsible for the system architecture and solution design of Tivoli and will help in understanding how to deal with the challenges in designing a logical solution of Tivoli in complex environments.

This redbook is divided into three parts: Part 1, "Tivoli Logical Design fundamentals" on page 1, where we provide the reader with a great deal of information related to the logical design of a Tivoli solution and its various elements and a number of perspectives from which this challenge can be approached; Part 2, "Case studies" on page 163, where we provide examples that demonstrate the concepts and processes learned in the previous chapters; and Part 3, "Appendices" on page 237, where the configuration files used in this redbook are provided.

The examples in this redbook are documented in a way that service providers can use them as a start in client implementations. The scenarios provided will also demonstrate a suggested schema of the components involved in the logical design of Tivoli.

The information held in this redbook is not a replacement for the detailed product information contained in the Tivoli management software product manuals.

The team that wrote this redbook

This redbook was produced by a team of specialists from around the world working at the, Austin Center.

Edson Manoel is an Advisory ITSO representative working as a project leader at the International Technical Support Organization, Tivoli Group, Austin Center. He applies his extensive field experience as an I/T Tivoli Specialist to his work at the ITSO where he writes extensively on all areas of enterprise systems management. Prior joining the ITSO, Edson worked in IBM's Brazil Professional Services Organization as an I/T Architect where he was involved in numerous projects, designing and implementing systems and network management solutions for major IBM Brazil customers.

Baldemar Damian is an IT specialist working for Laboratorios Magneticos, an IBM business partner based in Mexico. He holds a Communications and Electronics degree from the IPN. Baldemar is a Tivoli Certified Consultant and has several years of experience working with the Tivoli core products. His areas of expertise include the deployment and availability areas and Unix and Windows NT system administration.

William Leung is a System Management Consultant with IBM Global Services System Management Group in Sydney, Australia. He graduated from the University of Sydney with a Bachelor degree in Electrical Engineering and Commerce. Over the last few years he has been involved in numerous, local Tivoli implementation projects with IBM Global Services in Sydney. His areas of expertise in Tivoli include Framework, Software Distribution, Inventory, Distributed Monitoring, and Remote Control on Windows NT, Windows 95, and AIX operating platforms.

Terri Rose is a Senior Enterprise Systems Management Consultant at PSW Technologies, Inc., in Austin, Texas. PSW Technologies is a Tivoli Premiere Business Partner. As a Tivoli Certified Enterprise Consultant, Terri's recent projects include setting up the Tivoli solution for a large national retailer. He has been active in the IT industry since 1979, starting out in software development and moving into enterprise systems administration. Since the mid-1990s, he has focused on teaching and implementing Tivoli solutions.

Thomas Sant'Ana is an IT Specialist for Engesoftware Consultoria de Sistemas in Brazil. He has several years of experience in Tivoli deployment and application development. He holds a Bachelor of Computer Science degree from Universidade de Brasilia. His areas of expertise include network management, system security, database administration, and object-oriented application design and implementation.

Thanks to the following people for their invaluable contributions to this project:

Caroline Cooper
Manager, International Technical Support Organization, Austin Center

Yoichiro Ishii
Project Leader, International Technical Support Organization, Austin Center

Theo Winkelmann
Project Leader, International Technical Support Organization, Austin Center

Ingo Averdunk
Consultant, Tivoli Systems

Richard Hawes
Product Manager, Tivoli Systems

Stefan Uelpenich
Principal Engineer, Tivoli Systems

DInesh Kumar
Project Leader, International Technical Support Organization, Austin Center

John Owczarzak
Editor, International Technical Support Organization, Austin Center

Comments welcome

Your comments are important to us!

We want our Redbooks to be as helpful as possible. Please send us your comments about this or other Redbooks in one of the following ways:

- Fax the evaluation form found in "IBM Redbooks review" on page 289 to the fax number shown on the form.
- Use the online evaluation form found at `http://www.redbooks.ibm.com/`
- Send your comments in an Internet note to `redbook@us.ibm.com`

Part 1. Tivoli Logical Design fundamentals

Chapter 1. Introduction

In this chapter, we explain the fundamentals of an architecture and solution design, the key challenges in designing an architecture for a Tivoli deployment, the Tivoli Logical Design fundamentals, and best practices information.

We do not explain the product details of Tivoli applications in this redbook; however, we assume that the reader is reasonably familiar with the Tivoli concepts and Tivoli applications.

We also do not provide or explain an out-of-the-box solution in this redbook that can be used to automatically deploy a Tivoli architecture and solution without any effort. One of the main intentions of this book is to make the reader aware of that such a solution does not, and can not, exist. The creation of a high level design and architecture of a Tivoli solution is part science and part art, as the number of aspects that need to be considered vary from customer to customer.

We provide the reader with a number of perspectives from which this challenge can be approached, explain the elements involved in the logical design of a Tivoli solution, and have a look at the best practices performed.

The information provided in this chapter illustrates the elementary prerequisites of the architecture that must be considered and all other parameters that influence such a solution design. In addition, we introduce the main components of a Tivoli logical design, thus, giving the reader basic information on how they interact within the design, and introduce the chapters where additional information can be found.

1.1 Architecture and solution design fundamentals

In this section, we provide a brief overview of an architecture and the solution design fundamentals.

In a high-level view, an architecture development process for systems management involves three distinct steps:

1. Understanding the requirements and drivers for the architecture

   The term *drivers*, as used here, means the input specifications and the context information. By capturing the drivers for the architecture and understanding the information relevant to the architecture, we will learn the architecture requirements.

2. Creating architectural alternatives

   Using the information you have collected, you should be able to define several potential solution architectures.

3. Evaluating the solutions

   Now that you have one or more potential architecture solutions, it is time to compare each other and choose the best alternative.

Figure 1 shows an illustrative view of the high-level steps of an architecture process for systems management.

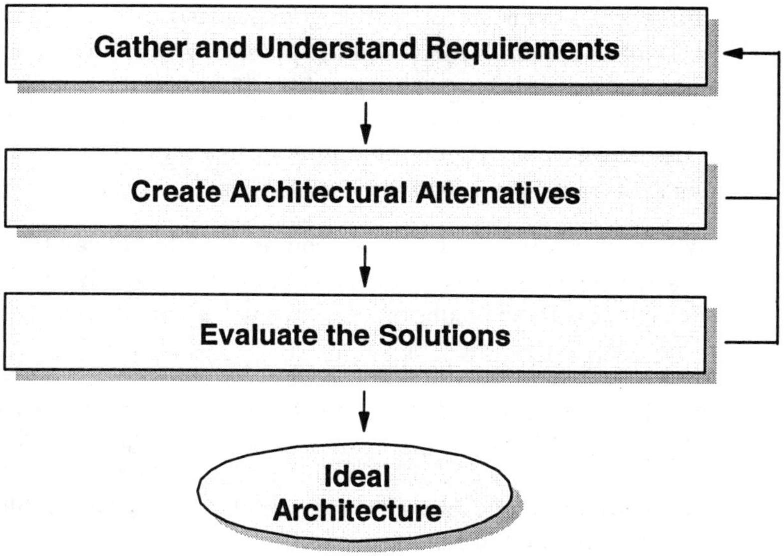

Figure 1. Architecture process - High-level view

The arrows that loop back illustrate a very important point: This is an iterative process. If a significant new requirement surfaces after you have developed the architectural alternatives, you may need to go back and redevelop the alternatives. Similarly, if during the evaluating the solutions phase, you find the customer indicates none of the alternatives really meets their requirements, you will need to go back and re-gather the requirements.

1.1.1 Gathering and understanding the requirements and drivers

The challenge of designing a system management solution begins in the requirements gathering phase, a process that discovers needs and purposes. The requirements you gather act as a foundation upon which the rest of your solution will be constructed. It is these requirements that are the basis for the selection criteria used when choosing an architecture.

Gathering requirements sounds like an easy thing to do, but it is not. It requires that you have knowledge of both the customer and systems management solutions, and that you are skilled in asking questions and listening to the answers provided. It also requires that you use your customer's time efficiently.

During the requirements gathering phase, all customer requirements are identified and documented. Drivers provide requirements for the architecture, help in prioritizing, and help predict the systems management disciplines that will be used in the solution. This will help to establish the scope of the solution and help the IT architect to analyze the information and create a System Architecture and Design document.

The requirements gathering phase allows the IT architect to be able to do a high-level design based on, but not limited to, the information that clarifies:

- An understanding of the customers' computer environment.
- A definition of the resources (systems, users, applications, and networks) involved in the solution and that should be managed.
- The way each resource will be managed.
- The one responsible for managing and monitoring those resources.
- The processes and procedures to manage those resources.
- The management software to be deployed and are required to perform the management functions.

1.1.2 Creating different solutions

Creating a high-level design requires special skills and experience. The people in charge of the design must be able to work on both technical and highly abstract levels.

Functional specifications should now be grouped, and functionality aspects should be analyzed. When effective solutions already exists, brainstorming them and learning the best practices applied may help in finding a partial or total solution that meets all the requirements.

An individual can produce an architecture and solution design, however, the best approach would be that a team of peers, subject matter experts, should review the solution in order to gain solid acceptance of the requirements while validating the basic architecture and design at a high level.

1.1.3 Evaluating the solutions

Several alternative architectures and designs may be developed, and a structured decision analysis can identify the best one.

Decision analysis is a structured method for making correct repeatable decisions. In our case, we want to pick the best architecture and design from a set of alternative solutions.

Given that solution XY is better than solution WZ, we might be tempted to choose it with no rule and be over with the subject. Still, solution WZ is not that much worse. One way to figure out the best one and decide one over the other is by using risk analysis.

What-if, or risk analysis, can be used to test the design on paper. The process invents changes in the design and tests its functionality, scalability, reliability, and suitability. The idea is to expose the solution to some fundamental design limits. For example, we may invent a scenario with twice the number of client machines than originally specified. A paper analysis may suggest small changes to the architecture and design to accommodate this possibility.

In addition, an implementation plan must be defined, and a disaster recovery plan should be created, or adapted, to an existing one to support the continued operation of the systems management solution. Both plans are part of the solution delivered to the client.

1.1.4 The complete flow

Figure 2 on page 7 shows how information flows from the initial specifications to the final validated design.

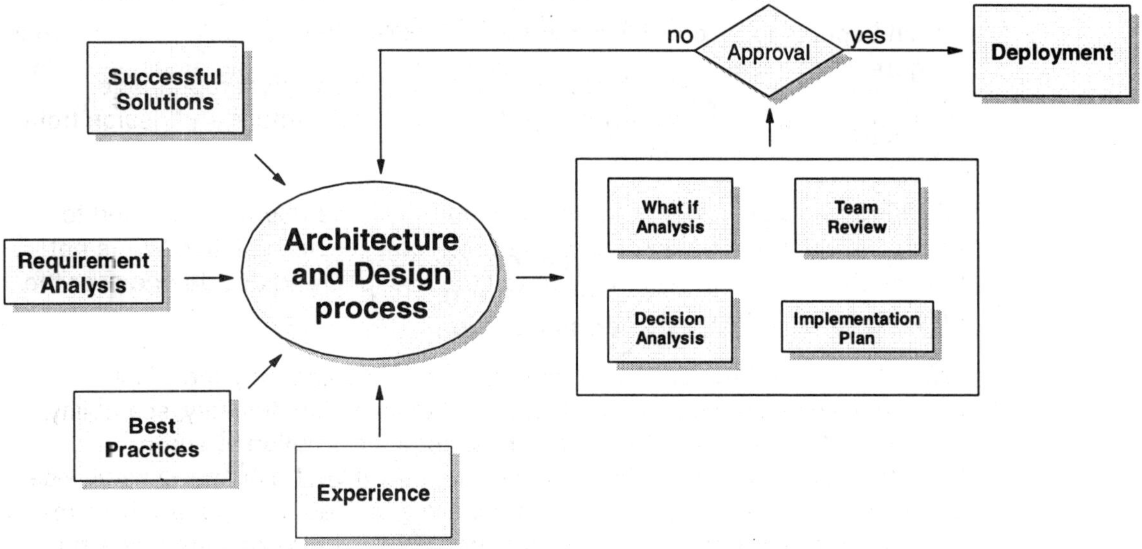

Figure 2. Architecture design process flow

We begin with our inputs and experiences, analyzing and recognizing requirements and drivers, and with lessons learned from successful solutions and best practices that have been used on such solutions in order to develop an architecture to support the requirements. The architecture is a high-level description or model of what parts and processes are needed. The design that follows the architecture and design process is initially a breakdown of these parts and processes, how they inter-operate, what standards to use, what components should be chosen, and what parameters should be assigned. The implementation plan consists of planning the installation, configuration, testing, and acceptance of the solution.

1.2 Tivoli architecture and design considerations

The best Tivoli architects design their solution by taking advantage of time-tested methodologies and principles. A complete understanding of Tivoli principles is a prerequisite for architecture and design to proceed.

Tivoli is a complex application that has a number of components, each of which need to be carefully placed into the system architecture and solution design of the customer.

In order to create an optimal Tivoli architecture and solution design, a careful and thorough understanding of the environment where Tivoli is to be deployed is required. Inside this environment, a number of factors can influence the architecture design and are different for each organization. The main aspects to be considered will be mentioned in this section. As shown in Figure 3, a typical design process might start with the basic architecture in respect to the physical and logical considerations according to the information gathered in the requirements gathering phase.

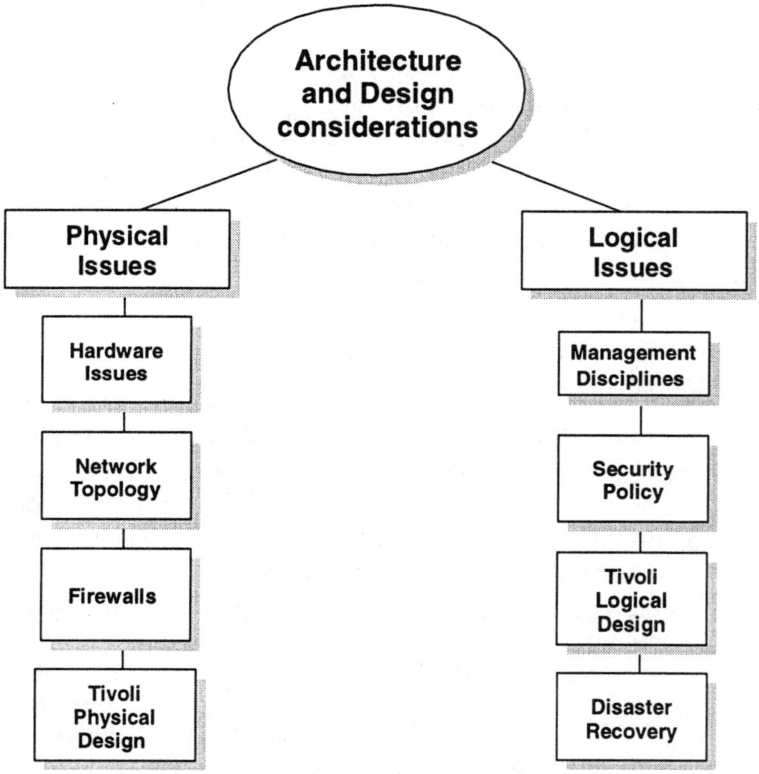

Figure 3. Tivoli architecture and design considerations

1.2.1 Physical issues

The issues involved on a physical level comprise the physical network structure on which Tivoli should be deployed, network protocols used, the speed of each network connection, existing firewalls, systems configuration, the existing hardware to be managed, and so on.

Hardware issues and Network topology structure should be addressed as soon as the basic requirements of the project are known. These items are part of the critical path on any systems management project.

The physical considerations are crucial for the whole systems management architecture. It is based on this information that the IT architect can prepare a Tivoli physical design.

The following list is a brief introduction of the activities involved in a Tivoli physical design:

- Identifying the number and configuration of Tivoli Management Regions (TMR)

  The TMR is the physical and functional building block of the Tivoli solution. All Tivoli managed resources and management functions are centered in the TMR. In addition, there is a physical resource requirement, for example, Tivoli management servers and the communication between Tivoli management servers, for each TMR you create. Understanding the number and relationships of TMRs needed for the solution is critical to designing the overall solution as well as in ordering the required hardware.

- Identify the required Tivoli management servers as well as their physical location.

  There are some types of management servers to be considered as you create the base physical architecture. Other than the TMR servers, the requirement of other servers, such as, TEC servers, GEM servers, RIM servers, Endpoint Gateways, and Software package repository server, will depend on the Tivoli management software being installed and, in some cases, the size of the installation.

- Analyze the network topology and structure in which the Tivoli solution will be deployed.

  Because a TMR server communicates with each managed node in the TMR, the amount of network traffic between the TMR server and managed nodes in the network can be considerable and might be a limitation to the number of managed nodes that can be serviced by a TMR.

  Also, the network traffic between the endpoints and endpoint gateways has to be considered. This can sometimes lead to the introduction of additional endpoint gateways and, therefore, additional managed nodes.

- Identify and analyze firewalls and their physical location.

  The major architectural concern for Tivoli operating across firewalls is one of port availability. The number of ports required is about three times the number of managed nodes that live on the other side of the firewall and are part of the same TMR or connected TMRs.

- Consider the size of the hardware to be used by the Tivoli management servers.

The Tivoli management servers demand some amount of memory and CPU resources of the machine they run on. These limited resources represent a practical limit to the number of Tivoli resources that can be reasonably serviced by a single server.

1.2.2 Logical issues

Based on the systems management strategy, an architecture has to be designed to best meet the requirements.

Tivoli Management Software consists of an underlying infrastructure, known as the Tivoli Management Framework, and a growing set of management applications that utilize this framework to manage heterogeneous systems and applications.

The management disciplines that are to be applied in the solution, such as Deployment Management, Availability Management, Operations and Administration Management, and Security Management, have to be determined. Once the management disciplines are defined, they need to be translated into Tivoli products so that within the Tivoli Management Environment numerous Tivoli applications can be deployed to attend the systems management requirements.

Another concern of analyzing the logical issues is to get the organization's security policy document. This document should describe what types of security measures are used and how these should be implemented. It will inform you about the company's security standards and guidelines. This information will help you to verify, adapt, and translate the security policy into activities required to create the Tivoli Logical Design.

As organizations have become more and more dependent on information and communication technology to conduct their business, and the more reliance an organization places on Tivoli to manage the enterprise, the more important it is to have a business recovery plan in place. In order to assure reliability to the Tivoli environment, a backup/recovery, disaster recovery plan or high- availability design should be defined or at least covered by the organization's existing processes, if any.

At this point, the IT architect can start planning the Tivoli logical design. We will dedicate the next section for a detailed explanation and description of Tivoli logical design components.

1.3 What is a Logical Design

In this section, we provide a definition and look at what is actually in place in the Tivoli logical design.

The Tivoli Logical Design is a broad concept that involves several elements. This redbook describes Tivoli Logical Design as follow:

Tivoli Logical Design Defines how the organization's managed resources are arranged to meet its operational requirements. It defines how resources are grouped to allow effective executions of administrative activities without compromising security.

The logical design is composed of the following elements:

Resources Correspond to the systems, devices, services, and facilities in a distributed system. Some examples of Tivoli resources are workstations, software, and Tivoli administrators.

Naming Convention Establishes consistent, efficient, and unique identification of the resources throughout the enterprise.

Policies Define the rules that govern the management of resources. Chapter 7, "Policies" on page 117 provides a great deal of information on how to work with policies and how they are related to the elements of the logical design.

Policy Region Schema Defines the policy region structure, what resources are stored in each policy region, and how they are related in the policy region hierarchy.

Profile Manager Schema Defines the profile managers to be created, which resources are contained in each one, and how they relate to each other.

Administrators Schema Defines the Tivoli administrators and what access they should have to resources.

Logical designs are more flexible than physical designs. It is much easier to change a logical design after it has been implemented. Nevertheless, as a logical design evolves, making big changes to the design becomes more and more difficult. For this reason, a good logical design should be able to cope with changes in the organization. A good logical design must be flexible and complete.

1.3.1 Developing a Logical Design

Developing a Tivoli Logical Design is a complex task. If you are an IT architect or have the task of developing a logical design, you may wonder where to start, what aspects to include, what elements are involved, and so on.

Your objective is to create an understandable and scalable design that facilitates management of organizational processes. You have to achieve a model that, at the same time, behaves similarly to the enterprise organization and provides effective TME management. The logical design identifies how the logical structure of the enterprise framework's object database will be configured to meet the organization's operational requirements.

Through the use of policies, policy regions, and profile managers, you can decide which Tivoli administrator can perform what functions and on what managed resources.

This section continues by providing a brief introduction of the activities involved in a Tivoli Logical Design. This activities are:

- Gather and consolidate detailed requirements
- Decide on a naming convention
- Construct a Policy Region schema
- Construct a Profile Manager schema
- Set the Tivoli administrators
- Review and evaluate the design

Figure 4 on page 13 provides the basic flow of high-level activities that should be followed by anyone in charge of the logical design of a Tivoli solution.

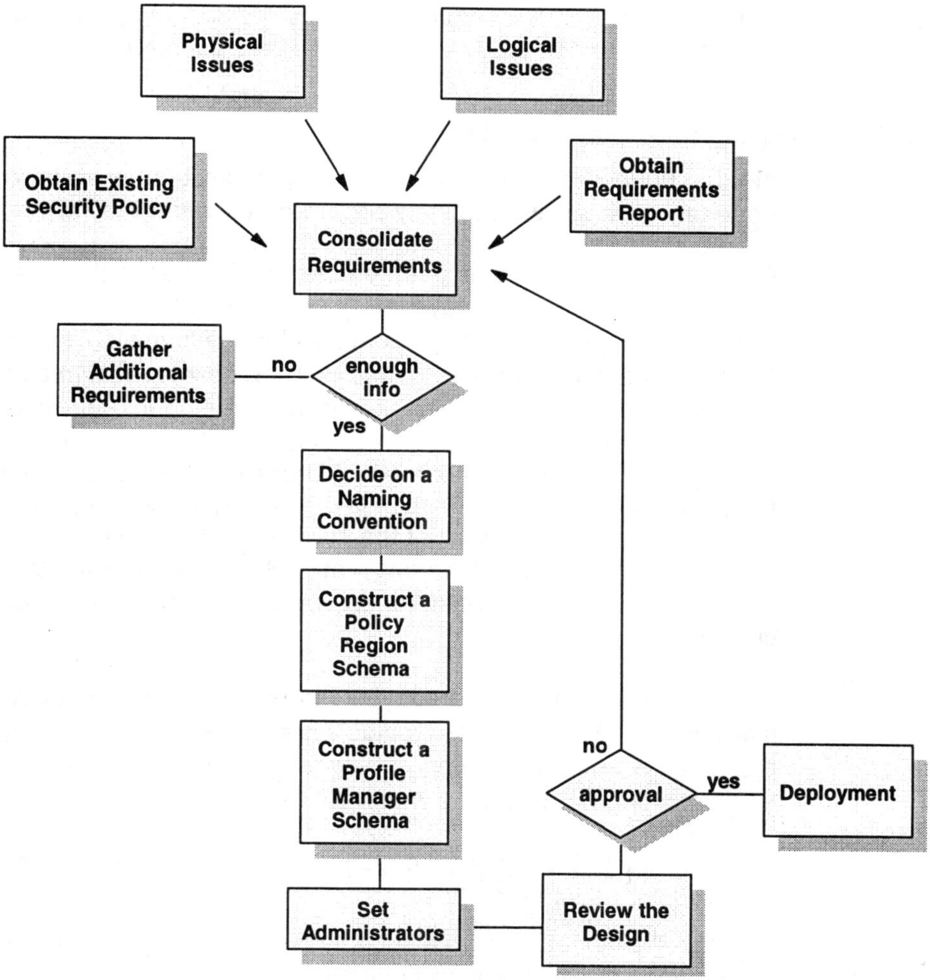

Figure 4. Logical design high-level activities flow

Chapter 9, “Creating a logical design” on page 143 is dedicated to providing you with a suggested approach on how to create the Tivoli Logical Design.

1.3.2 Gather and consolidate detailed requirements

An effective design depends on the quality of the information that has been gathered previously. The first step to be performed by the IT architect is to identify the minimal required information and to get all the information they think might be important for the design.

Requirements come in many forms: Business, technical, personal, and political, to name a few. In this phase of the approach, we should consider all forms, but we need to focus on business requirements and technical requirements. The relationship you have with the customer will largely determine how well you understand the personal and political issues that might be present.

Along with gathering requirements for the new Tivoli solution, you will also need to understand the customer's existing environment. New solutions are not often developed completely separate from what is already in place.

Gathering requirements is not a process that occurs only once, but rather is an iterative process that may recur several times as the Tivoli Logical Solution evolves through the phases described in this document. The objective here is to gather sufficient requirements to develop several design alternatives for consideration.

The IT architect needs to consider all physical and logical issues of the solution and, at this point, he/she should have, in hand, a requirements report of the Tivoli physical design of the solution and all the customers' requirements for Tivoli. If there is a security policy already defined, it also has to be available and analyzed; otherwise, the Tivoli consultant personal should create one.

As requirements are gathered, you should structure them to define management domains or to provide a justification for separating management applications from each other, managed resources from each other, or applications from resources within the logical design.

The answers to the following questions may be part of the information that help you define some of these domains:

- Does the company have a security policy? If so, can it be used without any changes, or will it require additional security policies?
- Do certain administrators need to control all aspects of some resources and not others? That is, the workstation support team should have no access to servers.
- Do certain administrators need to access specific applications and not others? That is, should people who distribute software not be able to change user IDs and passwords?
- Is there a multi-tier TMR structure and where do humans interact with the design? For example, will all administrators be defined at the top TMR or enterprise level, or will some operators be working at a regional TMR level?
- How are administrators and operators grouped?

- Is the physical design adequate and contain enough detailed information?
- Does the requirements report contain enough detailed information? Can all customer's needs for Tivoli management software be identified?
- What are the Remote Control security requirements?
- Do specific aspects of application usage need to be isolated? That is, software file pack creation, subscriber creation, file pack distribution, monitor creation versus distribution, and so on.
- Do specific resources need to be isolated from all other resources? For example, payroll servers versus print servers.
- Is there a need to distribute application code, and if so, how it will be done?
- Do you need a recovery plan for this Tivoli environment, or will it be covered by your organization's existing processes?

Careful thought should be performed in developing the logical design because once it has been deployed, it will get more complex over time and become difficult to modify.

The IT architect should now consolidate all the information gathered and evaluate if it is necessary to obtain additional information in order to proceed with the base logical design.

For additional information on gathering information and requirements for a Tivoli logical design, refer to 9.1, "Gathering information and requirements" on page 144.

1.3.3 Decide on a naming convention

Naming conventions are essential to keep order within a complex and growing environment. Defining a naming convention is not a trivial part of the systems management architecture. The naming convention should cover all resources that may eventually be part of the Tivoli solution. This includes Policy Regions, Profile Managers, Profiles, Jobs, Tasks, Administrators, Managed Nodes, and so on. In an ideal case, the naming convention already implies the underlying structure and gives a good term definition. Detailed information and proposal for convenient naming conventions will be discussed in Chapter 2, "Naming convention" on page 19.

1.3.4 Construct a Policy Region schema

The TMR is the physical grouping of resources in a Tivoli Solution, while policy regions are the logical grouping. This might sound abstract at first, but it simply provides a possibility to create groups of resources independently of how they are physically connected. In this way, you can create a policy region that contains only those resources a specific administrator is responsible for without considering the platform or type. The policy region is closely attached to the security functions to ensure that no one can get access to resources that he or she is not allowed to use. As many policy regions as needed can be created. You can also build a hierarchy of policy regions. You can get a better overview of the resources this way, and they will be easier to find in large environments. Detailed information on how to build a policy region schema can be found in Chapter 3, "Policy region design" on page 27.

1.3.5 Construct a Profile Manager schema

A profile is a collection of application specific information that can be manipulated and distributed to machines in the Tivoli environment. Even though profiles are part of the Tivoli Framework infrastructure, they are Tivoli management application specific. In other words, each Tivoli application will define specialized profile types used by that application.

A profile manager is a collection of profiles and the resources they can be distributed to. These resources are called subscribers. A profile is a logical set of data that might contain, for example, configurations, software, commands, or just simple data files. A major benefit of a profile manager is that a lot of different information can be distributed in one single action. Let's say you add a new server to the network. By distributing a profile to the new node, software, configurations, users, and setup scripts can all be distributed in one action. The quality will also be controllable as you will know that it is the same data that is distributed every time. We will dedicate Chapter 4, "Profile Manager design" on page 41 to provide a detailed description on how to design the Profile Manager schema.

1.3.6 Set the Tivoli Administrators

A Tivoli Administrator is someone who has been given authorization to perform management task in the Tivoli environment. Roles can be given to Tivoli administrators in order to restrict their scope of authority. These roles can be granted at the resource level or at a global TMR level. When granting roles at the resource level, you provide an administrator with authority on resources across policy regions. When granting roles at the TMR level, you provide an administrator with authority over all resources across the entire Tivoli environment.

Each administrator has his or her own Tivoli desktop that reflects the access and control he or she has been given. The contents of an administrators desktop is stored in the TMR database; therefore, the administrator will see the same desktop independent of the physical system that they are using.

Chapter 5, “Administrators’ considerations” on page 67 is dedicated to provide you with detailed information on how to plan, design, and deploy your Tivoli administrator schema. In addition, we present the input requirements for the creation of Tivoli administrators. Thereafter, the input requirements for Tivoli Administrator design, as a whole, are discussed. This chapter also provides a great deal of information, suggestions, tricks and tips on granting administrators suitable access to resources which fall under their responsibilities while, at the same time, restrict them access to all other resources that are not related to their activities.

1.3.7 Bringing it all together

The final relationship between the elements involved in a Tivoli Logical Design will result on how Tivoli will perform in the customer environment. Chapter 8, “Bringing it all together” on page 131 provides further information on how these elements interact with each other and discusses some of the issues when integrating such elements into the Tivoli Logical Design.

1.3.8 Review and evaluate the design

Several logical design alternatives may be created. This is valuable because they provide a forum in which to discuss the Tivoli components relative to the requirements. It is usually, at this point, that additional requirements or issues arise.

Once a set of architectural solution alternatives has been developed, the next phase is to decide which alternative is best suited to the customer environment. All solutions should be evaluated by a team of Tivoli consultants, which can validate and check if the solutions meet all the requirements.

Experience has shown that if you have reached this phase, very few additional issues will be raised because most issues will have come out of the architectural alternatives and will have been resolved during that phase. However, if additional issues do surface, they will need to be resolved. Ideally, these issues should be resolved, with Tivoli consultants present, during the same session that is evaluating the solutions. For additional information, please refer to 9.3, “Checking the result” on page 161.

1.4 Best practices

The term *best practices* is one of the most over-used phrases in consulting nowadays. In a generic way, it can be defined as a way of performing a task or function that is considered to be effective in improving a company's business processes. A best practice should continually add value to a company's products and services while ensuring the efficiency of the company's daily operations.

Tivoli best practices can be defined as follows:

Best practices Common, consistent, and repeatable methods used to perform required functions, providing real world value to the customers. Addressing a wide range of business processes that are, at the same time, critical and supportive from the initial planning phase to the operation and maintenance of the Tivoli management software.

Tivoli's best practices are effective ways of accomplishing certain tasks within the disciplines of systems and network management with Tivoli management software.

The best practices initiative is an ongoing strategy developed by Tivoli to discover, apply, and broadcast the best in Tivoli software product practices and experiences that relate to functional customer processes. It is the goal of Tivoli to keep their professionals, partners, and customers aware of such practices so that they can benefit from what the Tivoli professionals community is doing with Tivoli products. In addition, Tivoli's best practices are able to align people, process, and technology to achieve the desired state of functionality at the lowest cost. It is not only a matter of doing tasks better, but of distinguishing the tasks that really make a difference to the quality and effectiveness of the work.

It is our goal in this redbook to provide the best practices performed when laying out an Tivoli Logical Design. However, as described in this section, best practices are a product of several years of experience of Tivoli consultants, partners, and customers on how they are working with the Tivoli family of applications. This redbook was written with the input and experience of many people, and the result is a suggested approach that may apply directly to your situation or can be a guide to anyone involved in outlining a Tivoli Logical Design.

Chapter 2. Naming convention

Users and applications often access resources and objects, such as computers and applications, by using the name assigned to the resource. If there is a naming convention, where the names are consistent for all variations of resource types, it helps the user to quickly select the proper resource for their work. This means the administration can be simplified and more effective.

There are several requirements to defining an appropriate naming for Tivoli resources. From the point of view of a Tivoli administrator, resource names should be easy to keep in mind, and the type of resource should be easily determinable from the name. In order to automatically execute business tasks implemented through programs and scripts, the names may also be configured within programming variables.

This chapter describes the importance of defining a naming convention when planning the design of a Tivoli environment. In addition, we provide some examples as reference and best practices information.

2.1 Naming convention for Tivoli Enterprise Software objects

It is extremely important that a naming convention for each element of the Tivoli Logical Architecture be defined. Even more, it is essential that all personnel involved in creating new Tivoli resources, Tivoli administrators, or Tivoli management functions, understand and be devoted to the naming convention in context. The Tivoli administrators, support team, and help-desk personnel, will be always off track of the internal structure of the solution unless the naming convention is not followed by heart.

The naming convention should cover all resources that are part of the Tivoli systems management solution. Each Tivoli product may have many different resources types, for instance:

Tivoli Framework — TMR, Generic Collection, Administrator, Policy Region, Subregion, Managed Node, Endpoint, Profile Manager, Task Library, Task, and Job

Distributed Monitoring — Sentry Profile, Indicator, and Indicator Collection

Tivoli Enterprise Console — Event Source, Event Group, and Event Classes

Logfile Adapter	Adapter Configuration Profile
User Administration	User Profile and Group Profile
Security Management	Security Profile
Software Distribution	File package and AutoPack profile

One benefit of following a well constructed naming convention is that the solution becomes almost self-documenting, and limited additional documentation is required in order to understand the relationships of the different parts of the solution. In addition, a good naming convention within Tivoli helps you in the rapid deployment of the solution once it lends itself to automation through scripting.

A new object can be created for each Tivoli resource type. The TMR server guarantees that the object identifier for this resource is unique in the whole TMR even if other TMRs are connected (so long as resources are exchanged between connected TMRs). The reason is that when you create a new resource and give a name to it, the resource name will be registered with the Tivoli Name Registry (TNR). In addition, every resource in Tivoli is identified by its name and type. For instance, a policy region called Austin-Region.pr has a name Austin-Region.pr and is of type PolicyRegion.

The name registry does not allow two resources of the same type to have the same name within a single TMR. However, the name of objects of different types represented by the name field can reside several times in the TMR or even within connected TMRs. Therefore, it is possible to have various resources on the desktop with identical names. For instance, it is possible to have a profile manager called Help Desk, as well as a Tivoli User Administration group profile called Help Desk.

The type of object in use may or may not be obvious from the context of the desktop, but it may not be clear when working with the command line. For this reason, it is recommended to implement a naming convention that specifies the object type within the name, such as HelpDesk.pm, where pm indicates a profile manager.

Uniqueness of naming makes it much simpler to manage the environment. In a multiple TMR scenario, when an object's name is not unique, Tivoli will append a string of the format #TMR_name# to the object. This string forces the object to be unique within the Tivoli Name Registry.

When working in a multiple TMR environment, once the name registry is updated between the TMRs, Tivoli prevents you from creating a new resource that has the same name in the same resource type in another interconnected

TMR. However, this name will not be apparent to operators, and the wrong object could be selected for the operation, or a naming conflict could occur, and the operation would fail to execute.

Uniqueness of the names across the enterprise will also able the combining of TMRs, if required, by the organization in the future.

There are times when the Tivoli administrators have to deal with a Tivoli management environment via the command line, or the support group has to look at traces or log files. In these cases, it is essential to quickly know exactly what type of object you are dealing with, which can be achieved by following a common naming strategy.

2.2 Best practices

Experience has shown that the following should be a good approach when defining the naming convention:

- A group or individual within the organization responsible for defining and maintaining the naming convention should be identified.
- The name must refer to only one resource; it must be unique.
- If the name should be created in some standard way, the number of fields, each field contents, and the delimiter to be used for separation should be identified. For instance, a Tivoli administrator's name may be composed of the first four characters of their operating system user ID and their first four characters of their last name, or a resource name may include some indicator of its location, its type, and a unique part, each separated by a period (.). Some other possibilities to the field contents would be operating system type, physical location, organization or department, application name, TMR server name, object designator, and so on.
- A mechanism to validate the uniformity of names for newly defined resources may be defined. In the Tivoli enterprise software environment, you can use validation policies to enforce this.
- All dependencies on other naming conventions should be checked, such as the one that may already be in use in some other context within the organization. For instance, TCP/IP names, Microsoft-style domain names, and so on.
- Limitations for the group of characters used and length of names should be considered. As a recommendation, restrict names to alphanumeric characters, dashes (-), and underscores (_), while avoiding blanks, slashes (/, \), colons (:), semicolons (;), and At-signs (@) that might lead to trouble later.

- The need for a platform-specific naming convention for certain resources should be considered.
- Consistency and predictability should be present.
- All names should contain a TMR designator.
- Names should make sense when read either from right to left or from left to the right. The method to be defined will really depend on the organization-specific culture. However, it is advised to put the most significant value on the left hand side, since some dialogs (for example, table gadgets) do not show the entire name but only part of it. For example, you can decide to have names that go from the generic on the right to specific on the left, such as WinNT.desktop-subscribers.TI4011.pr representing a policy region in the TMR server TI4011, composed by desktop subscribers with a Windows NT operating system.
- The naming convention should be designed in a way that scalability should be considered as top priority.
- Command Line Interface (CLI) operations should be considered. Since the icon view is not available, objects must be immediately and readily identified by name only.
- All names should contain an object designators indicator. The object designators should be defined previously. Naming conventions for managed nodes need to be the hostname or the full-qualified domain name for lookup purposes. According to IOM settings, Tivoli tries to do a name resolution, and in case the name is not mapped, it falls back to IP addresses. In general, the managed node label should resolve to the correct IP address from the TMR server as the managed node as well. For endpoints, this process does not apply, however, we recommend following the same standard as for managed nodes for simplicity reasons. The following table provides an example of the object designator indicator code usage:

Table 1. Naming convention - Object designator code example

Object Designator	Recommended Usage
Administrator	adm
Administrator Collection	admc
AutoPack	apk
File Package	fpk
Gateway	gw

Object Designator	Recommended Usage
Group Profile	gpf
Indicator Collection	ic
Indicator Collection Policy	icp
Job	job
Policy Region	pr
Profile Endpoint	pfep
Profile Manager (database mode)	pm
Profile Manager (dataless mode)	dpm
Query	qry
Query Library	qryl
Remote Control	rc
Scheduler	sch
Security Profile	spf
Security Profile Endpoint	spep
Sentry Collection Maker	dmc
Sentry Profile	dmpf
Task Library	tklb
Task Repository	tkrp
User Profile	upf

2.3 Sample naming convention

The naming convention that should be adopted varies from environment to environment. In this section, we provide a sample naming convention that will be used later in this redbook. This naming convention can be the case of a single TMR environment with reasonable amounts of policy regions and profiles, profile managers, and administrators, as well as multiple TMR environments.

For the logical construction of the naming convention provided here, we followed the recommendations described in the Section 2.2, “Best practices” on page 21.

The name structure is composed of four locating fields separated by a period as shown in Figure 5.

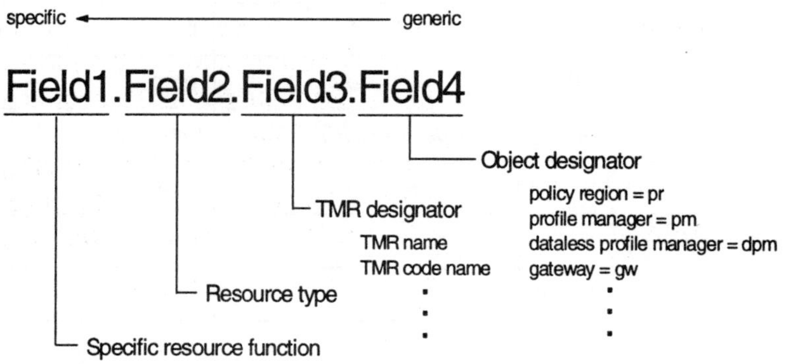

Figure 5. Naming convention structure fields

Field4 This field will hold the Tivoli object designator. In this naming convention, this is the most generic attribute of a particular resource that is being identified. An example of an object designator usage is shown in Table 1 on page 22. Certainly, this table can be adapted to best fit the environment in which this naming convention should be applied.

Field3 This field will be used to identify the Tivoli Management Region. Even if you are planning a single TMR design, you should consider using a TMR designator. It provides scalability for future growth. This field can be the TMR name, TMR hostname, geography, specific location, division, or anything that can identify different management policies, and so on. For example, the name Field1.Field2.BRZ.upf identifies the user profile resource defined in the BRZ TMR.

Field2 This is used to identify the resource type. For example, if you define Appl.BRZ.pr identifying the application policy region under the BRZ TMR, you can define DM-Appl.BRZ.pr, SD-Appl.BRZ.pr, and INV-Appl.BRZ.pr identifying the Distributed Monitoring, Software

Distribution, and Inventory sub policy regions of Appl.BRZ.pr under BRZ TMR. The hierarchy would be as follows:

Appl.BRZ.pr
    DM-Appl.BRZ.pr
    SD-Appl.BRZ.pr
    INV-Appl.BRZ.pr

Field1

This field describes the function of the resource. In this naming convention, this is the most specific characteristic of the object to be named. It should give a clear idea to the administrator about the resource function. For example, the name Notes-Mail.DM-Appl.BRZ.pm identifies a profile manager defined into the DM-Appl.BRZ.pr policy region that will contain Lotus Notes Mail distributed monitoring profiles.

Chapter 3. Policy region design

This chapter outlines some considerations in designing policy regions for your Tivoli Logical Design. Policy region definition, usage, hierarchy issues, best practices, and a design approach are provided.

3.1 What are policy regions?

One of the main elements used in the logical design of administrators' desktops are policy regions. It is important to understand what they are and how they should be used in order to produce good designs.

The simplest abstraction regarding policy regions is that they are a container for objects. This does not reflect the real nature of policy regions, though. One of their functions is to contain objects; however, policy regions will do more than serve as containers.

In Chapter 5 of the *Framework 3.6 User's Guide*, GC31-8433, policy regions are defined as:

Policy Region Tivoli maintains and enforces policies within policy regions. A policy region is a special collection of resources that share one or more common policies. Policy regions are abstract entities meant to enable you to model the management and organizational model of your distributed computing environment.

This description contains some important considerations about policy regions. As the name indicates, they are related to policies, defining a region where certain policies apply. Policy regions also serve as containers for the objects and resources that should be submitted to that policy.

3.2 Why create policy regions?

It is possible to create every kind of management object within a single policy region. Other than for demonstrations, however, this will be unworkable in real life use since there would be too many apparently unrelated icons in a single window. There is no particular threshold of icon clutter available. However, as for the effect on an administrator viewing screen, loads of icons will certainly be distracting. In addition, there is a display time factor involved for Tivoli Version 3.6.1 endpoints. That is why endpoint icons are not created by default.

That said, you should have a reason to create policy regions. What purpose does it serve? Should you have an international region if you only have two international distributors? Should you be satisfied with only one Western region, even when you know there are 12,000 desktops to be managed there? Would this region be subdivided further? How? By desktop type, by operating system, by job role, by applications used, by geography, by site, or by subnet? The answer to this question is, of course, YES!

Policy regions are used to:

- Contain and group managed resources
- Contain subregions
- Control access to resources
- Insure that policies are enforced before the use of the resources starts
- Supply defaults and validate values for fields used during resource creation and editing

Most Tivoli Management Environment (TME) applications are policy based. This means that they have certain policies governing their operations. These policies are defined on the policy region that contains the object.

Almost all managed resources within a Tivoli environment are created directly or indirectly within a policy region. They will be part of only one policy region. Tivoli Management Agents (TMA) endpoints are not created initially within a policy region but they can be added to a policy region later. Profiles are created within profile managers that are contained in policy regions (thus, they are indirectly created within policy regions).

A policy region is used to enforce four policies. Some policies are defined on the policy region itself, and others for the Tivoli administrators' characteristics. These policies are:

- Managed Resources
- Attribute Value Validation
- Attribute Defaults
- User Access

The first three policies are defined on the policy region itself. The last is defined on the Tivoli administrator object.

The Managed Resources policy defines which objects can be created or contained in a policy region. Each object refers to a real world resource being managed. This you allows to control which resource type can be grouped within a policy region.

The Attribute Value Validation and Attribute Default policies allow a certain level of customization on the behavior of the objects contained in a policy region.

The Attribute Default policies are used to inform the objects of a given type that default values can be used for the attribute. The Attribute Value Validation policy is used to check the values supplied by a user.

For the User Access policy, the access is controlled by stating what type of access a user has to a given policy region.

If the policy changes on a policy region, the new policy is not checked immediately. The policy must be manually checked. When checking a policy, the administrator specifies what should be done with objects that do not comply to the new policy. Some possibilities include linking the objects to a collection or listing them to a file. For more information, see Chapter 7, "Policies" on page 117.

All these aspects must be considered when designing the policy regions within the Tivoli environment.

3.3 Policy region hierarchy

Within a policy region, it is possible to create other policy regions. These regions within a region are called Policy Subregions. Policies of a subregion are copied from the parent region at creation time; subregions have the same policies of their parents' region at creation time. After they are created, the subregions policies can be changed.

Subregions allow some design options. Among them are:

- Specialization of policies
- Logical grouping of resource
- Creation of a region hierarchy

Since subregions, at creation time, have the same policies of their parent, they will be able to use the same validation and default policies and the same managed resources and administrator rights. After the creation, changes on the subregion's policies will allow a policy specialization. Note that the access control can only be extended in subregions, but never limited. In other words, if an administrator has a certain role in the parent policy region, this administrator will have the same role, by containment relationship, in all the subregions. Therefore, you should only grant the least necessary access to the parent policy region and extend an access to an administrator on demand for a subregion.

Since subregions can differ from their parent with regards of managed resources, they can also allow different resources to be grouped. In other words, a subregion may contain resources that could not be placed in the parent region. A careful and meticulous manipulation of this can help to organize and restrict the creation of resources.

The last use of subregions is the creation of a hierarchy. This hierarchy is a tree-like structure with the root being the top most policy region, branches being the subregions, and leafs being the managed resources. The hierarchies' design must be carefully done because access control and visibility of resources will be dictated by this tree.

Figure 6 shows a sample policy region hierarchy. The top most region represents the TMR specific region. Under it are three regions representing departments. Under the accounting policy region (acc.tmr.pr policy subregion), there are two subregions handling and holding different kinds of resources related to the accounting department: Accounting servers (server.acc.tmr.pr subregion) and accounting desktops (dsk.acc.tmr.pr subregion).

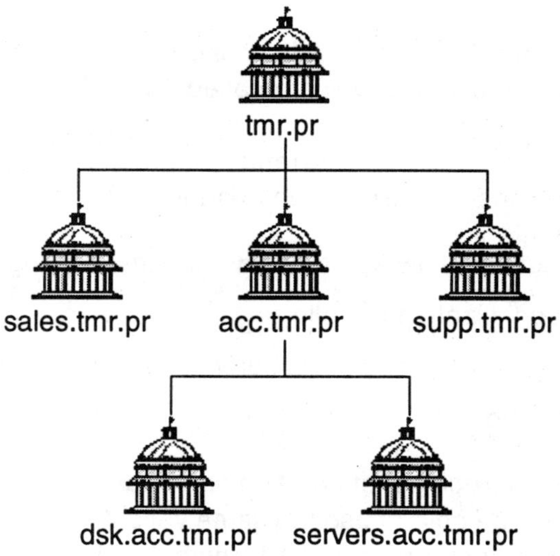

Figure 6. Sample policy region hierarchy

At the time the subregions were created, each one of them had the same policy as the parent region; however, each of these subregions might have its own policies defined according to the organization's policy. For instance, the dsk.acc.tmr.pr policy region may be designed to accommodate only endpoints, while the acc.tmr.pr policy region may contain many other resources, such as profile managers containing file packages to be distributed to the desktops endpoints.

The actual permission on each region may be set differently for each Tivoli administrator. However, any Tivoli administrator with access to a region will, at least, be able to visualize subregions. In our example, if a Tivoli administrator can visualize acc.tmr.pr, he or she will also be able to visualize both dsk.acc.tmr.pr and server.acc.tmr.pr. Both restricted visibility and Tivoli administrator access to regions and subregions must be considered when designing the policy region schema.

3.4 Best practices and design considerations

The essential issue concerning the design of the policy region schema is how the resources will be grouped so that Tivoli administrators can perform their functions without compromising security. This activity will lead to several questions, such as:

- How security constraints will affect the design?
- What policies may be needed and applied?
- How granular should the policy region hierarchy be?
- How many and which resources should each policy region accommodate?
- How to have access control done satisfactorily?
- How are the Tivoli applications to be involved and how do they affect my design?

Unfortunately, there is no single design that can handle that can handle all aspects of Tivoli Solutions all. Many different design options can be used with their advantages and disadvantages, and they will vary depending on the environment to be deployed. Some designs may look good on the test environment and prove bad on the production environment.

Policy regions can be used to group resources according to:

- Platform type
- Operating system
- Job function

- TME roles
- Application
- Geography
- Location
- Sub-networks

This is not an exhaustive list. Mixed grouping can be used. With all these options, it is easy to create a ineffective or extremely elaborated design, which eventually leads to very difficult operation and maintenance of the Tivoli environment.

One common design is to group all the required resources according to the tasks and jobs being done. As for resource grouping, one common approach is the use of geography, location, or organizational structure to group resources.

Depending on how resources are grouped, the final result will not operate properly. Another common problem faced when designing the policy region schema is that very often the company will suffer organizational changes, which will result in changes in the way resources are managed. The design should be flexible enough to absorb these changes.

Whichever design is to be used, there are some generic best practices that should be considered as follows:

- Keep hierarchy short and wide. For instance, although the structure being mapped has seven levels, the actual TME structure may have only three levels. This depends on how fine grained the control over the resources must be.
- Policy regions play a key role in administration creation and management; so, be sure to keep the number of policy regions as minimal as possible. It can lead to the easiest management and administration of the Tivoli environment.
- When creating endpoints, it is important that the endpoints be linked with a `wln` command into the policy region that the endpoint would have belonged to if created as a managed node instead. This is required to allow policy region role security to be enforced for management of endpoints objects. As an alternative, you may also create a policy region exclusively to accommodate endpoints as shown in 3.5.1, "Nodes policy region" on page 34.
- When analyzing the policy region schema, check if it provides flexibility in the following aspects:

  - Who can create, delete, and modify the resources.
  - Who can group the resources for management purposes.
  - Who can execute management functions on the resources.
- If Tivoli Remote Control is part of the solution, its specific security needs should be addressed. Whether a Tivoli administrator can take control or not over a specific resource can be handled by logically organizing the endpoints within policy regions.

A good design should be capable of handling organizational and individual changes with only slight alterations in administrator definitions and subscriptions. It should be flexible, open for expansion, and meet different security requirements.

Even though there is no such design that can handle all situations, experience has shown that the schema presented in the next section is often used as a base starting point of the policy region schema. Variations of this schema have been used in many successful Tivoli deployments in very large and complex environments. You should consider this schema as a starting point in designing the policy region schema and then adapt it to best fit the requirements of your environment.

3.5 Nodes, applications, and subscribers policy region design

This section describes one specific policy region design that has been very successful. The design consists of having three top-level regions or subregions. These regions will manage individual applications, subscribers, and managed nodes. These regions serve an unique purpose, the same purpose in every connected TMR. This gives clarity of structure and complete predictability within the enterprise. These regions are:

Nodes
This region only contains all managed nodes, Netware managed sites, PC managed nodes, or further subdivided subregions containing the same. It can also contain a subregion to group endpoints, if necessary.

Applications
This region will contain application specific subregions. Each of these subregions will contain all resources for a certain application.

List or Subscribers
This region will contain an effective hierarchy of Profile Managers and Collections used to create subscription lists and grouping of managed resources.

In Figure 7, the nodes, applications, and subscribers policy region schema is shown. Obviously, there are other plans, but this is a clear, simple, and logical one.

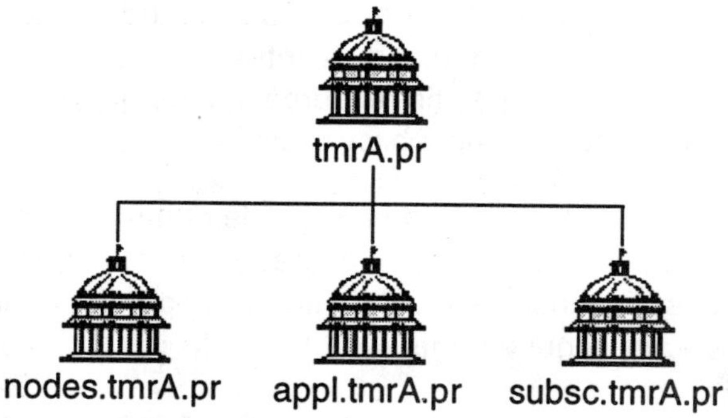

Figure 7. Top-level policy regions

This model provides several benefits when dealing with the management of the environment. First and foremost, it makes restricting users' access much easier. It is very simple to configure the administrators so that they are restricted to accessing what is needed to perform their jobs.

Another advantage is that while administrators can do their activities, it is not required to give them access to the entire picture. The view of the administrator can be easily restricted to only what he or she needs to know to perform his or her activities. This model also allows policies to be tailored, taking in consideration the activities that should be handled in each region.

3.5.1 Nodes policy region

This region and its subregions will contain the managed systems, that is, managed nodes, endpoints, PC managed nodes, Netware sites, and other final profile subscribers. The nodes region must only contain these kinds of managed resources. No application resource or subscribers list should be placed into it. Figure 8 on page 35 shows an example of the nodes policy region.

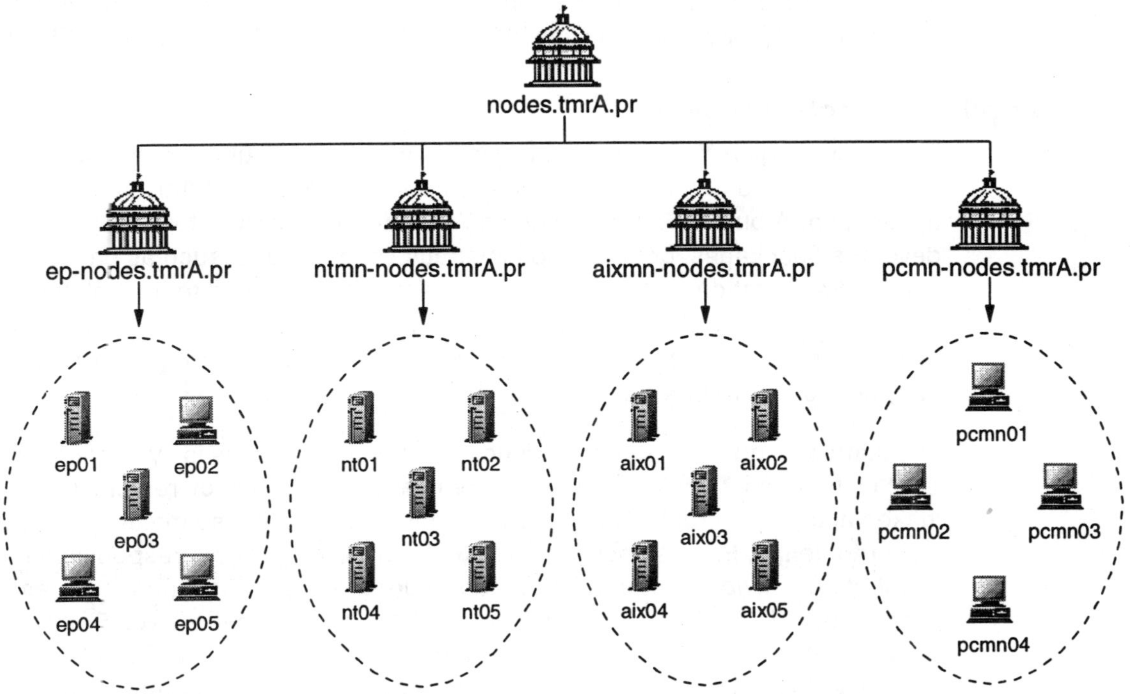

Figure 8. Nodes policy region schema example

The resources can easily be grouped into subregions. The way you group the resources will depend on the demands of the environment. Geography, location, and organization can be some of the reasons for the grouping. However, the grouping is not designed for distribution purposes. The key concern on the grouping in this region is to allow policy region role security to be enforced for management of these managed systems.

Tivoli Remote Control is not governed by a subscription list. All resources visible to an administrator can be controlled by it. The only way to restrict it is to not allow the administrator to have access to certain resources. If there is a need to restrict the administrator, the restrictions should be considered when grouping the resources. For example, let's suppose an organization that has a security policy that allows the system administrator unhindered control of any machine, both servers and desktops, and the help desk personal access only to desktops. In this case, desktops and servers should be grouped into different policy regions with different policies. The policy for the servers policy region has to deny access to help desk administrators.

Besides the remote control security requirements, there are not to many other serious constraints to the design of this region. However, the general policy region best practices should be considered, that is, as few regions as possible, and a wide and shallow hierarchy tree should be the goal.

3.5.2 Application policy region

This policy region is designed to group all applications subregions, each of which is devoted to the comprehensive management of each business application. A business application can include third-party, internally developed packages, or purely administrative applications, such as backup or Tivoli administration, for example. This policy region is used to host all the application specific resources so that the application's resources, such as FilePackage, SentryProfile, Remote Control, Task Libraries, and so forth, can be grouped and held within this region.

The simplest and most effective grouping of these resources is by application. That is, for each Tivoli application, there is a respective policy region. This makes access control to the applications much easier. It also makes policies easier to define. For instance, if you have Tivoli administrators responsible for distributing software, but not authorized to perform other functions, such as defining user IDs, these administrators will have access to the Tivoli Software Distribution policy region but will have the access denied to the Tivoli User Administration policy region. Figure 9 on page 37 shows an example of the Application policy region. Again, you should consider this schema as a starting point to designing the Application policy region schema and then adapt it to best fit the requirements of your environment.

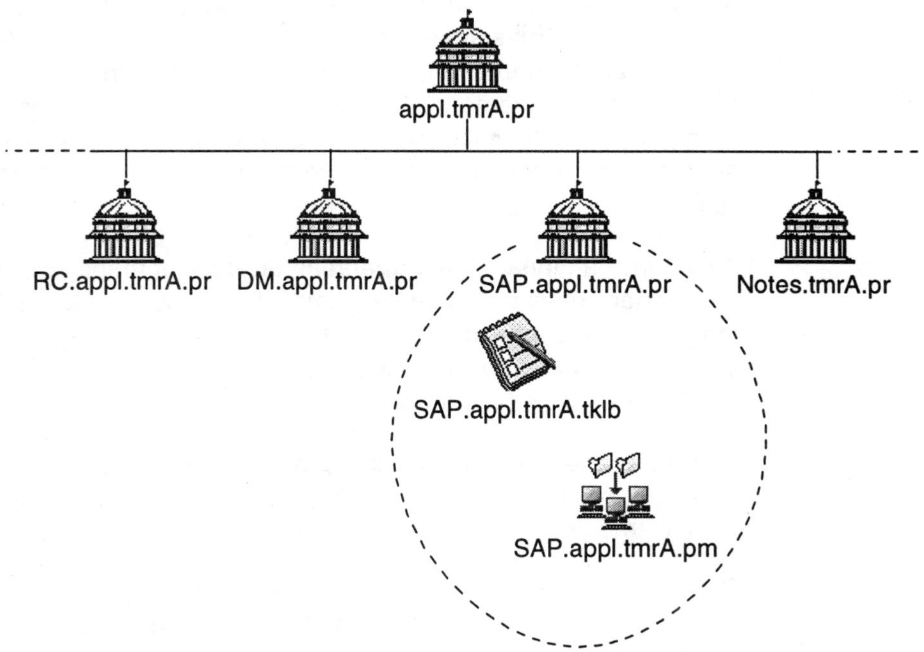

Figure 9. Application policy region schema example

Endpoints and managed nodes associated with these applications should not be defined into these regions. This is frequently referred to as *management by subscription*. A Profile Manager defined into any of these subregions will contain only Profiles for the subregion's specific application. The subscribers for these profile managers will be defined in the subscribers region.

This design is very logical but is not always the most "operator friendly". The administrators desktop can become confusing, and finding resources can become difficult. However, the solution lies not in relaxing this design. Instead, intelligent use of the Desktop Navigator, collections, and an effective naming convention will make the desktop more user friendly.

Some applications may have requirements that will not fit within this design. However, the general model should be used because it makes management much easier in the long run.

3.5.3 Subscribers or List policy region

A comprehensive tree of profile managers should be created in this policy region in order to allow subscribers to be addressed anonymously by their membership in some generalized category of entity. In other words, managed resources are grouped into groups that will likely require the same management operations to be performed on them. Anonymity is essential to avoid the hard-coding of individual machine identities into the distribution architecture. For instance, all machines with Windows NT Version 4.0 installed as the operating system can be grouped into a profile manager in order to receive the new Service Pack maintenance software. This profile manager would be subscribed to the Windows NT Version 4.0 maintenance software profile manager defined in the Tivoli Software Distribution policy region.

To perform a management operation on a set of managed systems, the subscriber profile manager can simply be subscribed to another profile manager that contains an application profile. When the application profile is distributed to the intermediate profile manager, the profile will, in turn, be distributed to its subscribers.

By placing these subscriber only profile managers in their own policy region structure, you can define administrative roles by policy region to control which administrators are authorized to maintain these subscriber's lists.

Only profile managers should be allowed in this region, and policies can be adjusted to restrict the way subscriptions are made. The actual content of the subscriber's profile managers, as well as the best approach when designing them, will be discussed in Chapter 4, "Profile Manager design" on page 41.

Another advantage of creating these regions is security. The region can be managed so that only certain administrators can manipulate its contents. This allows an effective control on how resources are grouped and how they are subscribed in the application policy region.

Figure 10 on page 39 shows an example of the subscriber's policy region.

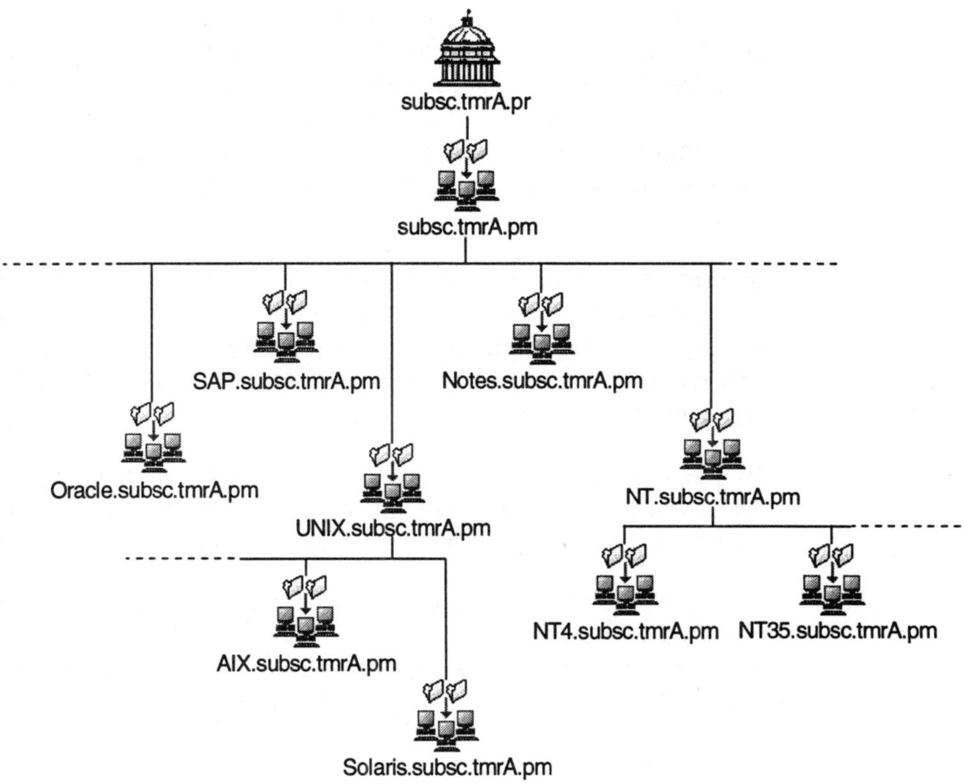

Figure 10. Subscribers' policy region schema example

When you add a new machine, you must define it in the appropriate nodes policy region and subscriber list in the subscriber policy region. Since these subscribers' lists are used by the applications policy region, no further action is required to enable the distribution of services to the new machine.

Chapter 4. Profile Manager design

Profiles and profile managers construct the configuration management portion of the Tivoli Management Framework. Together, these objects organize, create, and distribute information to remote systems. A strong understanding of profile and profile manager concepts, and the ways to design them is essential for anyone in charge of the Tivoli Logical Design.

In the following sections of this chapter, we describe the feature of profiles and profile managers as well as mention some of the most general guidelines to follow when designing the profile managers schema for the Tivoli Logical Design.

4.1 Overview

Designing a profile manager schema, at first thought, does not look to be such a difficult and important task to achieve. However, profile managers, along with policy regions, are the way Tivoli architecture uses to make all resource management, organize groups of profiles and locate resources so that the way you design your profile manager schema influences all the performance, control, and security you may have over all off your Tivoli solution. This procedure is, then, one of the key steps to follow when designing any Tivoli solution.

A profile manager schema can be made in many different ways, always according to the environment where Tivoli to be deployed, the way the administration should be done, and the security control requirements. You can have profile managers containing application profiles in one policy region, profile managers containing profile managers in a second policy region, and profile managers grouping TMA endpoints in a third policy region. Or, you could simply have all of your profile managers in one single policy region. The way you design depends on the logical structure you are following. Nevertheless, there are certain design considerations you should be aware of, for example, security, control over the resources, performance, changes in the design, and so forth.

4.2 Profiles and profile-based applications

A profile is a managed resource within the Tivoli environment that is related to a Tivoli application. That is, every Tivoli profile based application will define specialized profile types used by that application.

The profile object is the collection of all information required to perform a certain management function. It contains the configuration information that says what and how that specific profile does its management functions.

The profile class (or profile type) also contains all the information required to distribute and apply the profile. The distribution is a general procedure and is mostly the same for all the profiles. Once the profile has reached its final destination (its target), some activities must be performed. These activities are defined by the profile type and its configuration.

Profiles are created and maintained in profile managers. Profiles can be edited without immediately putting the changes into effect on the managed machines.

As stated above, profiles are created in the context of a profile manager. Once created, profiles can be distributed through a hierarchy to the managed systems. You can choose to have the profiles distributed in such a way that they are immediately applied to the managed systems, or you can have the profiles distributed to intermediate locations where another administrator may have the authority to modify the profiles before distribution to the managed system continues. Using this hierarchy of profile managers allows organizations within the enterprise to customize the information in the profiles if desired. In addition, the local administrators can decide when to actually apply the system changes represented by the profile.

Since profiles are application-dependent resources, one of the first steps to take when designing a logical Tivoli structure is to define which Tivoli applications are involved.

Within the Tivoli environment, we have the following profile-based applications with their specific profiles:

Tivoli Inventory	InventoryProfile
Tivoli Software Distribution	FilePackage, Autopack
Tivoli User Administration	UserProfile, GroupProfile
Tivoli Distributed Monitoring	SentryProfile
Tivoli Security Management	SecurityProfile
Tivoli Enterprise Console	Adapter Configuration Profile

The Tivoli architecture manages profiles according to policies. Every profile or profile type has a specific set of default and validation policies that, according to the Tivoli architecture, are used to rule the way a profile is created, the contents it may have, and the way it is associated with a profile manager. These profile policies can be used to avoid them to be modified by a subscriber, thus, enabling these policies to be enforced throughout a logical design for a Tivoli solution.

Application profiles store system configuration information in platform-independent profile databases, that is, the profile configuration information is stored in the distributed object database of the Tivoli architecture. When the profiles in a profile manager are configured, the configuration information is stored in the associated profile database. When a profile is distributed, the configuration information is copied from the object database and sent to the subscribers; so, what the subscribers get into their profile database is a copy of the original profile.

A profile manager may contain as many application profiles as you may want. That is to say, there is not an established limit for the number of profiles inside of a profile manager. The number of profiles you create inside a profile manager depends on the Tivoli applications you are working with and the resources that act as subscribers for that profile manager as well as the security and control level you decide to have within your Tivoli solution.

4.3 Profile managers

A profile manager is another managed resource within the TMR environment. This managed resource is created in the context of policy regions and acts as a container of other managed resources. Profile managers are the way used by the Tivoli architecture to store, organize, and control profiles and subscribers.

Profile managers do more than just contain profiles. They provide a place to create and organize groups of profiles and groups of subscribers so that you can specify to which subscriber groups the profiles will be distributed to.

Profile managers can be of two type:

Dataless The distribution is done directly to the system files of its subscribers. No local copies of the profiles are established.

Database The distribution is done to the subscriber's database, resulting in an existence of local copies of the profiles being distributed.

The difference between the two types will be described in more depth in subsequent sections.

4.3.1 Subscribers

Subscribers are entities that receive profile records from the profile manager at the time of its distribution. They can be of two types:

Profile endpoint These represent the final targets of the profiles, also known as target machines.

Profile manager Either dataless or database profile managers can be subscribed to profile managers.

Profile endpoints represent the resource to where a profile will be distributed. The most common profile endpoints are TMA endpoints, managed nodes, and proxy endpoints. Some applications will create new profile endpoints, such as Network Information Services (NIS) domains, databases, and DB2 partition groups, to name a few.

The other subscribers will be profile managers themselves. Only database profile managers can have profile managers as subscribers.

4.3.2 Database profile manager

The database profile manager may be a container of the following resources acting as subscribers:

- Profile manager (database or dataless)
- Managed node
- PC managed node
- Netware managed sites
- NIS domains
- Proxy endpoints

Note that a database profile manager cannot contain TMA endpoints as subscribers.

All of the database profile manager subscribers have their own profile database. This feature enables the database profile manager to distribute the information (the profiles) to its subscribers by storing the information in the profile database of each subscriber and writing the profile information into the system files of the subscribers.

That is, when distributing a profile to a profile endpoint, what actually happens is that a copy of the profile is converted to the proper format of the subscriber platform and located at its profile database, and the profile information is placed into the configuration files of the profile endpoint.

If a profile is distributed to a subscriber profile manager, this subscriber profile manager now contains a local copy of the profile into its profile database. This feature enables us to make local modifications that may be necessary to copy the profile definition before distributing the profile down to the hierarchy.

4.3.3 Dataless profile manager

The dataless profile manager may be a container of the following resources acting as subscribers:

- TMA endpoints
- Managed nodes
- PC Managed nodes
- Netware managed sites
- Proxy endpoints

Note that a dataless profile manager cannot contain database profile managers as subscribers.

Although we can have different managed resources as subscribers for dataless profile managers, such as managed nodes, it is always recommended to have only TMA endpoints as subscribers.

There are few reasons why you may consider having managed nodes as subscribers for dataless profile managers. We found the following two reasons to be most important:

1. When having dataless profile manager distribution actions over managed nodes, the distribution process changes. The distribution of the profile's records is first converted to the proper format and installed directly in the configuration files of the managed node without touching its profile database. The distribution performance may be increased, but it also may lead to inconsistencies between the profile's databases. This distribution format may be helpful during installations that do not require the exchange of information between profile databases.
2. Another reason why you may want to subscribe managed nodes to dataless profile managers is to keep consistency in the distribution behavior. If an environment uses endpoints and managed nodes, the distribution semantic changes as described previously. Experience has shown that, in order to keep a consistent semantic, it is recommended subscribing managed nodes to dataless profile managers. A design

document needs to clearly detail the use of managed nodes and the respective subscription.

4.3.4 Profile manager hierarchy

When defining profile managers as a subscriber of another profile manager, a hierarchy is created. Unlike the policy region hierarchy, profile manager hierarchy is not a tree-like structure. Policy regions can only belong to one policy region, while profile managers can be subscribers of any number of profile managers.

This creates a much more flexible structure similar to the UNIX file system and to the WWW. Circular subscription is not allowed, though.

Figure 11 shows a typical example of profile manager hierarchy design. The top-most level represents the entire corporation, the second level (austin.corp.pm and dallas.corp.pm) represent locations. Within each one of these profile managers, there are two other profile managers. One is defined to contain all TMA endpoints in such location, being a dataless profile manager. The other one is defined to hold all managed nodes of such location.

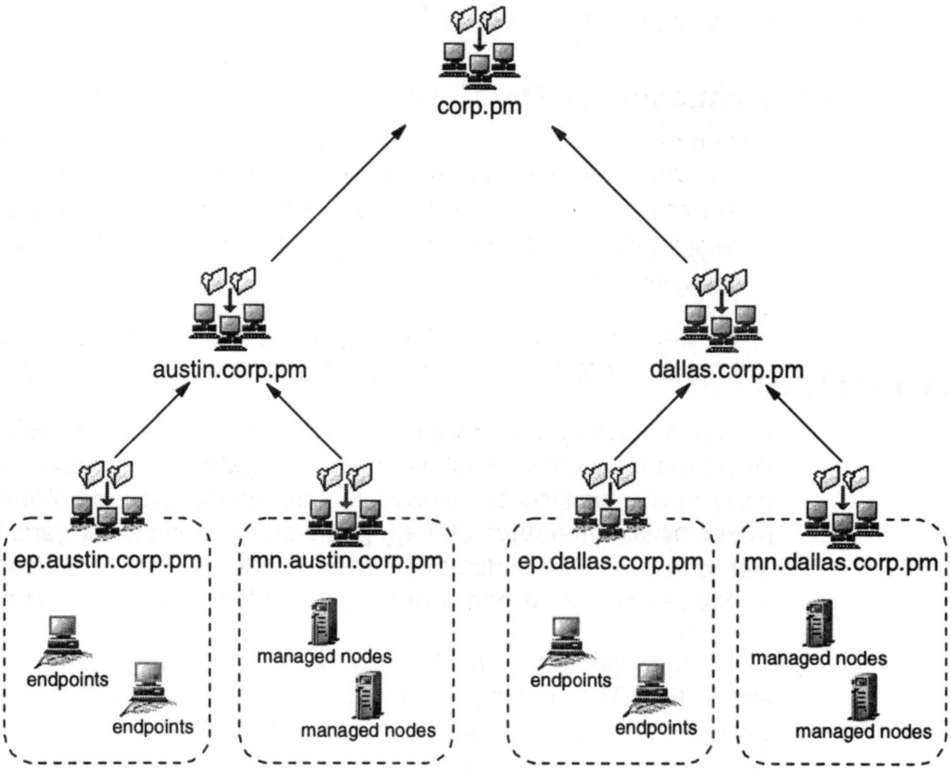

Figure 11. Sample profile manager hierarchy

The hierarchy dictates how distributions are executed. There are two key consideration that should be observed when this hierarchy is established:

- Distribution can be done to all subscribers of a given profile manager.
- Roles are checked at subscription time.

When any profile is distributed, all endpoints that are subscribed to them, directly or indirectly, can receive the profile. If a profile is distributed to corp.pm, all endpoints and managed nodes that are part of the hierarchy may receive the profile. Essentially, any endpoint within the hierarchy is visible, and any visible endpoint can be distributed to.

The other important aspect of profile manager hierarchies is that resource roles are checked only at subscription time, *not* at distribution time. This means that if a senior administrator subscribes corp.pm to a profile manager, where a junior administrator can distribute profiles, the junior administrator can distribute to all the resources under corp.pm.

Reckless usage of the profile managers can cause serious security problems and potential trouble on the managed resources; however, in general, these characteristics allow:

- Senior administrators to control subscription and, hence, the distribution of profiles.
- Administrators that do not have access to the resources to distribute to the resource without having to be granted excessive access to resources.
- Resource grouping to be done in several ways to suit the distribution needs.

4.4 Profile managers and profile distribution

Profile distribution is overruled by the profile manager hierarchal schema. Distribution can be done to all subscribers of a profile manager, and there is no security checking at distribution time. In other words, by taking the hierarchy shown in Figure 11 on page 47, for instance, if a profile is to be distributed to the corp.pm profile manager, all managed resources subscribed to this profile manager may receive the profile.

The actual distribution mechanisms varies a little for each profile-based application. The GUI implementation is somewhat different, although the general procedure is logically the same. When using the GUI the resource selection allows the following:

Distributed Monitoring Select the profile managers that are subscribed to the current level. In our example, from corp.pm to austin.corp.pm and dallas.corp.pm.

Inventory Select any of the profile endpoints subscribed to the current level. It is not possible to a group within these groups.

Software Distribution Select any object within the profile manager hierarchy, including other profile managers or just a profile endpoint.

Even if you are using the command line interface (CLI), Distributed Monitoring can only distribute to all levels or to one level at a time, following the hierarchy. In our example, it is possible to distribute from corp.pm to dallas.corp.pm, but not directly from corp.pm to ep.dallas.corp.pm without dallas.corp.pm getting involved in the distribution.

Software Distribution and Inventory can distribute to any profile endpoint or profile manager within the hierarchy.

These differences can influence the design of the profile manager schema. Distribution of the profiles of each application may require additional details in the design.

One issue that can potentially influence the design are the local profile copies that some profile based applications generate during distribution. The following Tivoli applications make use of local copies of its profiles:

- Distributed Monitoring
- User Administration
- Security Management

For these Tivoli applications, the profile manager design can be used to provide additional configuration for specific resources. For example, the local copy could be used to disable a specific monitor on a managed node while keeping the same monitor active on other managed nodes. See “Distributed Monitoring” on page 63 for additional information. In addition, for these applications, the profile distribution can be done either to all levels or only to the next level of subscriptions. This facility allows local administrators to modify a particular portion of the profile before distributing it again to the next levels. However, it is important to keep in mind that a profile copy will be replicated in every profile manager that belongs to the hierarchy, causing redundancy of data storage. Specially in the Tivoli user Administration case, a flat and shallow profile manager hierarchy is recommended, as the user data may use a large amount of space, and every profile copy holds the entire data-set. As a general rule, only introduce an additional layer to the profile manager hierarchy if it is really necessary. Please refer to *Framework 3.6 User's Guide*, GC31-8433 for additional information on how distribution to multiple levels works.

TMA endpoints can only be subscribed to dataless profile managers. These dataless profile managers can also contain managed nodes as subscribers. In this case, managed nodes will behave as TMA endpoints, that is, they will not have a local copy of the profile. Even though it can make the distribution faster, it does lead to potential inconsistencies in the behavior of the application on these managed nodes.

Since the subscribers of a dataless profile manager do not have an object database, it should not be used in the case of the managed nodes. Distribution to them results in a slightly different behavior. Once the profile reaches the dataless profile managers, the profile is converted into a sequence of data and actions before being pushed to the endpoint and executed. The actual execution of the actions is a responsibility of the endpoint gateway.

4.5 Designing the profile managers' schema

The profile manager schema will govern how distributions will be done, thus, preventing the distribution of specialized profiles to systems that do not support them while ensuring that those systems will receive all profiles that they need. It also determines the security of the distribution process. For all these reasons a good design for profile managers is critical. This section explores design aspects and considerations that lead to an effective profile manager design.

4.5.1 The goals

Any effective profile manager design must meet, at least, the following minimal goals:

- Administrators can distribute profiles to the correct targets.
- Administrators don't have to remember which endpoints they have to distribute to. The profile manager hierarchy should be done, keeping in mind that the profile managers associate the configuration management information to its targets. Therefore, for a given profile manager, any profile defined on it may be distributed to any subscriber of this profile manager without doing any harm to the environment. This design rule is much more preferable than having the Tivoli administrator require the knowledge of which profile is applicable to which subscriber. The later choice is a very error prone solution, and delegation of tasks doesn't seem to be feasible in such a scenario.
- Administrator can only distribute to the endpoints they have authority to.
- Distribution can be made to subgroups when performance is an issue.

Meeting these goals will lead to a much more appropriate design. One important difference between a profile manager and policy region hierarchy is that the profile manager is not a tree like structure; it's more of a hyper tree. This allows several profile managers to be shared and several distribution paths to exist at the same time. Figure 12 on page 51 shows an example where multiple paths are available to the profile distribution. The darker lines indicate subscriptions.

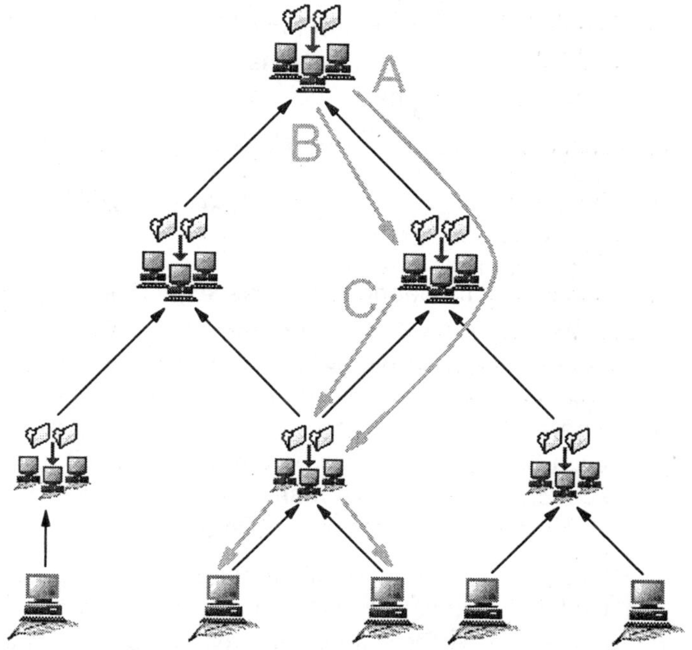

Figure 12. Profile distribution paths

In this example, the profile can reach the endpoint in a variety of ways. For example, a Tivoli administrator can distribute a Sentry profile by either using path A, or path B-C, or even any other convenient path. The distribution can be done in a two step operation by first using the next level of subscription, as indicated by path B, and then a second distribution would be done by using path C. This is the case when a particular parameter must be changed before distribution to a specific group of endpoints.

A very effective design of profile managers is to have a group of profile managers that contain only the endpoints as subscribers and another group that contains application profiles. This approach complements the subscribers and application policy regions as described in Section 3.5, "Nodes, applications, and subscribers policy region design" on page 33. This will be discussed in more detail in 4.6, "Subscribers' and applications' profile manager design" on page 53.

4.5.2 Best practices

The profile manager schema will depend heavily on the policy region design. Depending on how you have used policy regions to group resources, applications, and data, the appropriate design of profile managers will need to be developed to match resources with the appropriate profiles. As you can see, there are no specific steps to follow or specific design parameters when designing a profile manager logical structure within a Tivoli solution. However, there are some common features a good and practical profile manager design must have. Among these, we may mention the following:

- Define the application profile manager hierarchy and the managed resources list of subscribers profile manager hierarchy in different policy regions so that you have differentiated control and administration policies over these resources.
- Number of managed resources subscribing to a profile manager. When subscribing managed resources to profile managers, make sure you do not exceed a certain number of subscribers. Experience has shown that it is a good approach not to have more than 500 in a single profile manager; whereas, this is a database profile manager or dataless profile manager, even though it may also be a good approach to have a minor number of subscribers per profile manager, not because of performance issues, but for organization and control issues.
- Limit the number of profile managers a managed resource is subscribed to. Although you may subscribe a managed resource to any number of profile managers within your environment, the more number of profile managers a managed resource is subscribed to, the more the complexity to manage that managed resource.
- Subscriptions of managed nodes to dataless profile managers. Since managed nodes have their own profile database, if you subscribe a managed node to a dataless profile manager, when a distribution process is initiated, the profile attributes will be directly applied to the configuration files of the managed node, thus, passing by its profile database.
- Avoid subscriptions of profile endpoints that belong to other TMRs to local profile managers. Instead, once the resources' exchange takes place, you can subscribe profile managers of other TMRs to local profile managers. This is suggested because of the authentication operations across TMRs boundaries. The more authentication operations you have, the less performance of your environment.
- Limit the number and type of application profiles created in a single profile manager. If you are working with multiple Tivoli profile based applications, it is recommended for you to have a specific profile manager for each of the Tivoli applications in order to keep the security and control policies of your environment.

4.6 Subscribers' and applications' profile manager design

This section describes the profile manager design according to the policy region schema presented in 3.5, "Nodes, applications, and subscribers policy region design" on page 33.

4.6.1 Subscribers' profile manager design

Subscribers' profile managers are used to provide grouping for distribution of profiles. Resources should be grouped according to the needs of the profile distribution. Since the logic and characteristics of distribution differ among applications, this profile manager schema tends to have specialized parts for each application.

Subscribers profile managers can be grouped according to several classes. Among them are:

- Platform type
- Operating system
- Job function
- Application
- Geography
- Location
- Sub-network

A combination of these groups can also be used. The actual resource grouping should be made according to the distribution required. Any subscriber profile manager schema must be able to handle all distribution modes for all applications.

Let's use a simple example to illustrate these considerations. Our corporation wants to make usage of Tivoli Inventory and Tivoli Software Distribution. This corporation has two sites: One located in Austin, and the second one in Dallas. The corporation wants to collect inventory information from all of its systems (endpoints and managed nodes). It also needs to distribute software to its endpoints and managed nodes. In order to make things easier, in our corporation, all managed nodes are AIX machines, and all endpoints are Windows NT machines. Therefore, different versions of software are distributed to endpoints and managed nodes.

The first subscriber profile managers schema that comes into mind is the one shown in Figure 11 on page 47. This profile manager schema handles the inventory task very well. Inventory information of the entire organization can be collected from corp.pm profile manager, and if there is the need to collect information by location, it can be done by using any one of the two profiles manager, austin.corp.pm or dallas.corp.pm.

However, this profile manager schema cannot handle software distribution properly since there are different kinds of software for managed nodes and endpoints. Any file package intended to be distributed to an endpoint from corp.pm would end up on all the machines. A non-practical solution would be that the administrator select ep.dallas.corp.pm and ep.austin.corp.pm to distribute only to endpoints. This solves the problem but forces administrators to select only sub profile managers, which can potentially lead to problems if administrators are not careful.

With slight changes in this profile manager schema, it can support the software distribution requirements. In this case, defining the profile managers, all-ep.corp.pm and all-mn.corp.pm, in order to accommodate all endpoint and managed nodes, respectively. Figure 13 shows the updated design.

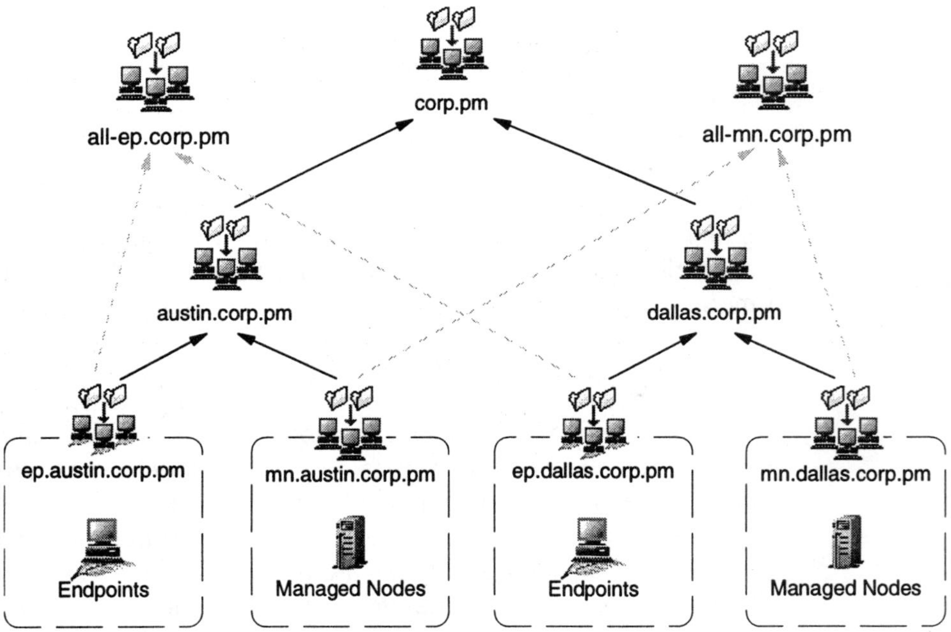

Figure 13. Changes in the profile manager schema

The new profile managers, all-ep.corp.pm and all-mn.corp.pm, are used for the software distribution profiles. Subscribed to them are the endpoints or managed nodes of both sites. Distribution can also be made for the endpoints or managed nodes of only one site, but the difference between the two platforms is preserved. This design does not require the administrators to remember which profiles to distribute to.

The profile endpoints could have been subscribed directly to the profile managers. Since the need to distinguish the sites is not critical, this would have created a shallow hierarchy. However, this would add more places to control the subscription of profile endpoints. For example, a new managed node is added to the Dallas site. By using the design shown in Figure 13, adding the managed node to mn.dallas.corp.pm automatically makes it a subscriber of all-mn.corp.pm as well. If the subscription were done directly, both all-mn.corp.pm and mn.dallas.corp.pm would have to be updated.

The actual design must also take into consideration some of the characteristics of each application being deployed. In the next section, we describe some of these considerations for each core application. Some applications behave differently, but in general, profiles should not be distributed directly to final profile endpoints (managed nodes, TMA endpoints, and so forth).

4.6.1.1 Software distribution

Both through the Tivoli desktop and the CLI, a distribution of a file package profile can be done to any endpoint or profile manager within the profile manager hierarchy. If the endpoint or profile manager is visible within the hierarchy the profile can be distributed to. The desktop even allows the hierarchy to be seen like a “directory tree” and any “directory” to be selected for distribution. For this reason, the design of the subscribers profile managers for Tivoli Software Distribution should be according to the grouping used to distribute software. If a company distributes a file package to a department one site at a time, the profile managers should allow both site and department to be selected by the operator at the time of the distribution. Figure 14 on page 56 shows some examples of such a design.

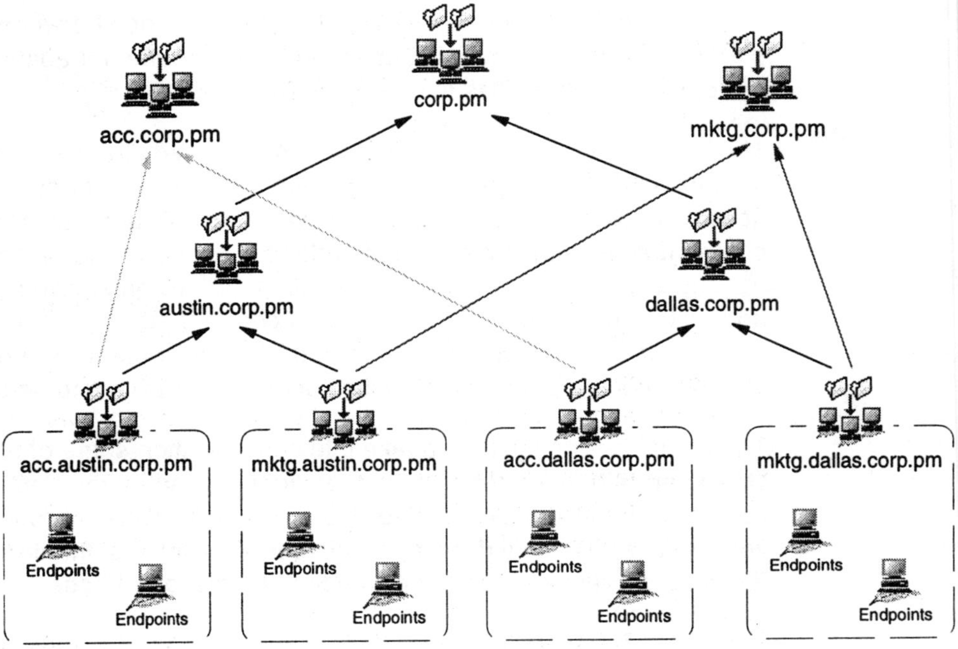

Figure 14. Profile design for staged software distribution

4.6.1.2 Inventory

Inventory is normally used for two types of distribution:

Scheduled — Collection done periodically, usually in an automated fashion. Regular collection of information to support asset control, decision support, and subscription queries.

On demand — Used to collect information for a specific moment, normally without any predictable order, such as a help desk person scanning for a specific requirement or an auditing team doing a flash scan to check for possible violations.

In the same way as Software Distribution, the CLI allows profiles to be distributed to any profile endpoint or profile manager within the profile manager hierarchy. However, the desktop does not allow the actual tree to be browsed, therefore, forcing the administrator to know where the target is within the hierarchy.

For example, let's assume the profile manager schema as shown in Figure 14. Using the desktop, the administrator would display a list of all profile endpoints, independent of which profile manager they are located in. This can be confusing for a block distribution but is perfect for on demand scans. If scheduled scanning is done in an automated fashion, by using scripts of the scheduler, for instance, the corp.pm profile manager can be used to distribute the inventory profile to all systems.

4.6.1.3 Distributed Monitoring

There are two important characteristics of Tivoli Distributed Monitoring that may require a specific design for subscriber profile managers as follows:

- Distributed Monitoring profiles tend to be very specialized, frequently having only a few valid endpoints to be distributed to.
- Local copies of profiles are generated during distribution. This may cause performance problems if the distribution path is too deep.

Profile managers are usually created to group a set of similar functions. It is always useful to categorize the monitors into similar types. By doing that, very often the monitors will fall into a category of some kind and provide a logical grouping of functions.

The simplest grouping of resources for Distributed Monitoring is the operating system platform. Most generic monitors are only significant within a specific platform. For example, a monitor that verifies free space in the /usr file system is only logical for UNIX, while space available in logical drive only makes sense for Windows NT. Thus, one natural grouping is by platform type.

Another grouping can be done using the applications that run on the servers, specially those with Tivoli Plus Modules. It may be useful to have a group that represents all the Lotus Notes servers, for example.

In order to avoid excessive local copies to be made, the subscription profile managers for Distributed Monitoring should not be placed in a deep profile manager hierarchy. Figure 15 on page 58 shows what happens when a Sentry Profile is distributed to all levels. In this example, from the original profile, another three copies were created after distribution. This can be a cause of performance and administration problems. Therefore, the subscriber distribution path should be as short as possible.

When local copies differ from the master copy, it may be necessary to have additional levels. However, this could be better done in the applications' profile manager than in the subscribers' profile manager.

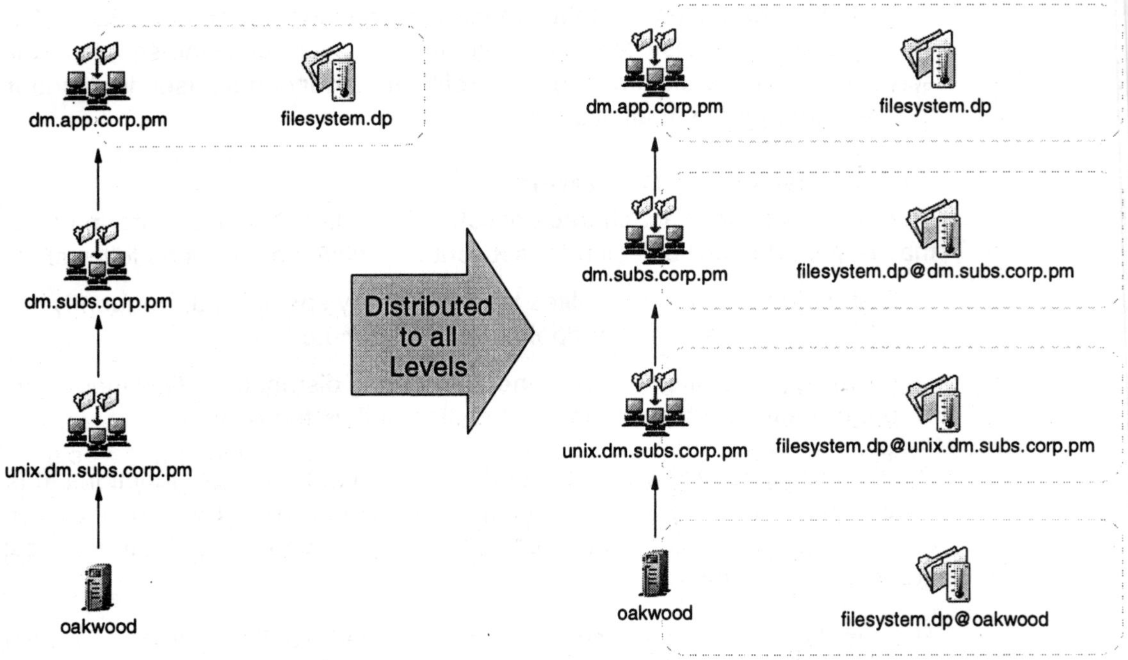

Figure 15. Local copies of a profile

4.6.1.4 Security Management

Security Management also generates local copies during distribution. However, unlike Distributed Monitoring, profiles tend to be much broader in scope so that the profiles can potentially reach hundreds of machines when distributed.

Since Security Profiles can be extremely restrictive, the only subscribers should be in the subscribers of profile managers. Profile endpoints should be grouped according to the profiles they will receive. So, if a profile enforces a desktop security, only desktops should be subscribed to it.

In the real world, it is often possible (and more practical) to identify distinct groups of machines that can be secured together. Each group is managed separately, and machines do not belong to more than one group. For example, all the machines in the Publications group can be managed together, as can all the machines in the Accounting department, the Telesales team systems, and so on. It is possible to manage different operating system types from the same profile, that is, to define UNIX resources for protection in the same profile as OS/390 resources, or OS/2 resources, or whatever. The same data is distributed to all targets, and at the target, the decision is made as to whether any of the data applies to that particular target type or not. The decision on whether to mix platform types in a profile may depend on how you organize your profile hierarchy for other products and whether the frequency and size of the changes that take place would result in excessive network traffic.

In any case, the consideration must be that a change to any of the four Security Management resource types will be sent to the correct set of systems to implement that change. The four resource types are security group, security role, security resource, and system policy. The last of these, system policy, can be treated as a special case. This resource is used to ensure certain machine-wide security policy rules are kept consistent. Usually, the same rules are required for every machine of that type in the enterprise. For example, you may want to ensure consistent password strength rules on all Windows NT domains. Security policy resources are typically created in their own profile that can be subscribed to all targets across the enterprise, similar to the use of Inventory demonstrated in Figure 11 on page 47. Whether the same security policy profile is used for multiple system types (Windows NT, AIX, Solaris, HP-UX, or whatever) will depend on how often you expect to need to distribute this profile.

4.6.1.5 User administration

The subscribers' profile manager should be created in order to contain all machines that will receive a specific set of profiles. They may be grouped by NIS or NT domains, by location, department, and so forth. This is determined by how the users are created and maintained in the environment.

Another way of thinking about the subscriber's profile manager design is through the way you need to distribute the user profiles. When distributing a user (or group) profile to a managed node using the exact copy option, the user (or group) entries from that profile are merged with the user (or group) entries residing in the downstream profile copies previously distributed to the same managed node. This merge is possible because all copies reside on the managed node's local database. This is done to avoid (during the exact copy distribution) deleting users from the system files that are managed by Tivoli residing in different user profiles.

For instance, if your NT server, called DocServer, is used by 100 sales users and 100 marketing users, the users system file on the NT server will contain 200 users. Imagine that you define two user profiles to manage these users (*SalesUsers* profile and *MarketingUsers* profile). If you decide to distribute the SalesUsers profile to DocServer using the exact copy option, you expect to have the exact copy of the Sales users attributes in the NT user system file, but you do *not* expect to delete all the Marketing users. That is why Tivoli

User Administration merges the entries of the MarketingUsers profile with the SalesUsers profile before distributing to the target machine.

The merge behavior described previously is not guaranteed for TMA endpoints because they do not have a local database in which to store downstream copies of distributed profiles. The merge behavior only occurs when there is a profile manager that serves as a consolidation point for distributions to a given TMA endpoint. Since TMA endpoints can only be subscribers of a profile manager in dataless mode, the merge for TMA endpoints occurs in a dataless profile manager.

Moreover, if you want the merge behavior to occur for the exact copy distributions to a TMA endpoint, you need to arrange the subscription hierarchy so that a TMA endpoint is a subscriber to *only one* dataless endpoint profile manager. This dataless profile manager will be a subscriber to all the profile managers containing user profiles that will be distributed to the given TMA endpoint.

For instance, imagine that the SalesUsers profile and the MarketingUsers profile reside in two different profile managers, PM1 and PM2, but the same TMA endpoint is a subscriber to PM1 and PM2. In this scenario, merging will not occur, and the exact copy distribution of the SalesUsers profile, for instance, will result in the deletion of all the Marketing users.

The solution is achieved by performing the following steps:

1. Create a dataless profile manager NTboxesPM
2. Subscribe the NT DocServer to NTboxesPM
3. Create a profile manager PM1
4. Create a profile SalesUsers in PM1
5. Subscribe NTboxesPM to PM1
6. Create a profile manager PM2
7. Create a profile MarketingUsers in PM2
8. Subscribe NTboxesPM to PM2

The merge will occur in the dataless profile manager NTboxesPM.

4.6.2 Applications' profile manager design

Applications' profile managers refer to the profile managers that will contain the actual application profiles. They should only have other profile managers as subscribers. This allows different administrators to handle application and subscription to the application profiles as well as prevents the distribution of specific profiles, such as user lists and file packages, to systems that do not support them. The security for this separation can be enforced by means of policy regions. Figure 16 shows how the application and subscriber profile managers work together.

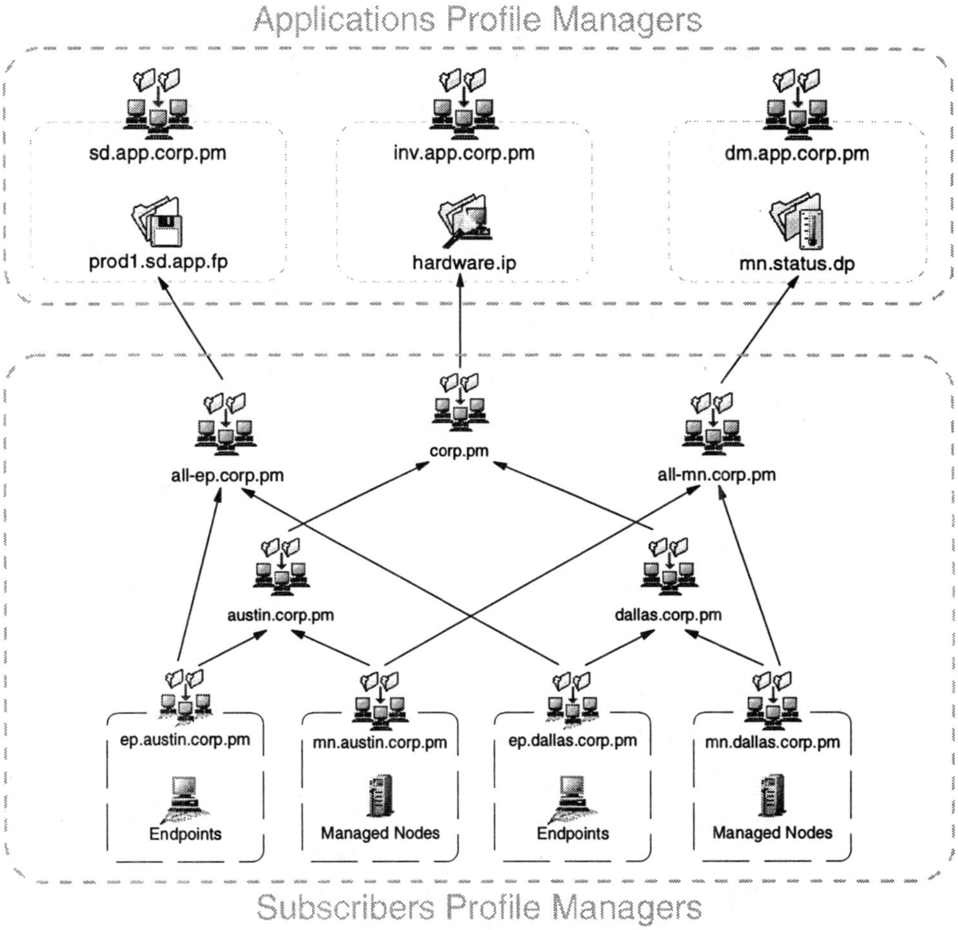

Figure 16. Application and subscriber profile managers

Application profiles are only created in the application profile managers, and the subscribers are only defined in the subscriber profile managers. Notice that there are two groups of resources: Applications' profile manager schema and subscribers' profile manager schema. These resources can be created in different policy regions so that different Tivoli administrators can be responsible for managing them.

The majority of the profile managers will be defined in the subscribers' profile managers; nevertheless, some important design possibilities exist for the applications' profile managers. In the next sections, we will describe these possibilities per application.

4.6.2.1 Software Distribution and inventory

For Software Distribution and inventory applications, profile managers are simply profile holders. Besides the application specific profile, the subscribers profile managers should be subscribed to the applications' profile manager. A given subscriber should be in the profile manager only if it can receive all the profiles. This way, administrators do not have to remember which profile can be distributed to what.

To illustrate this concept, we use a sample distribution requirement. A company has three departments that are targets for software distribution (DEP1, DEP2, and DEP3). Five products are involved (products A through E). Table 2 shows which products are distributed to which departments.

Table 2. Sample software distribution mapping

Product	**Departments**		
	DEP1	**DEP2**	**DEP3**
A	X	X	X
B	X	X	
C		X	X
D		X	X
E	X		X

Each product is distributed to at least two departments, and two products (C and D) are distributed to the same departments. The profile manger schema shown in Figure 17 on page 63 is a valid grouping to handle the distribution requirements. Each distribution group combination has a profile manager, and those that are distributed to the same departments are placed in the same profile managers.

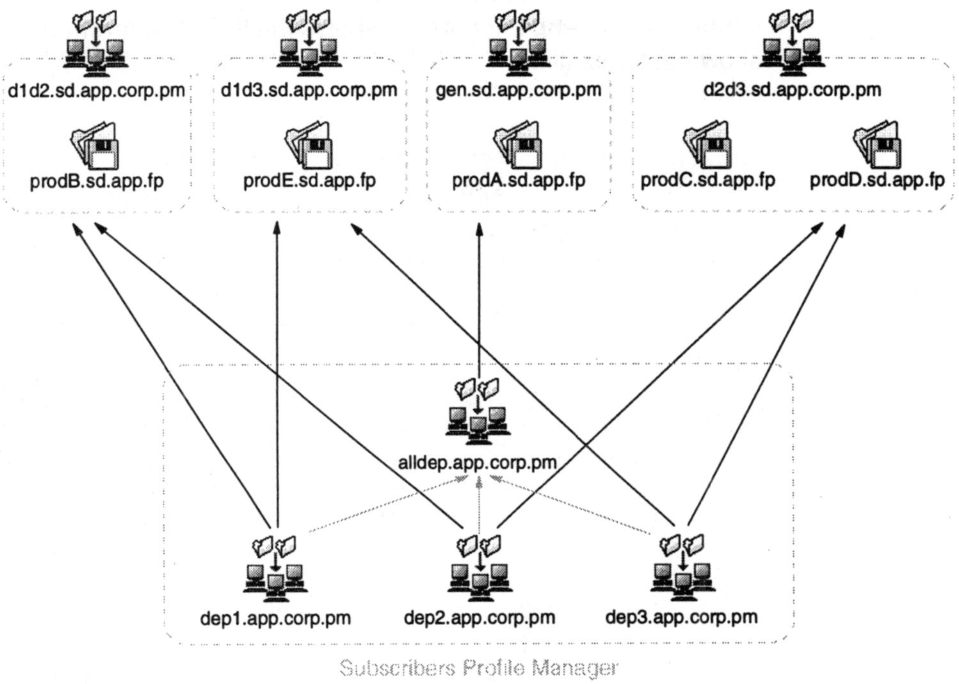

Figure 17. Profile grouping for software distribution

In general, if grouping can be made, it should be made. This may not seem significant in a small example like the one used here. However, if the number of groups and products increases, having a profile manager for each product would lead to excessive profile managers and more complexity to manage the environment.

4.6.2.2 Distributed Monitoring

The same profile grouping considerations used for Software Distribution are valid for Distributed Monitoring. Profiles should only be together if they have the same targets.

Distributed Monitoring profiles will generate local copies of themselves upon distribution. This means that having a very long distribution path can easily lead to several copies of profiles. However, this can be used to increase the flexibility of the tool.

Local copies of a profile can be modified to reflect local differences. For example, a group of machines has to be monitored for file system space. A global profile sets all the file systems to monitor. However, a subgroup of these machine does not contain one specific file system. Instead of creating two different profiles, the local copy for that group could be modified to make up for the difference. Figure 18 shows the use of different profile managers to allow customization.

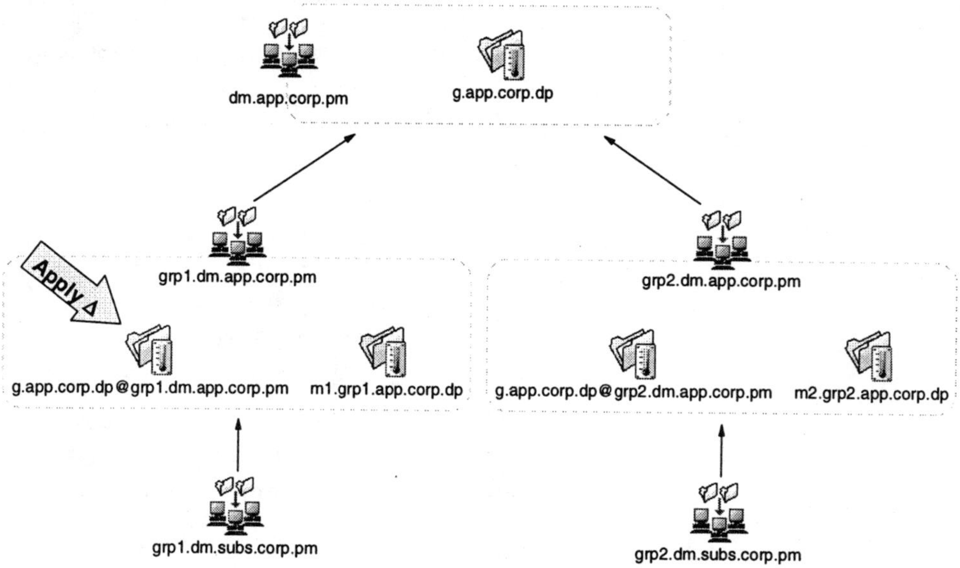

Figure 18. Distribute Monitoring customization through profile manager

The global profile, g.app.com.dp@dm.app.corp.pm, contains the file system monitors for all machines. After distributing to the first level of subscribers, the copy, g.app.corp.dp@grp1.dm.app.corp.pm, can be changed and then distributed to attend to the requirements of the subscribers on grp1.dm.subsc.corp.pm.

Another alternative, also shown in Figure 18, is the creation of profiles in the group profile managers. This is much more flexible but effectively creates more maintenance points in the structure. If changes are simple, such as disabling a specific monitor, it may be easier and more consistent to modify the local copies.

Modification in the local copies can be preserved. If new monitors are added to the master copy, the next distribution will add these monitors to the copies also. However, if a monitor in g.app.corp.dp is modified in a local copy and then modified in the master copy, the change to the master will not be sent to the local copy if distribution is not done in the make exact copy mode.

4.6.2.3 User Administration

User Administration functions similarly to Security Management. That is, profile are copied, and local copies can be edited to insure local differences are considered. It is possible to create a global profile that contains all central users and then have local user defined in the copies of the central profile.

For the application profile managers, a hierarchy of profile managers can be used so that there is a top-level central profile, and each sub profile contains the profiles for a local area. Figure 19 is an example of this design.

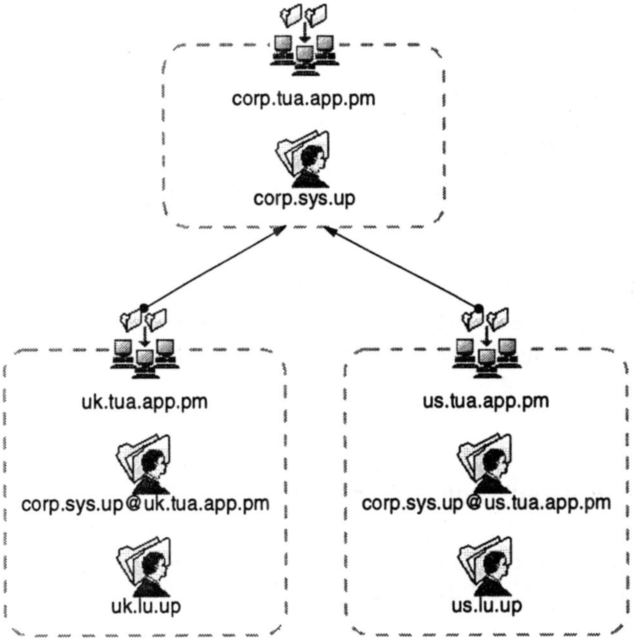

Figure 19. User administration profile manager schema

The profile, corp.sys.up defines all accounts used by application and central administration. Local copies of it (such as, corp.sys.up@uk.tua.app.pm) can be changed to hold local differences.

The local users are kept in the local profiles (uk.lu.up and us.lu.up). These can be kept by local personnel. The profile managers, uk.tua.app.pm and us.tua.app.pm, will be distributed to the appropriate endpoints.

4.6.2.4 Security Management

The choice for a Security Management profile hierarchy will depend on how your organization's security policy will be implemented. An ideal Security Management implementation will be heavily “role-based”. That is, you would use Security Manager roles to define the access rights for people based on something, such as their job function. A security role (which is distinct from a TMR or Resource role used for Tivoli administrators) can define the access requirements across multiple platform types. As an example, we can assume the role, "Printer Operator," requires certain access rights to print-related resources in Windows NT domains, UNIX servers, and the AS/400 in our organization. Any update relating to this role must reach all the necessary target machines to ensure the correct access is granted. In this example, subscribers need to be grouped according to how they may be affected by a particular role. This might appear to be very complicated on the surface; certain roles may need to go to most machines in an enterprise, and other roles may only affect a very small group.

4.7 Profile manager policies

As with other managed resources within the Tivoli architecture, profile managers are also controlled with default and validation policies.

The default policy defines which managed resources can become subscribers to a profile manager. The following are the default policies methods provided by the Tivoli architecture for profiles managers:

- pm_def_subscribers
- pm_def_profile_types
- pm_def_profile_managers

The validation policies govern profile manager subscriptions. The following are the validation policy methods provided by the Tivoli architecture for profile managers:

- pm_val_subscribers
- pm_val_subscription
- pm_val_remove_subscribers
- pm_val_remove_subscription

When designing the profile managers schema for a specific Tivoli solution, creating custom policies for profile managers may be helpful for subscribers control and performance purposes. Additional information on policies and policy methods for profile managers is provided in Chapter 7, “Policies” on page 117.

Chapter 5. Administrators' considerations

The goal of this chapter is to provide readers insight into the considerations that should be taken when designing administrators within a Tivoli management environment. Through the Tivoli management framework and its suite of management applications, system administrators will be able to manage their enterprise-wide environment with one single graphical user interface. This would greatly reduce the number of interfaces that system administrators are forced to deal with, thus, allowing them to manage their environment more efficiently.

Administrator design is relatively straight forward for systems environments where systems are homogeneous and administrator structure is small. However, the task of developing a design for Tivoli administrators becomes difficult for heterogeneous systems environments where the number of system resources and system administrators are large. The final design should be easily deployed and managed, while accountability and authorities for administrators must be provided and defined for each administrator.

In this chapter, we present the input requirements for the creation of Tivoli administrators; thereafter, the input requirements for Tivoli administrator design, as a whole, will be discussed.

In designing a Tivoli administrators' strategy, there is no one best solution because different organizational structures and/or administrative responsibility requires a different strategy. While a given administrator strategy might work in some environments, it might not be effective in another. Therefore, rather than providing the best solution, this chapter will provide considerations, recommendations, hints, and tips to assist readers in designing an effective administrator strategy for a given environment.

The chapter will examine the required Tivoli administrator roles by Tivoli application. Administrative tasks for each Tivoli core application and their required administrative roles will be defined.

5.1 Input requirements

For an organization consisting of a large number of multi-disciplined administrators and heterogeneous system resources, the roles assigned to each administrator must be clearly defined in accordance to the job responsibilities of the specific administrator and the organization administrative policy. In line with the organization administrative policy, the roles assigned to administrators must allow them access to resources in order to perform their normal administrative tasks but restrict them from gaining access to resources that they should not have access to.

By assigning appropriate administrative roles and policies to policy regions, and moving and associating resources to Tivoli policy regions, administrators can perform system management tasks without having the system root account or the NT Administrator account. This capability of authority delegation by resources, together with the desktop design, gives senior administrators complete control over who can perform specific administrative tasks on different sets of resources. In addition, administrators can be granted the required access on *all* resources at once in the TMR rather than by resources.

Throughout this section, the reference to system root account refers to the UNIX root account and the NT Administrator account. In addition, Tivoli administrators will be referred to as administrators throughout this chapter of the book. A Tivoli administrator is a person with a network user account delegated to manage one or more Tivoli policy regions and/or to perform Tivoli administration functions depending on the context.

5.1.1 Single administrator

Input requirements in the context of a single administrator refers to the input required when creating an administrator. The information required when creating an administrator is best summarized in Figure 20.

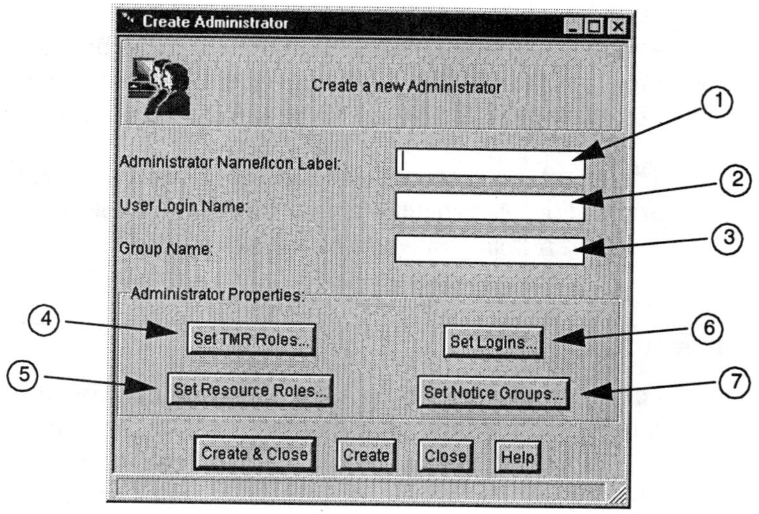

Figure 20. Creating a single administrator requirements

where:

1. Administrator Name/Icon Label

   The content of this field will be used as the Tivoli object name and the administrator icon label for the administrator to be created

2. User Login Name

   An existing user account name on the TMR server and all Tivoli targets where the new administrator will perform Tivoli activities on.

3. Group Name

   Group name that the user account above belongs to.

> **Note**
>
> The user login name and group name must exist on the TMR server and all targets used by the administrator. This allows the requesting administrator to run tasks and/or applications on targets where access to certain resources are required. For example, starting a Tivoli desktop session where an xterm session is required or backups and writing log files where write permission to directories are required. This information will also be used by Tivoli tasks where the user name and user group is specified as asterisk (*).

In cases where one administrator may manage system resources spanning several operating systems, Tivoli provides an ID mapping utility that allows administrators to assume a different user account name and group for each operating system, for example, AIX's system root account and Windows NT's Administrator account. The `widmap` command can be used to create and edit user and group ID mapping under different operating systems. For usage of the `widmap` command, refer to 5.4.1, "ID mapping" on page 97 and/or the *TME 10 Framework 3.6 Reference Manual*, SC31-8434.

If the use of ID mapping is required for the new administrator, instead of entering a specific user login name or group name, an ID mapping name can be specified by preceding the map name with a dollar sign ($).

Example

Two new ID mapping profiles (*ops_user* & *ops_group*) have been created for user bill_leung. If user bill_leung belongs to group ops on AIX (aix4-r1) and in group Users on WINNT (w32-ix86), the following steps must be taken:

a. On the Administrator Login Name field, enter **$ops_user**.

b. On the Group Name field, enter **$ops_group**.

c. Using the `widmap` command, add the following entry to the ops_user map: aix4-r1 bill_leung and w32-ix86 bill_leung

d. Using the `widmap` command, add the following entry to the ops_group map: aix4-r1 ops and w32-ix86 Users

The ID mappings for these two groups are shown as follow:

```
# widmap list_maps
# root_user root_group ops_user ops_group#
# widmap list_entries ops_user
aix4-r1 bill_leung
w32-ix86 bill_leung
# widmap list_entries ops_group
aix4-r1 ops
w32-ix86 Users
```

4. Set TMR Roles...

   This is where TMR-wide roles are granted to new administrators. By granting new administrators TMR-wide roles, administrators will assume the given roles (and the authorities that come with the roles) on *all* resources within the TMR.

Note

Roles are not hierarchical. For example, having a senior role does not imply roles of administrator and user. To be sure, always assign the required roles as listed by the product documentation.

5. Set Resource Roles...

   This is where administrator roles can be granted over system resources. By granting administrative roles by resources, tighter restrictions can be placed on the TMR where resources can only be administrated by the appropriate administrators.

Note

With resource roles, administrator roles need to be added to each administrator managing the resource each time a new resource is created.

In setting the TMR roles or the resource roles, the administrator designer must have detailed information on what job responsibilities and resources access each administrator is entitled to have. For example, if a specific administrator's job responsibility is to support all workstations and servers within a TMR, she/he would require TMR-wide roles remote_control. Whereas, for an administrator whose job responsibility is to support workstations only, she/he would require remote_control roles on resources/collections that are associated with all workstation class machines only but not server class machines.

6. Set Logins...

   This determines who and where a person is allowed to log in to the system as this administrator. For the example, in Figure 21 on page 72, the user *bill* can log in to the system from either the managed node shark.austin.ibm.com or cologne.austin.ibm.com.

   If an administrator is allowed to log in into the TMR from any manage node within the TMR, only the user account name is required for this field as shown as the first entry in Figure 21 on page 72. For administrators in an NT domain, domain name and user name can be entered as NT_DOMAIN_NAME\user_name.

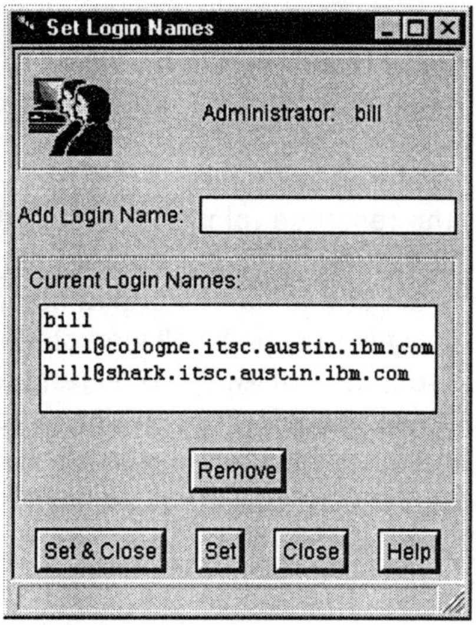

Figure 21. Set login

7. Set Notice Groups...

   This allows the appropriate notices to be assigned to the new administrator (by management application).

   The Tivoli Framework and each of its management applications comes with their own set of administrative notices. Notices are posted on the respective notices each time a task/operation is performed within the application discipline. Administrators can have access to the application notices to which they are responsible for by subscribing them to the appropriate sets of notices.

Note

Tivoli notices are expired after 168 hours (one week) with the exception of the Tivoli Scheduler notices, which expire after 72 hours by default. However, this can be shorten by using the `wexpnotif` command together with Tivoli scheduled task. Refer to *Framework 3.6 User's Guide*, GC31-8433 and *TME 10 Framework 3.6 Reference Manual*, SC31-8434 for usage of `wexpnotif` command, and creating scheduled Tivoli task

5.1.2 Organization

The input requirements in the context of an organization are similar to that for a single administrator as discussed in 5.1.1, "Single administrator" on page

68. However, in creating each individual administrator, consideration must be given to the effect that the new administrator design may have on the other administrators in the environment. For example, the label for each administrator in the TMR must be unique for distinguishing between different administrators. A strong naming convention should be placed and followed when defining Tivoli Administrators. Hence, the complexity of administrator design will increase as the number of administrators increases. Thus, a detailed level of planning and roles definition should be derived before administrators are created.

This section of the chapter will describe the inputs that the redbook team had identified and considered essential for the development of a complete administrator design strategy.

5.1.2.1 Administrator name/icon label

The content in this field will be used as the label for the administrator icon on the desktop, which will be used to distinguish between administrators. While an administrator is being created, an object is generated within the Tivoli object database using the entered administrator name as the object name. Therefore, this entry must be unique within the TMR in which the administrator is created. For details, refer to Chapter 2, “Naming convention” on page 19.

The inputs required and considered essential by the redbook team are:

Administrator list

A list containing the names of the administrators and their corresponding account user name in the organization. This is necessary in order to determine the unique administrator name/icon label for Tivoli to ensure that no two users have the same user account name on different NT domains and in order to derive a different naming convention if this does occur.

Physical design

The number of TMRs and their connectivity in the environment should be considered when developing a design for administrators. While an administrator label may be unique within a TMR, it may not be so when two or more TMRs are interconnected. On the other hand, if the physical design was not to have TMRs interconnected, then it is possible to have two administrators with similar administrator label names on two different TMRs.

5.1.2.2 User login name

The input requirements for a user login name in the context of organization design is similar to that for a single user as described in 5.1.1, “Single administrator" on page 68. The user account name must exist in the system resources where Tivoli tasks/operations will be executed.

The `widmap` command can be used to create/edit mappings for users with different user account name under different operating systems.

Administrator list
A list containing the names of the administrators and their corresponding user account name for each operating system that they will manage.

5.1.2.3 Group Name

The input requirements for group names in the context of organization design is similar to that for single user as described in 5.1.1, "Single administrator" on page 68. The group name that the specific user belongs to must exist on the system resources where Tivoli operations/tasks will be executed.

The `widmap` command can be used to create/edit the primary group to which the users belong under different operating systems.

The inputs required and considered essential by the redbook team is:

Administrators group list
A list containing the administrators' names and the corresponding administrative group to which they belong to under different operating systems.

5.1.2.4 Set TMR roles

The input requirement in the context of organization design is similar to that for a single user as described in 5.1.1, "Single administrator" on page 68. Administrators who have been granted admin TMR roles will have admin roles on *all* resources within the TMR. This also applies to all resources that are yet to be created.

The inputs required and considered essential by the redbook team are:

Organization's security policy
This document is used to determine whether administrators should have specific administrative roles on *all* resources within the TMR. It should explicitly state the access that personnel has on the organization's system resources and its business applications. For example: An administrator who is supporting all desktop workstations *only* in an environment should not have the remote_control TMR roles because it would enable the administrator remote control access on all resources in the environment, with server class machines included.

Administrators' job responsibilities

This document is used to determine the essential (minimum) administrator roles that administrators require to perform their usual administrative tasks. This document should explicitly state the type of resources that administrators are responsible for. For example, operating systems, machine class (desktops X servers), location site, business application, etc.

5.1.2.5 Set resource roles

Where administrators do not have the required authority to perform certain administrative tasks on *all* resources within the TMR, they could be granted their required access based on available resources (collections). Tivoli provides the facility to create policy regions where system resources can be associated to. Access to the required resources are granted by assigning the appropriate administrator roles to the policy regions that associate with the required system resources. This requires an adequate policy region design, which was described in Chapter 3, "Policy region design" on page 27.

As with setting resource roles based on available resources. administrative roles for administrators need to be updated each time a new application or resource is installed/created within the TMR. The input requirements the redbook team considered essential for assigning resource roles are:

Policy region design

This will contain all available policy regions/collections that exist within the TMR. Where system resources are grouped and associated to policy regions according to their properties, administrative roles can be assigned based on available policy regions in the TMR and system resources that are associated with these policy regions.

Organization's security policy

This document determines whether administrators should be granted TMR roles or roles by resources. Should administrators be granted roles based on resources? This document should provide details on resources that specific personnel is off-limited to.

Administrators' job responsibilities

This document is used to determine the essential (minimum) administrator roles that administrators require to perform their usual administrative tasks. This document should explicitly state the type of resources that administrators are responsible for. For example: Operating systems, machine class (desktops or servers), location site, business application, etc.

5.1.2.6 Set logins

Setting logins for administrators in the context of organization design is similar to that for a single administrator as described in 5.1.1, "Single administrator" on page 68. Different login names to those used in user login names can be used to log in to the system. This allows administrators to perform administrative tasks on system resources without the necessary privilege on that resource. The input requirements the redbook team considered essential are:

Administrators' privilege

This should highlight the privilege that each administrator should have within the organization for each system resource or groups of system resources.

Administrators' job responsibility

This document should highlight the administrators' job responsibilities within the organization. It should explicitly state the required roles required to perform the administrative tasks.

5.1.2.7 Set notice groups

Notice group subscription in the context of an organization design is similar to that for a single administrator as discussed in 5.1.1, "Single administrator" on page 68. Administrators can be subscribed to Tivoli notices by selecting the appropriate notice groups corresponding to each management application. Subscription to notices are mutually exclusive, that is, subscription of one administrator does not affect the subscription of another administrator.

The input requirements the redbook team considered essential in setting the notice group subscriptions are:

Administrator job responsibilities

This should highlight administrators' job responsibilities by Tivoli management application. Administrators can then be subscribed to the appropriate notice groups based on the management applications that they manage.

Event loads

This is used to determine how long the Tivoli notices should be kept in the Tivoli object database. The `wexpnotif` command can be used to alter the expire duration from zero hours to 186 hours.

Events reporting

This is used to determine whether administrators should save all notices from the Tivoli notice board. For events reporting purposes, administrators have the option to save notices after they have been read.

Events generating applications

Any in-house generated application, which can execute command-line-like commands, can forward events to Tivoli notices by using the `wsndnotif` command. Refer to *TME 10 Framework 3.6 Reference Manual*, SC31-8434 for usage of the `wsndnotif` command.

5.1.3 Summary of input requirements

In this section, all input requirements that the redbook team have considered essential for the design and development of an administrator strategy for a single administrator and for an organization have been identified and discussed.

In section 5.1.1, "Single administrator" on page 68, detailed description on each entry field relevant to the creation of an administrator has been provided. In the context of a single administrator, design and implementation of an administrator design can be performed disregarding its effects on other administrators within the environment. Thus, the input requirements for a single administrator requires little or no planning effort.

In Section 5.1.2, "Organization" on page 72 then expanded on the descriptions provided in section 5.1.1, "Single administrator" on page 68. Additional documentation and information, that the redbook team had considered essential in the development of administrators design, were introduced and described.

In the sections that follow, the team will examine the considerations that need to be addressed in developing an administrator design strategy.

5.2 Critical considerations

In the previous section, the team had identified the input requirements in the form of documentations and relevant information, which administrator designers should take into consideration when developing an administrator design for any system environment. Having gathered all the information required, the designer can then proceed to plan and develop the administrator design for a particular environment.

As mentioned in the beginning of this chapter, we will not attempt to give the readers a solution in developing a administrator design. Rather, the team will identify relevant considerations for designers to look out for when developing a design for administrators. The reason for doing so is because there is no single *best solution* for an administrator's design. A particular design might work well in certain environments and poorly on others. With this in mind, administrators' design may be different for different environment s to which the design is based on. The remainder of this section will describe the considerations that the redbook team had identified that may be of help to designers when developing an administrators' design.

All considerations described in the this section will be treated independently. While they might affect other considerations described here, they are treated independently to allow readers to understand the effects of each consideration.

The considerations that the redbook team had identified to be relevant are described in the following sub-sections.

5.2.1 Interview the workers

Very often, designers fall into the trap of assigning administrative roles to administrators based on their job title or administrator groups to which they belong. Experience has shown that administrators' effective roles and the kind of tasks that administrators actually perform rarely matches those that have been specified for them by their job title. Thus, assigning roles based on job titles often results in administrators not having adequate access to perform their day-to-day tasks, or administrators having access to resources that they are not suppose to. These factors can discourage administrators to use the product.

In order to match the administrators' roles to their administrative needs, administrator designers should understand the type of tasks and resources that administrators will need to manage. From these, they should determine the roles that specific administrators should be assigned.

Where the number of administrators is small (less than twenty) in an environment, the designer should conduct interviews with each administrator to create a profile for each administrator. The profile should specify an administrator's current job description and their access to various system resources and applications.

In an environment where the number of administrators is large (larger than twenty), an individual interview is not feasible. An approach would be to select administrators from representative administrator groups in the environment, and then create profiles for administrators to which the profiles are best suited.

The profiles created can be used in two ways:

- To identify discrepancies between the level of access administrators currently have and the level of access that management has specified, thereby, redefining the administrators access and roles.
- To help define administrators' roles within the TMR.

5.2.2 Number of administrators and system performance

In an environment where there is a large number of system and local administrators, the number of Tivoli administrators will also be large. Administrator designers should consider the effect that having a large number of administrators has on the performance of the TMR server. An object is generated within the Tivoli database each time an administrator is created. Where an operation requires cross-referencing of database objects against each administrator in the TMR, depending on the processing power of the TMR server, these Tivoli operations would require a longer period of time to execute.

Thus, in determining the number of administrators in the TMR, consideration should be taken on the resources available on the TMR server. In an environment where the TMR server is running on an machine that is inferior in processing power, the number of administrators should be kept to a minimum for higher performance. In an environment where the number of administrators is expected to be large, more resources should be allocated to the TMR server to sustain superior performance. This is also valid when you expect a large number of concurrent Tivoli Administrators with Tivoli desktops open. When the Tivoli desktop is opened by an administrator, a large amount of deamons (or processes) are spawned; therefore, the performance decrease can be much more noticeable.

5.2.3 TMR roles versus resource roles

Assigning TMR-wide roles to administrators in an TMR effectively grants them specific authorities on *all* resources within the TMR. In granting administrators resource roles, administrators only have specific authorities over resources to which they were assigned to. From the organization's security perspective, administrators' authority should be allocated through resource roles over TMR-wide roles because it allows senior administrators to assign authorities to junior administrators on an more granular level.

Assigning administrators roles using resource roles allows for more precise control over the authority on administrators. Consideration must be given to the additional capital required to manage administrators with resource roles. For administrators assigned with TMR-wide roles, the assigned roles will propagate to any newly created resources within the TMR. Thus, no additional effort is required before administrators can manage the newly created resource. For administrators assigned with resource roles, roles need to be added to these administrators for resources that have been created in the TMR.

In developing an administrator design for an organization, the organization's security policy, administrators' responsibilities, and organization structure must be evaluated when determining between TMR roles, resource roles, or a mix between both.

> **Note**
>
> The *user* TMR-wide role must be assigned to every administrator that will log in to the TMR through Tivoli desktop.

TMR roles should be used in assigning administrators roles where:

- The number of administrators is small (typically less than four). In such cases, administrators will likely manage all system resources in the environment. Thus, using TMR roles would be adequate for the environment.
- In assigning administrator roles to administrators who manage the whole subset of the same application, or by system management functionality. For example, admin TMR role for administrators responsible for Tivoli infrastructure roll-out, senior and super TMR roles for administrators who manage other administrators within the TMR, etc.

Resource roles should be used in assigning administrator roles where:

- TMR roles alone cannot provide adequate granularity in allocating system resources to administrators.
- Organization security policy requires that each administrators only be allowed access to those resource that they manage. For example: Administrators supporting desktop workstations cannot have access to business application servers.
- Organization structure does not allow administrators to access resources across the boundary of organization division and/or department.
- The TMR contains a large number of administrators with vastly different responsibilities. For example: An environment with groups of administrators managing machines and applications running on different operating systems.

- The environment prioritizes high availability. For this reason, administrators are given as little authority as possible on mission critical system resources to reduce the risk of unintended system tampering.
- System administration is distributed. For example: Local administrators only require access to resources within the local system environment.

Obviously, there are additional factors that must be considered when assigning administrators roles. As a rule of thumb, administrator designers should minimize the use of TMR roles and specify administrators roles by available resources. Administrator management complexity alone should not defer designers from assigning administrators roles using resource roles since this complexity can be reduced through the use of customized scripts.

It is all about finding the largest common denominator in-terms of administrator roles that gives the tightest access on resources. The larger the common denominator, the less the effort in managing administrators. However, extra care must be taken in determining this common denominator such that administrators won't have roles they should not have.

5.2.4 Avoid giving remote access

Having an unqualified current login name (user01) allows users access to the TMR from any managed node in the TMR. Using a qualified current login name (user01@machine_name) provides extra security by restricting users logging into the TMR through specified managed nodes. Users with unrestricted access to the TMR should only be allowed to log in through managed nodes with high securities features.

5.2.5 Unique current login name in an TMR

On setting current login name (Set Logins... -> Add Login Name) for an administrator. Tivoli (version 3.2 and later) had restricted use of an exact login name to more than one administrator. However, it doesn't restrict the use of a qualified name (user01@managednode) for one administrator and use of an unqualified name (user01) for another administrator. This should not be performed as the example that follows will demonstrate.

The following scenario was created in a test lab. An operating system user account *testuser* was created on two manage node systems (cologne.itsc.austin.ibm.com and shark.itsc.austin.ibm.com). Two Tivoli administrators were created: One with administrator named *user01* and its current login name as testuser, the other administrator named *user02* and its current login name as testuser@shark.itsc.austin.ibm.com. Both are shown in Figure 22 on page 82.

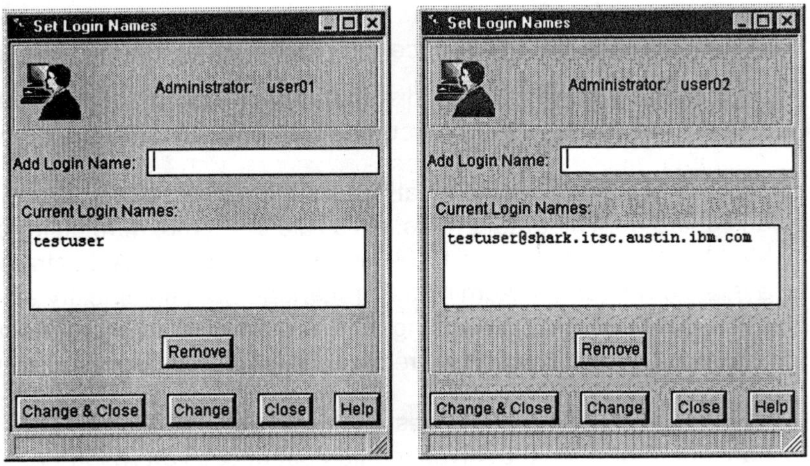

Figure 22. Current login name example

If the user *testuser* logs into the Tivoli desktop via the system shark.itsc.austin.ibm.com, Tivoli will interpret the user as administrator *user02*. If the user testuser logs into the Tivoli desktop via systems other than shark.itsc.austin.ibm.com, Tivoli will interpret the user as administrator *user01*.

Therefore, current login names should not be duplicated to more than one administrator; otherwise, scenarios similar to the example above may occur.

5.2.6 Avoid using default root user

A default root user should be created for each TMR server that is installed. This default root user will have full access to all resources within the TMR. It would have super, senior, admin, user, install_client, and install_product TMR roles on its list of assigned roles. Readers can use the `wauthadmin` command to get a list of administrators with the TMR root authority.

As a precaution, this default administrator account should not be used to perform any normal day-to-day operation in an TMR. Reason being: First, it is mapped to the UNIX root user and/or NT Administrator login name so that there is no way of keeping an audit on who had been performing operations using this administrator account. Second, it is because this account has full access on all resources within an TMR. Some tasks that have to be performed using this administrator are not reversible and/or cannot be undone by another user. Third, it is good practice to have an administrator with root authority who has the capability to create administrators and any other objects within an TMR if they were accidently erased by junior administrators.

The default root administrator account should only be used when:

- All administrators fail to perform some Tivoli administrative task. That is, it should only be used as a backup administrator if all else fails.
- To create and assign roles to those administrators who required access no other administrator can assign.

If administrators wish to have access similar to that of the default administrator, a new administrator account should be created with the default root administrator. Thereafter, assign all TMR roles and use the `wauthadmin` command to give the new administrator the root authority within the TMR.

5.2.7 Specify NT domain name in setting administrator login name

In setting the user login name for administrators (Set Logins -> Add Login Name) where the user belongs to an NT domain, the NT domain name should be specified as part of the user's login name. For example, for a user with user account name *user01* in the domain NTDOMAIN who can log in through managed node shark.itsc.austin.ibm.com, the login name should be \\NTDOMAIN\user01@shark.itsc.austin.ibm.com. Specifying the domain name in the user login name ensures that only users within a legitimate NT domain can access the TMR, while restricting users on different NT domains, but with the same user account, from accessing the TMR as the legitimate user.

5.2.8 Effective resource roles assignment

Administrators' resource roles are assigned based on available policy regions/collection in an TMR. Where an administrator is to be assigned resource roles to policy regions/collections that associate to one parent policy region/collection, administrator resource roles should be assigned to the parent policy region/collection since policy regions operate in a containment relationship. That is, resource roles assigned to one policy region/collection will also apply to resources that are underneath it in the hierarchy. This, coupled with an effective policy region design, can reduce the amount of effort in assigning administrators to resources within an TMR. This will be explained and demonstrated in Chapter 8, “Bringing it all together” on page 131.

5.2.9 Access resources without appropriate OS authority

Upon creating an administrator, a user account name on the local system or within a domain must be specified for the User Login Name field. The user name specified in this field will be used for accessing system resources during execution of Tivoli tasks. Thus, users who log in as this administrator can assume system access as the user specified in the User Login Name field when executing Tivoli tasks.

Tivoli allows multiple users to log in as the same Tivoli administrator. This is enabled by adding multiple login names (Set Logins -> Add Login name) to the same Tivoli administrators.

By combining these two Tivoli administrator features, users with non-administrative access can perform administrative tasks on system resources via the execution of Tivoli tasks.

Example

A user with user account *user01* on a system does not have write access to the /backup file system. Another user account *backup* has been created with appropriate access to /backup on the same system. A Tivoli administrator has been created with user *backup* as its user login name, and user user01@hostname has been added to its login name list. A customized backup task has been created to back up files to the /backup file system, with asterisk (*) as its privileged user. The user ID, *user01,* can now write backups to the /backup files system.

5.2.10 User login name auditing

The operating system user name that was specified under User Login Name field when creating administrators will be the default user that will be used for task execution when an asterisk (*) is specified as the privileged user name for the task. In the example in 5.2.9, "Access resources without appropriate OS authority" on page 84, the user backup was used when executing the task. The use of a generic user (backup) for task execution produced an undesirable feature on auditing at the operating system level. All administrators who run the task will be logged as user backup. Therefore, for accurate auditing of administrator activities, it is recommended to use the user's normal login when creating administrators.

5.2.11 Mapping administrators' user name

Tivoli allows users to manage several operating system as one administrator. If the user has different user names and group names for different operating systems, Tivoli provides an utility that contains the mapping of the user's different account names and groups under different operating systems. The `widmap` command allows senior administrators to create/edit the mapping for different administrators. Refer to 5.1.1, "Single administrator" on page 68 and the *TME 10 Framework 3.6 Reference Manual*, SC31-8434, for usage of the `widmap` command.

5.2.12 Single administrator for multiple users performing similar jobs

There may be situations where specific types of administrative users might manage the same resources (policy region/collection) and perform similar tasks (Task Libraries). For example; Call Center desktop support personnel whose job function might entail remote controlling of remote workstations and distribution of file packages to those workstations that have required periodic upgrade of application patches. In this case they would require similar authority on resources and to receive notices of the same class. As these groups grow, the management of users would become troublesome, as roles are changed periodically.

Using the Set Login -> Add Login Name function of Tivoli administrator, multiple users can log on as the same administrator and use its desktop to perform their administrative tasks. When a user needs to be added/removed from the specific job roles, it can be done by simply adding or removing entries to the Current Login Names (Administrator -> Edit Logins) list for the specific Tivoli administrator. This is much less troublesome than creating/deleting an administrator from the database each time a user needs to be added/removed from the environment.

Having multiple users assigned to one administrator does have its drawbacks. First, since all of the users share the same administrator, the subscription notices will be shared also. This means if the first user has closed a notice after it has been read, other users will not be able to read the same notice. Second, only one TEC console can be opened for a single administrator and its desktop, which means only one user can have the TEC console opened at a time.

Therefore, the decision on whether to use one user for one administrator or multiple users for one administrator depends on the needs and requirements for users of the same group. In general, designers can determine whether to use multiple users for one administrator or have one user for one administrator by asking the following questions:

- Do users need to read notices from the Tivoli desktop?
- If users will be reading notices from the Tivoli desktop, are missed notices an issue for the user?
- Do users' job descriptions require them to monitor events through the TEC console?
- If users are monitoring events through the TEC console, do these users all have to have the TEC console opened on their workstation?

If the answer to all of the questions above are *NO*, then multiple users for one administrator may be used. However, if the answer to any of these questions is *YES*, then one user for one administrator should be used.

Note

The decision between one user for one administrator and multiple users for one administrator can not rely solely on the manageability of its administrators. Other considerations should be taken into account. For example: Accountability of its administrators and/or administrator arrangement within the organization.

5.2.13 Tivoli desktop limit

A TMR can support a maximum of 30 concurrently active desktops, regardless of how the desktop is to be used (TEC consoles, remote control, etc.). This limit is driven by tests performed in a lab environment. In a TEC environment, the number of desktops is limited by the amount of traffic due to routing of events to consoles and updates against the database. For other desktop activities, the limits are driven by the TMR oserv deamon and the dsl activity associated with using the desktop.

A TMR server should be configured to support no more than 10 concurrently active Tivoli desktops. If more than 10 are required, additional administrative managed nodes should be added to the configuration. For performance reasons, desktops should not be run from the TMR server. A managed node should be used for this purpose.

5.2.14 Accountability

Accountability, in the context of system management, refers to the ability to identify the owner of a process or a method. This allows senior administrators to identify who, and at what time, initiated a task to run on an system. Accountability can used for the following purposes:

- Detect security breaches on system resources.
- Back track and understand the series of events that lead to application or system errors. This assists in identifying possible causes of errors.
- Allows senior administrators to appraise administrators' access to system resources against job responsibilities.
- Work tracking.

With each operation that has been initiated from the users' Tivoli desktop, a corresponding Tivoli notice is posted to the initiator's desktop and the appropriate notice group. For example: The user *user01* has decided to create a collection within its own desktop. Once the collection is created, a message will be posted to *user01*'s desktop as well as to the appropriate Tivoli notice group (TMR Administrator for this case). The notices for the desktop is shown in Figure 23.

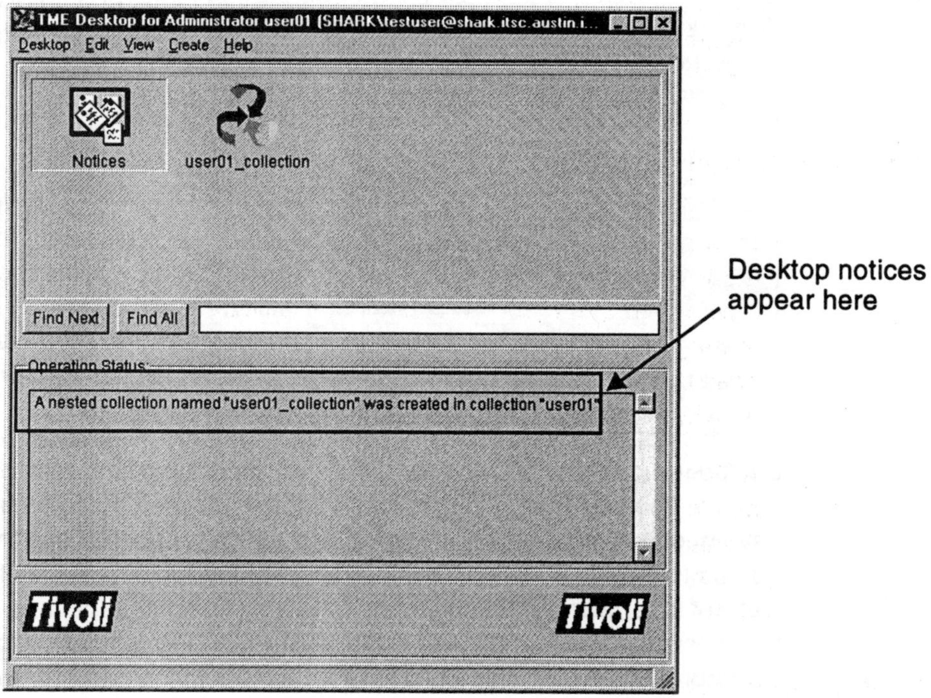

Figure 23. User desktop notice

The notice group is shown in Figure 24 on page 88.

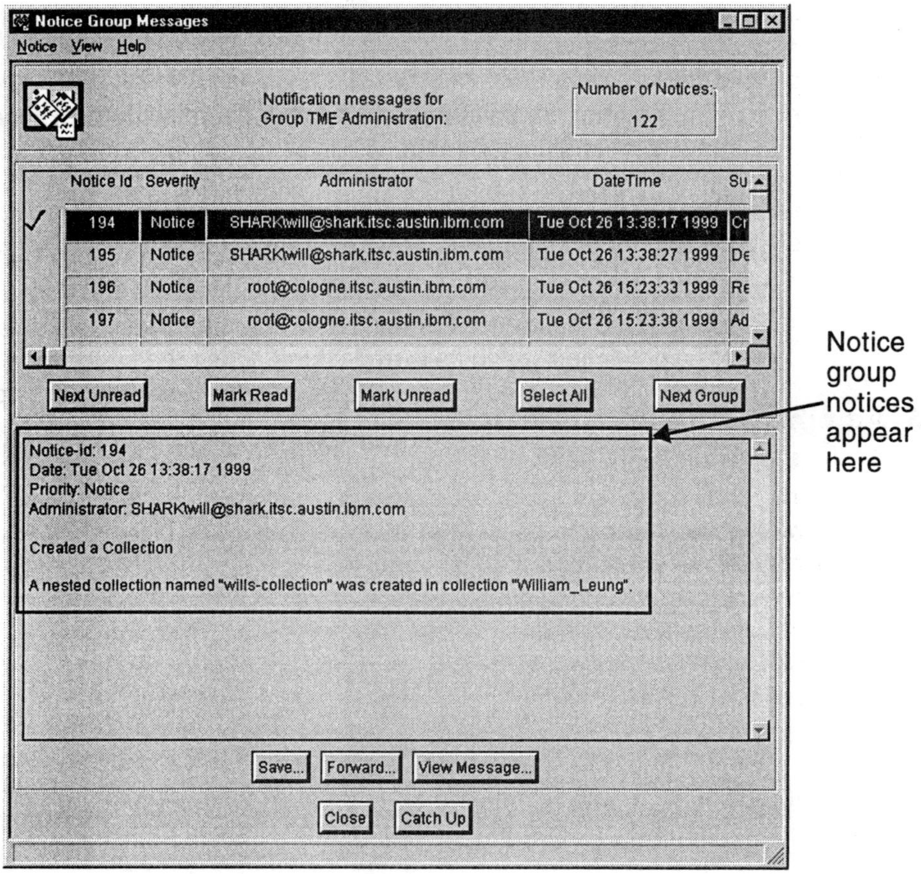

Figure 24. Notice group notices

The desktop notice is just a notice board that informs the administrators of any operations that have been performed via the current desktop. Notices that are posted to the Tivoli notices can be accessed by administrators who have been subscribed to the appropriate notice group. Notices that have been posted to the Tivoli notices will include the user login name (Set Login -> Current User Name), the time when the activity took place, and the body of the message. Therefore, in a multiple users for one administrator configuration as discussed in 5.2.12, "Single administrator for multiple users performing similar jobs" on page 85, each user can not be distinguished by their user login name.

Where organizations require accurate auditing information on its more senior administrators, Tivoli notices alone may not be appropriate since notices cannot be read by administrators once it has been closed. More accurate auditing of users for accountability can be achieved by using one user for one administrator configuration with user's normal operating system account mapped to User Login Name (Create Administrator -> User Login name) as described in "User login name auditing" on page 84. This allows logging of events on the operating system level, such as removal and creation of files.

Tivoli allows administrator designers to define the level of auditing on administrators for accountability. Where accountability is not a priority, as in cases where administrators do not have destroying roles (Event monitoring), the level of auditing provided by Tivoli notices may be adequate. On the other hand, more accurate auditing can be utilized for administrators who hold more destructive roles.

5.2.15 Administrators in collections

An administrator collection is created by default during the installation of the TMR server. When an administrator is created within the TMR, it is *linked*, or *referenced,* to this collection. In addition to the default administrator collection, Tivoli administrators can also be linked to Tivoli generic collections. A generic collection is a set of objects or reference to multiple objects, similar to that of policy region but without the features of the default policy and validation policy. As such, a generic collection can contain reference to virtually any type of object within the TMR.

A generic collection can be used for the following purpose in administrating administrators:

- It provides a hierarchical structure where senior administrators can coordinate specific administrators into smaller groups with common characteristics.
- It provides a shortcut for senior administrators to locate specific administrators among a large pool of administrators.
- By coordinating administrators into hierarchical structure, it allows senior administrators to delegate administrator functions to junior administrators based on their locality within the administrator hierarchy.

The advantage of using collections in coordinating a large number of administrators is demonstrated in Figure 25 on page 90. On the left, administrators are associated to the Administrator Collection by default, where administrators are not coordinated in any logical order. On the right, administrators are coordinated into smaller groups (level 2) based on their common characteristics. Common characteristics can be of locations where administrators are based, business units they belong to, alphabets of administrators' name characters, and many others.

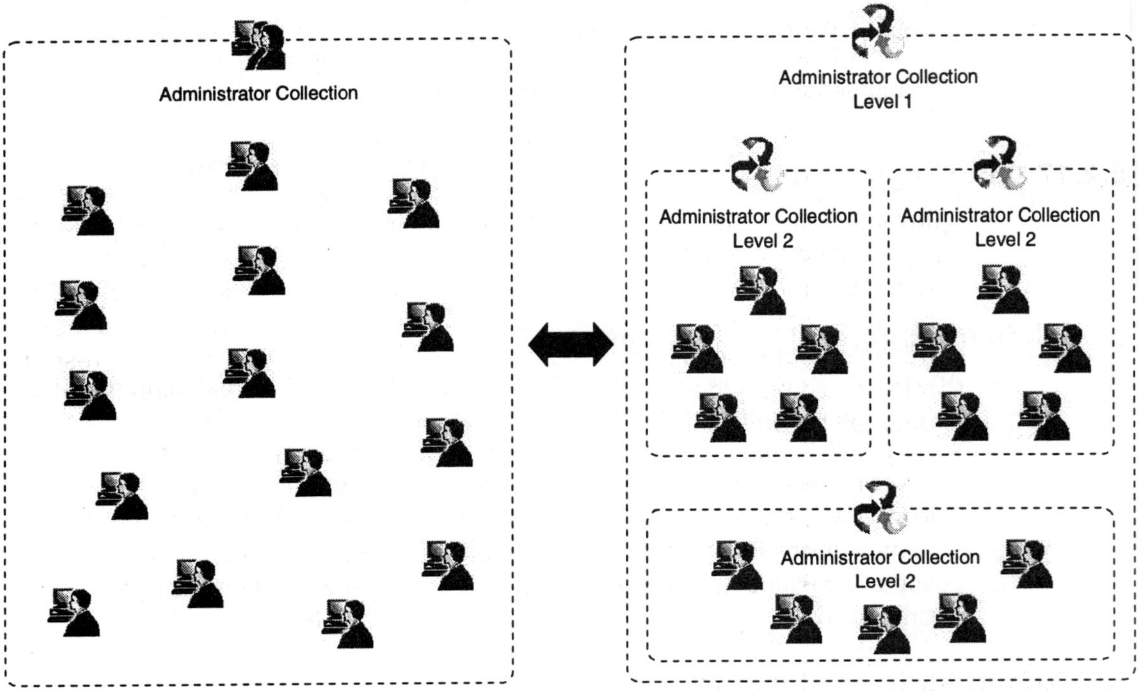

Figure 25. With and without collection comparison

5.2.16 Desktops icons: What to place on an administrator's desktop

The motivation of developing an administrator design was to ensure that administrators be given adequate level of access to system resources, which allow them to perform their required administrative tasks, thus, the concept of resource roles used by Tivoli. For resource roles, administrators are assigned roles to specific policy regions in order to manage resources that associate with these policy regions/collections. They should also be given *shortcuts (links)* to these policy regions. Given the same argument, administrators should not be given *shortcuts (links)* to those policy regions/collections that they have no access to since:

1. They cannot perform any administrative activities on these resources.
2. They still have the ability to see the resources within the collection, even though they cannot perform any tasks on them. This is a feature of the user TMR role.

Note

> With the Tivoli built-in navigator, administrators with the user TMR role can browse for all resources within the TMR. This accounts for all administrators who have access to the Tivoli desktop. In 5.3.2.1, "Adding security to Tivoli built-in navigator" on page 93, we will show readers how to add security to the Tivoli built-in navigator.

5.2.17 Inter-region administration

In situations where TMRs are interconnected, considerations must be given to the effects that interconnections have on administrators' roles. Resource roles within the local TMR would not be affected by the interconnection because these roles are assigned based on available resources. If a local administrator wishes to have access to resources on a remote TMR, resource roles could be added to the administrators after the resource type has been updated on the local TMR.

All TMR roles, with the exception of the super TMR role granted within the local TMR, are effective on an remote TMR as they are in the local TMR once administrator resources are exchanged between TMRs. In the case of a super TMR role, it will be effective as the user TMR role on remote TMR.

5.3 Administrators' desktop design

Tivoli desktop provide administrators with another alternative to manage Tivoli managed resources if they are not given CLI access to Tivoli management servers. It provides a logical view of system resources that are being managed by Tivoli. These system resources can be managed as Tivoli Framework clients (Managed nodes) or as Light Client Framework clients (Endpoints) and may consist of desktop workstation class machines, servers class machines, and mainframes. These resources can be managed individually or as a logical group by using policy regions and/or profile managers.

The objective of enterprise system management is the effective management of system resources performed by a number of system administrators within the system environment. Thus, system administrators must be allowed appropriate access to resources that fall under their responsibilities, while restricting them access to all other resources. This would prevent inexperienced administrators from performing destructive tasks on mission critical systems, thus, reducing the risk of an unintended security breach.

Tivoli administrator roles and Tivoli desktop working in combination would provide the level of restriction control that is required for effective management of system resources. This can be achieved by:

1. Assigning appropriate TMR roles and resource roles to specific administrators.
2. Restricting what administrators can "see" through the Tivoli desktop

5.3.1 Administrator role requirements for Tivoli desktop

Administrator access to resources within an TMR can be controlled by granting TMR roles and/or resource roles to specific administrators. Administrators that have been assigned TMR roles would have those specific roles on all resources within the TMR. For resource roles, roles would only be granted to administrators by individual resources or groups of resources.

For a detail description of administrator roles, please refer to the appropriate sections in 5.1, "Input requirements" on page 67.

We dedicate Appendix A, "Tivoli administrators roles" on page 239 in providing a complete set of tables highlighting the TMR roles or resource roles required when performing certain administrative tasks via the Tivoli desktop. Similar listings for Command Line Interface (CLI) can be found in the *TME 10 Framework 3.6 Reference Manual*, SC31-8434, and in each management application's reference manual.

Note

The redbook team discovered that different methods were executed between the Tivoli desktop and CLI, even when the same operations were performed. As each method may have different administrator role requirements for its execution, required administrator roles may be different between Tivoli desktop and CLI.

5.3.2 Administrators' visibility

Administrators' visibility, in the context of desktop design, refers to the number of objects that are associated to an administrator's desktop. Objects that are associated to an administrator's desktop will become *visible* to the specific administrator when he/she log in to the Tivoli desktop. By default, only the Tivoli notice board is associated to a newly created administrator desktop. Once an administrator is created, senior administrators can then associate the appropriate Tivoli resources to the new administrator desktop based on the accessibility of the specific administrator within the TMR. For considerations and strategies on object association with administrator desktops, please refer to 5.2.16, “Desktops icons: What to place on an administrator’s desktop” on page 90.

A feature that comes, by default, with Tivoli administrator desktop is the Tivoli built-in navigator. The Tivoli built-in navigator enables administrators with user TMR roles to browse for specific Tivoli resources within the TMR. Since all administrators must have the user TMR role to access the Tivoli desktop, administrators would have the ability to browse for resources that were not associated to their desktop. This then conflicts with point two: “*Restricting what administrators can see through the Tivoli desktop*” in 5.3, “Administrators’ desktop design” on page 91. The subsection that follows will detail the steps that may be taken to implement added security to the Tivoli built-in navigator.

5.3.2.1 Adding security to Tivoli built-in navigator

The Tivoli built-in navigator allows administrators with user TMR roles to browse through any resources within the TMR. Two strategies will be introduced here They are:

1. Change the TMR role required to open the Tivoli built-in navigator.
2. Another TMR role is added to existing set of TMR roles. Administrators must be granted this new TMR role in order to access the built-in navigator.

Change required TMR role for built-in navigator

This solution involves changing the TMR role required in order to open the built-in navigator. By default, TMR role *any* was assigned to the open-navigator method. The solution described in this section will allow senior administrators to alter the open-navigator, method-required TMR role to a more senior administrator role.

The script in Figure 26 on page 94 has been customized to alter the method-required TMR role for opening the built-in navigator to any one of the following:

- super
- senior
- admin
- user
- any

Note

The *any* entry means that administrators with any TMR roles will be able to open the built-in navigator. This is the default TMR role that was assigned for the built-in navigator.

```
#!/usr/local/Tivoli/bin/aix4-r1/contrib/bin/perl

# This script will query the user the TMR role that the open-navigator method should
# map to. Thereafter it will ask for users to re-confirm, and will proceed to change
# The required TMR role for the open-navigator method. The assigned TMR role can only
# be one of the following:
# super
# senior
# admin
# user
# any

%valid_roles = ("super", "*", "senior", "*", "admin", "*", "user", "*", "any", "*");

print "Enter the new TMR role for the built-in
navigator:\n[super/senior/admin/user/any] > ";
chop ($new_tmr_role = <stdin>);
if ($valid_roles{$new_tmr_role} ne "*") {
   print "invalid role entered\n";
   exit (0);
   }

$nav = `wls -o /Library/navigator`;
@nav=split(/\#/, $nav);
chop ($oid = `resolve $nav[0] open`);
chop ($old_tmr_role = `objcall $oid om_get_acl open`);
print "Required TMR role will change from '$old_tmr_role' to '$new_tmr_role'\n";
print "Are you sure ? [y/n] > ";
chop ($response = <stdin>);

if ($response eq "y") {
   objcall $oid om_set_acl open $new_tmr_role`;
   print "The TMR role for built-in navigator is now ";
   print ($nav_role = `objcall $oid om_get_acl open`);
   }
else {
   print "program terminated\n";
   exit (0);
   }
```

Figure 26. A Perl script to change built-in navigator role requirement

After this script is executed, the required role for opening the built-in navigator has been changed from the default of *any* to either super, admin, senior, user, or *any*. Thereafter, unless an administrators has the specified TMR roles above to use the built-in navigator, the administrator will get an "*insufficient authorization*" error when attempting to open the built-in navigator.

To reverse the required role change, the same script can be executed to change the required role back to the default entry of *any*.

Add another TMR role for opening built-in navigator

This solution involves the addition of another TMR role to the existing list of TMR roles and mapping of the open-navigator method TMR role requirement to the newly created TMR role. A customized script, as shown in Figure 27 on page 95, has been created to automate these tasks for users.

```
#!/usr/local/Tivoli/bin/aix4-r1/contrib/bin/perl
#
# This script will query user for the name of the new TMR role for use with
# navigator. Thereafter the new TMR role will be created, and the navigator
# role requirement will be assigned to the newly created TMR role
#
print "What will be the name of the new TMR role for built-in navigator > ";
chop ($newrole=<stdin>);
chop ($aco=`wlookup -o Administrators`);
`idlcall $aco add_supported_tmr_role '"$newrole"'`;
#
$nav = `wls -o /Library/navigator`;
@nav=split(/\#/, $nav);
chop ($oid = `resolve $nav[0] open`);
chop ($old_tmr_role = `objcall $oid om_get_acl open`);
print "navigator required TMR role will change from '$old_tmr_role' to '$newrole'\n";
#
`objcall $oid om_set_acl open $newrole`;
print "The TMR role for built-in navigator is now ";
print ($nav_role = `objcall $oid om_get_acl open`);
```

Figure 27. A Perl script to add TMR role and change navigator

Once the script shown in Figure 27 has been implemented, administrators who require assess to the navigator will require to have the newly created navigator TMR roles added to their assigned TMR roles.

To reverse the effect of the script shown in Figure 27, senior administrators can execute the perl script shown in Figure 26 on page 94 to change the open-method TMR role requirement back to *any*.

5.3.2.2 Removing all menu items from administrator desktops

To effectively prevent administrators from performing destructive operations through the Tivoli desktop, you can think about removing menu items from the desktop. The extreme, and sometimes most effective method, is to remove all available menu items from their desktops. This, together with the limiting of available Tivoli objects on their desktop, described in 5.2.16, “Desktops icons: What to place on an administrator’s desktop” on page 90, can limit the type of resources administrators can access, thus, preventing them from accidental removal or deletion of mission critical Tivoli resources.

Tivoli AEF provides additional commands that can be used to alter the dialog of each individual resources that appear on an administrator's desktop. Thus, Tivoli AEF, which is provided along with the Tivoli Framework CD, must be installed. The steps that follow will detail the actions required in altering the desktop dialog of one particular administrator's desktop:

1. Create a temporary directory, /tmp.
2. For security purposes, create a backup of the original dialog for resource Administrator desktop. The following command will create a compiled copy of the Administrator desktop dialog in the /tmp/Adm.desktop.original file:

   ```
   wgetdialog -r Administrator desktop > /tmp/Adm.desktop.original
   ```

3. Create an non-compiled copy of the Administrator desktop dialog. This file will be edited to remove the required menu items. The following command will create an non-compiled copy of the desktop dialog to /tmp/Adm.desktop.source.dsl file. An example of this file can be found in Appendix B, "Desktop design files" on page 259.

   ```
   wgetdialog -r Administrator desktop | rdsl > /tmp/Adm.desktop.source.dsl
   ```

4. Edit the *.dsl* file you have created. You can choose to remove certain buttons or menus from the Administrator desktop by removing their corresponding button or menu entries from /tmp/Adm.desktop.source.dsl file. Our file example can be found in Appendix B, "Desktop design files" on page 259.
5. Compile the edited .dsl file by using the following command:

   ```
   dsl /tmp/Adm.desktop.source.dsl > /tmp/Adm.desktop.compiled.dsl
   ```

6. Assign the compiled edited dialog to the appropriate administrators using the following command. In our example, the Tivoli administrator label is `helpdesk`:

   ```
   wputdialog -l @Administrator:helpdesk desktop < \
   /tmp/Adm.desktop.compiled.dsl
   ```

7. The Tivoli administrator help desk will now have the new desktop dialog according to the changes you have made.

You may choose to go further and change additional attributes on the Tivoli desktop. In addition to the Administrator desktop dialog, the following dialogs can also be changed by performing steps two through seven described above:

- PolicyRegion desktop

  Editable dialog file by issuing the following command:

```
wgetdialog -r PolicyRegion desktop | rdsl > \
/tmp/PolicyRegion.desktop.source.dsl
```

- TaskLibrary view_dialog

  Editable dialog file by issuing the following command:

```
wgetdialog -r TaskLibrary view_dialog | rdsl > \
/tmp/TaskLibrary.view_dialog.source.dsl
```

- ProfileManager main

  Editable dialog file by issuing the following command:

```
wgetdialog -r ProfileManager main |rdsl > \
/tmp/ProfileManager.main.source.dsl
```

Note

Some of the information contained in 5.3.2.1, “Adding security to Tivoli built-in navigator” on page 93 and 5.3.2.2, “Removing all menu items from administrator desktops” on page 95 were based on information found in the following Web site:

http://www.orb-data.co.uk

The redbook team have decided to present the material discussed in this section because of its relevance and the added flexibility to the overall Tivoli desktop design. In general, tempering of TMR roles and internal methods are NOT recommended by Tivoli, as they may affect the overall operation of a Tivoli environment.

5.4 How administrators work

This section describes how IDMAP (and the roles) is used to determine if an administrator can preform a certain activity and how this activity will be done.

5.4.1 ID mapping

The IDMAP is used to map a symbolic name to user ID on the destination platform. Whenever an administrator executes an activity on the target, there is a need to obtain a user ID for the task being executed. This can be done using static user ID names or using an IDMAP entry.

Figure 28 shows the general schematics of the IDMAP. On the left of the figure are the IDMAP maps. Each map is composed of a set of IDMAP entries (shown on the right side of the figure).

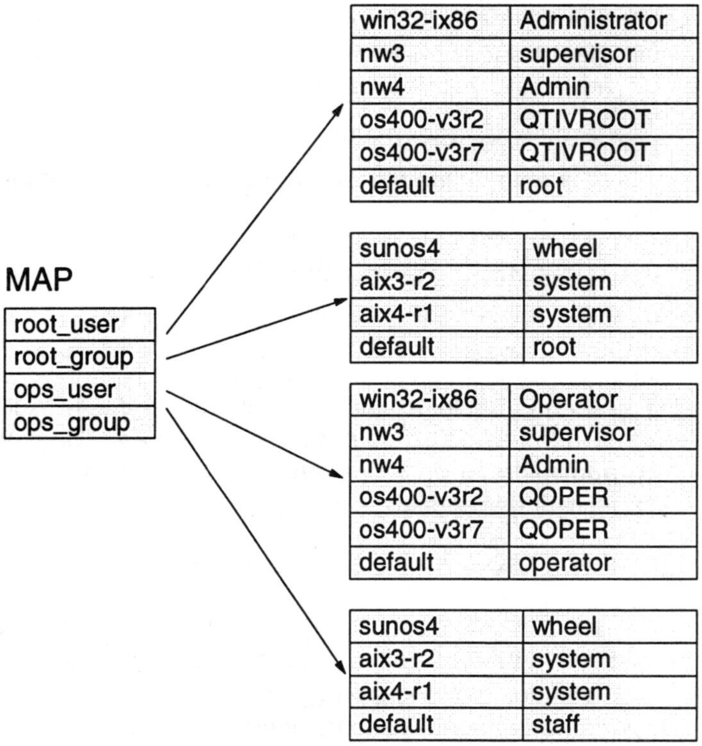

Figure 28. IDMAP structure

Whenever the user ID specified in a task is preceded by a dollar sign ($), the IDMAP will be used. The remainder of the name is the map to be used. Once the map has been determined, the entries are searched. If there is a entry that corresponds to the platform of the target, the values for that entry is used. Otherwise, the default entry is used. If the ID map or entry cannot be found, the task will fail.

Given the example shown in Figure 28 on page 98, let's assume a task states user $ops_user must run a task on three different platforms: os400-v3r7, win32-ix86, and sunos4. Since the name has a dollar sign, the IDMAP will be used. The ops_user map will be used, and the following user ID will be used:

- QOPER on the os400-v3r7 target.
- Operator on the win32-ix86 target.

- Operator on the sunos. This value is assumed using the default entry since there is no entry for sunos4.

Adding new maps can be very useful when not all user should have access to the root account. Setting the static user ID can be lead to problems in a heterogeneous environment.

Note, however, that the IDMAP will only distinguish operating system platforms. So, if a new map is created and administrators and tasks are using this new map, the account to be used must exist in all the machines of the same platform.

5.4.1.1 Editing the IDMAP

All the management of the IDMAP is done using the `widmap` command. This command can be used to create, update, and delete maps. The following section shows some examples on how to use it. All results are based on the IDMAP shown in Figure 28 on page 98.

Managing maps

The following options can be used to manipulate the maps on the IDMAP:

- To list the existing maps, use the following command:

  ```
  widmap list_maps
  ```

  The output should be similar to:

  ```
  root_user root_group ops_user ops_group
  ```

- To add a map, use the following command:

  ```
  widmap add_map newmap_user
  ```

- To remove a map, use the following command:

  ```
  widmap rm_map newmap_user
  ```

Note that the root_user and root_group maps should not be deleted. They are used for many of the TME activities.

Managing entries

To manage the entries in each map, the following operations can be made:

- To list the entries in a map:

  ```
  widmap list_entries root_user
  ```

  The output should be similar to:

  ```
  default root
  w32-ix86 Administrator
  nw3 supervisor
  ```

```
nw4 Admin
os400-v3r2 QTIVROOT
os400-v3r7 QTIVROOT
```

- To add an entry to an existing map, use the following command:

  ```
  widmap add_entry root_user os390 SYSPRG1
  ```

- To remove an entry from the map, use the following command:

  ```
  widmap rm_entry root_user os390
  ```

- To check which user ID will be used for a map on specific platform, use the following command:

  ```
  widmap resolve_entry root_user os390
  ```

  The output will be the name resolved using the IDMAP. If the map does not exist, an error will occur.

5.4.2 Checking security and executing

All the attributes of an administrator and the ID maps come together when administrators try to execute methods and run activities on machines.

Figure 29 on page 101 shows the flow used to determine whether or not an administrator can execute a given method based on the required Tivoli role.

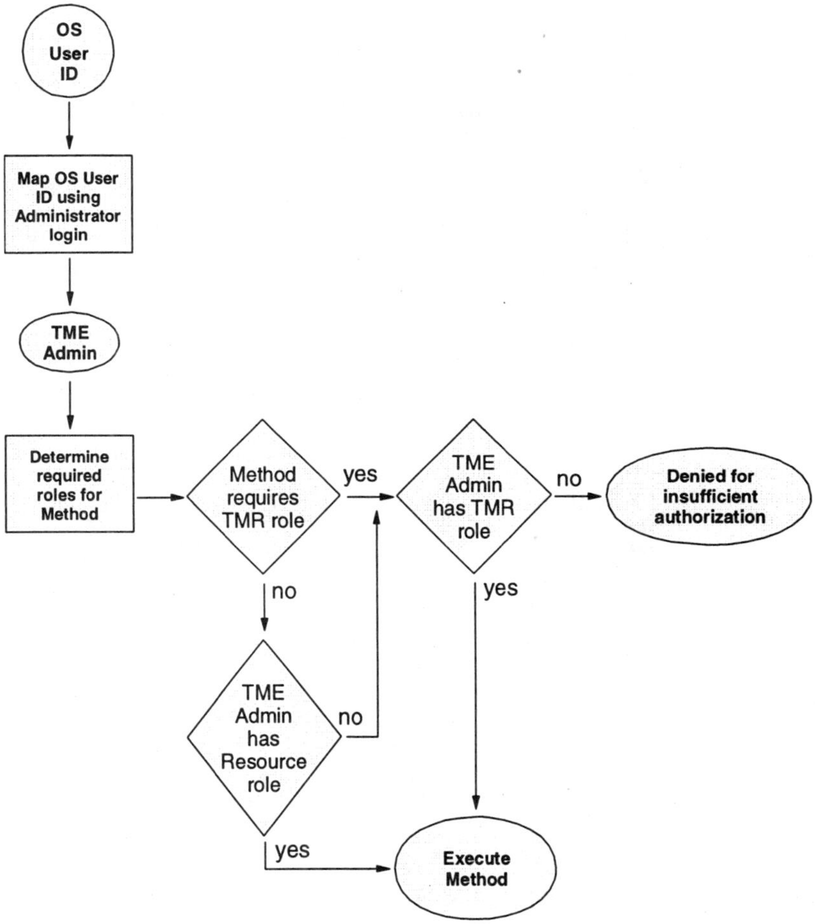

Figure 29. Checking administrator roles

The first step is to map an existing operating system user into a Tivoli administrator. This happens every time a CLI command is executed or when an administrator logs on to their desktop. This is done using the logon user ID and checking which administrator has this entry in their login list.

Once the administrator has been mapped into a TME administrator, he or she can execute his or her method. Each method has its own access control list (ACL) that determines which kind of roles are required. These roles can be either TMR roles, resource roles, or a combination of both. In order to determine which the roles are required to execute the method on an object, Tivoli first needs to find out where the object resides (normally policy regions), then, by knowing the method name, Tivoli can identify which roles are required to invoke the method.

When the method's ACL is determined, then the administrators' roles are checked against this ACL. If a resource role is required, the administrator must have these roles. If they do not have the resource roles, TMR roles are checked. If either the TMR or resource roles required have been granted to the administrator, they can execute the method. If not enough resource or TMR roles were granted, the method is not executed because of insufficient authorization.

Once the required authorizations have been checked, the method is executed. If the method requires that a given process be executed on a target machine, an user ID will have to be determined before executing the process. The determination of which ID to be used is done using the flow shown in Figure 30.

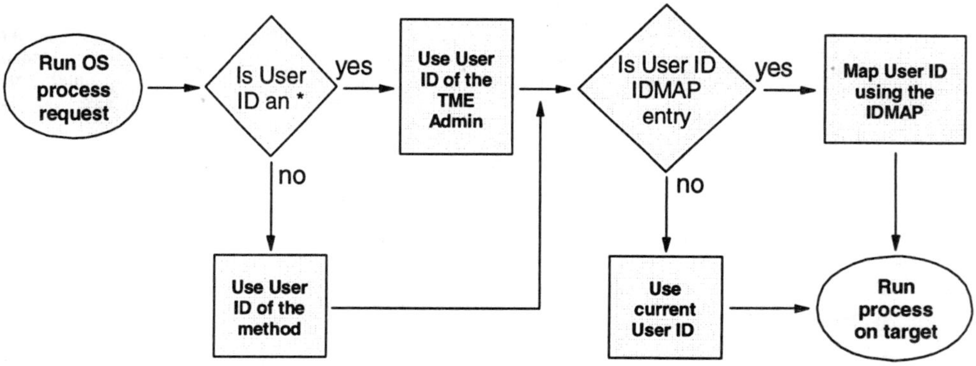

Figure 30. Running processes from a TME administrator

When a certain process must be executed, the method that requires its execution will contain some kind of user ID information. This information may be one of the following:

- User ID
- ID map entry
- Asterisk (*)

If the user ID is an asterisk, then the user ID of the administrator must be used. When an administrator is created, he or she will be given a user account name and a group name. This name can be either a static user ID or an ID map entry. The ID specified on the administrators' creation will be used in case the method's user ID is an asterisk.

If the user ID of the method is not an asterisk, that user ID will be used.

The next task involves determining if the current user ID is an ID map entry or not. It will be a map entry if it starts with a dollar sign ($). If it is a map entry, the ID map will be used to determine which user ID should be used for that entry in the target's operating system. If no entry exists with this name, an error is generated (not shown in the Figure 31).

If the user ID is not an ID map entry, then that user ID will be used in the target system.

The task is executed on the target system using the user ID determined by the flow as described above. If no user can be found with that user ID, the execution will fail.

Chapter 6. Interconnected TMRs considerations

The Tivoli Framework provides the ability to subdivide the Tivoli Management Environment (TME) into multiple, connected Tivoli Management Regions (TMR). In this chapter, we discuss some of the issues involved with the Tivoli Logical Design when the Tivoli physical design holds out a multiple TMR scenario. In order to do this, we choose the Hub-Spoke model architecture for interconnecting the TMRs. This model is widely used by Tivoli. The ideas exposed here may apply to other ways to connect TMRs as well.

6.1 The Hub-Spoke model architecture

The network topology and the management system's performance goals are the primary determinants influencing physical topology under which the Tivoli Management Environment will be installed and configured. In the case of customers with large network environments, experience has shown that a Hub-Spoke architecture is often a good recommendation.

In a Hub-Spoke architecture, the TME is segmented into several Tivoli Management Regions. The reasons for implementing this, for instance, can be for performance, scalability, and management reasons. For instance, each one of these TMRs can be placed to be responsible for directly managing a different physical segment of the enterprise, responsible for business units, or placed based on distributed management access purposes.

The way you plan to administer your Tivoli environment will dictate the way the Spoke TMR will be connected to the Hub TMR. In an one-way connection, the Hub TMR will act as a manager of the Spoke TMR. The Spoke TMR will not be able to view the Hub TMR managed resources. This means that no administrators defined in the Spoke TMR will be able to perform operations on the Hub TMR. In other words, the kind of TMR connection used in a Hub-Spoke model architecture will be defined by the way the administration of the Tivoli environment should be performed. This is required to determine if the environment will be managed in a centralized or distributed fashion. We previously discussed centralized or distributed administration in detail in Chapter 5, "Administrators' considerations" on page 67.

The Figure 31 on page 106 shows the typical design of a Tivoli Hub-Spoke model architecture.

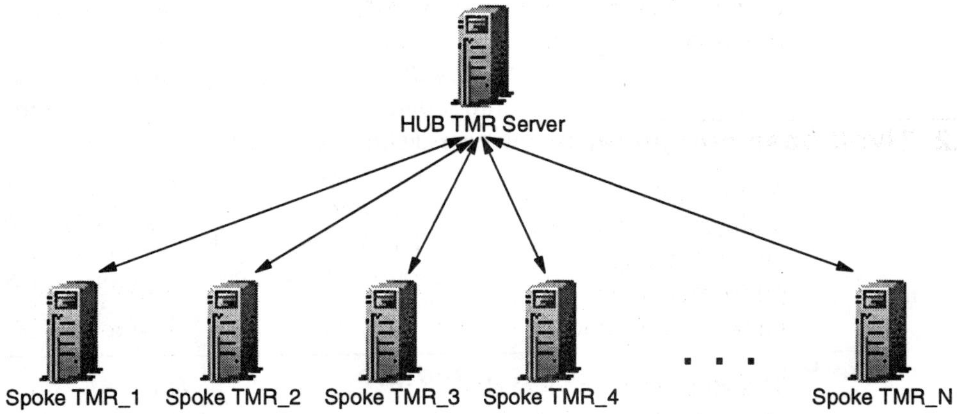

Figure 31. Hub-Spoke model architecture

The Hub TMR server has, as one of its roles, to provide a centralized management server in its own dedicated TMR. The Hub TMR server directly manages a limited number of resources so that it can be dedicated primarily to the support of analysts accessing the management functions in the TME. In addition, it can be the focal point for hub-wide activities such as required, for example, to configure and distribute monitoring profiles to any servers in the environment.

The Spoke TMRs provide the direct control function to all endpoints in the TME. Spoke regions can be used to group managed nodes by physical location in the network and to localize Tivoli functions to that physical location to improve network and system performance. Generally, Spoke TMRs are not used as entry points for administrators. (This is not a hard and fast rule). Tivoli administrators can use either the Hub TMR or any managed node strategically placed in the design as an entry point into the Tivoli management environment.

The discussion about why multiple TMRs can be used is very long, and several reasons can be found. Among these reasons are: Server loading, number of clients, network limitations, local administration, security, and the need for a single view of non-shared resources. The design parameters that go into a Hub-Spoke solution are almost exclusively definable by server loading and the number of client considerations.

This model supports a centralized management paradigm. All managed function operations are performed through the Hub TMR. Remote TMRs are placed and configured to optimize network utilization and system performance and to distribute TMR server loads. Scalability is achieved primarily through the use of gateways and TMA endpoints.

6.2 Tivoli base components in a Hub-Spoke model

As mentioned before, the main usage of a Hub-Spoke model in a Tivoli architecture is regarding performance improvements through distributing server loading. For instance, Spoke TMR servers help to improve performance when performing enterprise-wide inventory scans as well as allow the introduction of local TEC servers for special requirements.

The Hub-Spoke model does provide scalability when planning a Tivoli design solution. However, the TMR servers no longer serve as the primary tool for achieving scalability in a Tivoli 3-tier architecture. The primary role is now played by the endpoint gateway. Figure 32 on page 107 shows how Tivoli based components may be placed in a Hub-Spoke model.

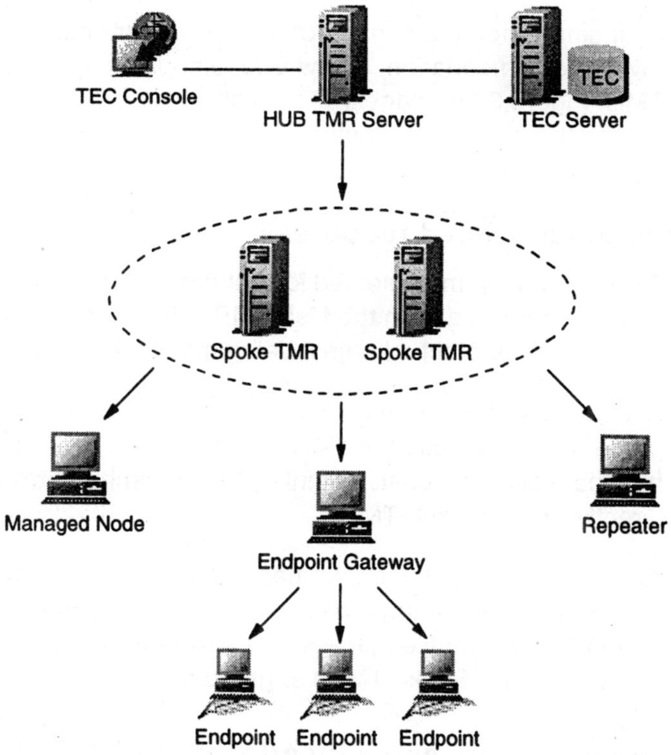

Figure 32. Tivoli base components in a Hub-Spoke model

The Hub TMR server forms the central administration point from which all managed functions are performed within an TME. Administrators' desktops and TEC consoles are defined and configured in this TMR.

The TEC server can be configured either as a managed node contained within the Hub TMR server or on a stand-alone TMR in the same layer as the Hub TMR server.

All managed systems are spread out into the Tivoli environment and connect to the Spoke TMR server most appropriate to that system based on the Spoke TMR server loading and on the physical network location.

Managed nodes will still be required in this environment. For example, we can have managed nodes to support remote Tivoli administrators desktops.

Endpoint gateways are installed throughout the Tivoli environment to host endpoints. In this TME hierarchy, all endpoint gateways are assigned to Spoke TMRs only. When adding endpoints to this environment, they will be hosted off of a gateway within a Spoke TMR that is placed close to the endpoint. When the number of endpoints per endpoint gateway exceeds the Tivoli recommendation, a new Endpoint gateway can be added to the Spoke TMR. Figure 32 on page 107 also shows how the Hub-Spoke model fits into the Tivoli 3-tiered architecture.

6.3 Organizing the managed resources

With a properly implemented logical design, virtually all TME-wide operations can be performed from the Hub TMR without concern for where in the Spoke environment the actual object being manipulated actually exists.

A logical layer of Policy Regions and Profile Managers combined with the proper interconnection of TMRs placed on top of this physical architecture will provide a simple, consistent interface to manage portions of the enterprise directly from the Hub TMR.

As a general rule, it is recommended that you construct your policy region and your profile manager design in a way that you keep as much of the policy region and the profile manager hierarchy in the Spoke TMRs as possible as well as use the Spoke TMRs to group similar systems.

6.3.1 Nodes, applications, and subscribers model

As shown in Figure 33 on page 109, when defining the nodes policy region, it should be done by creating a hierarchy of policy regions so that each Spoke

TMR hosts a second level policy region that is different from each other. While creating a managed node, it is important to be sure that it is being created inside a policy region that is defined in the Spoke TMR closest, depending on the network topology, to the managed node.

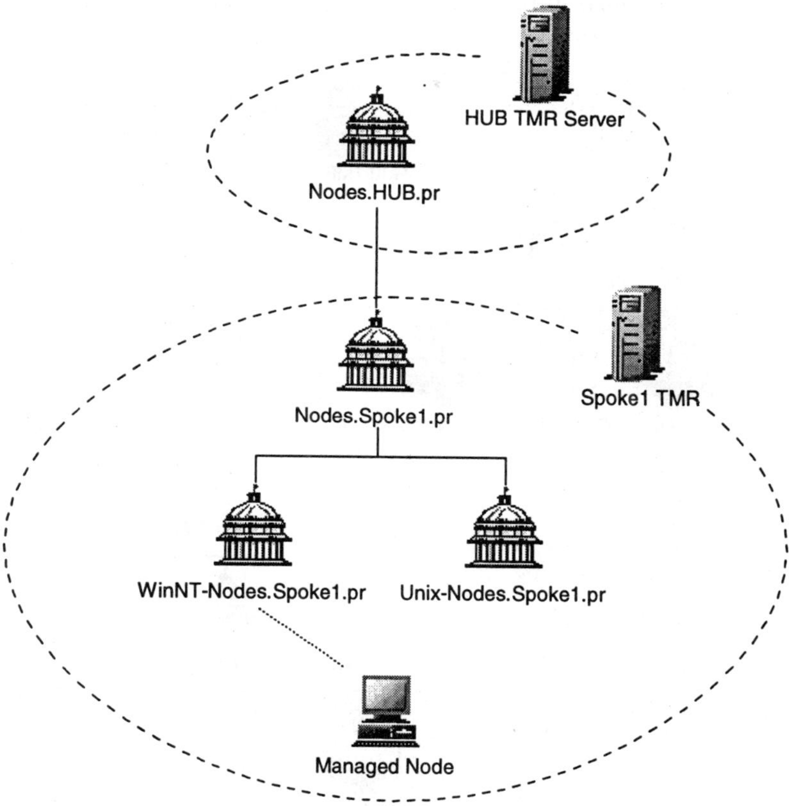

Figure 33. Nodes policy region example into a Hub-Spoke model

When planning the application's policy region, it is recommended that the policy region and the profile manager hierarchy should be created only in the Hub TMR. The subscriber to the application's profile manager schema would be the profile manager defined in the subscriber policy region defined in the Spoke TMR. This way will allow the Hub TMR to be the central point of operations for application functions. This schema is shown in Figure 34 on page 110.

In order to plan a subscribers' policy region design in a Hub-Spoke environment, you should consider the case of defining a subscribers' policy region for each TMR. By doing this, managed resources (managed nodes, endpoints, and so on) will not be subscribed to profile managers across TMR boundaries. As shown in Figure 34 on page 110, subscriptions should be made indirectly through profile managers in the Spoke TMR being subscribed across the TMR boundaries into the Hub TMR. This will force management to focus on profile manager as the managed objects instead of endpoint as managed objects. However, it is the goal of the logical design to attempt to minimize the profile manager across subscriptions as well.

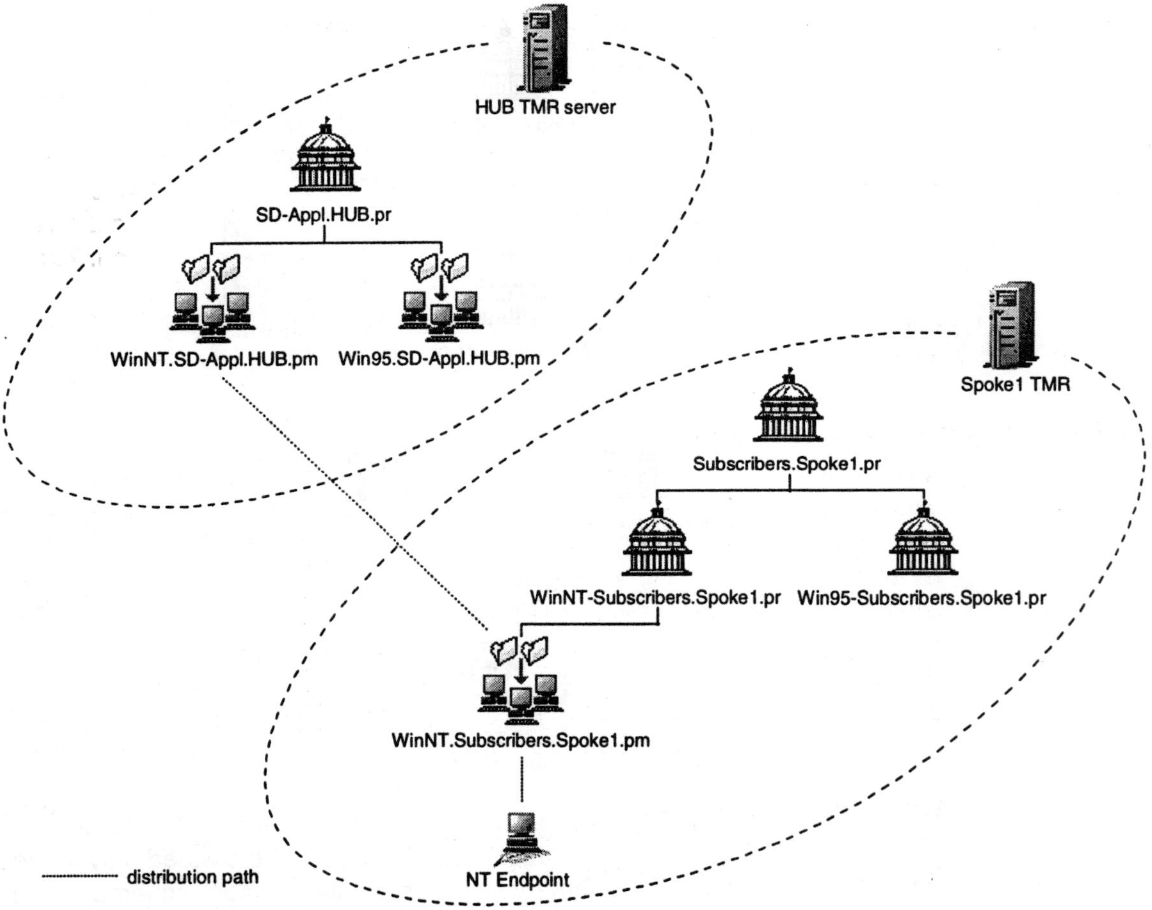

Figure 34. Subscription example in a Hub-Spoke model

Management through the profile manager provides better performance and scalability. One important point to watch out for is that all profile distribution should be done through the profile manager hierarchy. If the distribution is performed by selecting the profile and the target endpoint, the result will be as if the endpoint was subscribed across TMR boundaries. The distribution will go directly from the Hub TMR to the endpoint without passing any of the processing loads on the Spoke TMR. It increases the processing loads on the Hub TMR and increases the distribution times.

Another reason not to have endpoints subscribed across TMR boundaries is the Tivoli Framework database growth and maintenance. When performing a clean-up operation with `wchkdb` command, these types of cross TMR subscriptions require the Hub TMR server to check a much larger number of objects for consistency then would otherwise be required.

Experience has shown that, by implementing these recommendations, you get some operational difficulties. Operators will require well defined procedures when distributing a profile to a individual machine. An idea to relieve this impact to operations when performing these special procedures would be by using tasks to distribute profiles rather than distributing directly. The approach taken would be a function of the logical design chosen. There is no need for operations to be performed from the Spoke TMRs. All operations can be performed from the Hub TMR but require that a suitable logical design be put in place.

6.3.2 Subscription hierarchies

A subscription hierarchy with various levels results in a larger number of intermediate profiles being created for Tivoli profile based applications, such as Distributed Monitoring or User Administration. When a profile distribution is performed for the first time, a copy of it will be placed on each intermediate level of the hierarchy. When performing the distribution from now on, each a profile copy in the hierarchy must be compared against the current copy being distributed and updated as required before the distribution continues. This can not only cause performance problems when distributing profiles, but also the Tivoli Framework database can grow as the number of objects increases.

When designing subscription hierarchies, this performance impact should be understood. There is no fixed definition on the number of levels to define. Experience has shown that two or three layers deep within a TMR is fine, with the possibility of four or five layers being acceptable when you take the cross TMR subscriptions into account. Generally, flat and wide subscription designs will perform better than narrow and deep hierarchies.

6.3.3 Subscribing X exchanging resources

As mentioned in 6.3, “Organizing the managed resources” on page 108, it is very important in a interconnected TMR environment that you have the least number of subscriptions across TMR boundaries as possible.

Subscribing affects multiple objects in the framework database, and by consequence, the framework maintenance is also affected. Let's suppose there is a managed node subscribed to a profile manager across a TMR boundary. When performing a maintenance operation with the `wchkdb` command, the profile manager's check method will track down all of subscribers of this profile manager to check their status. This means a lot of cross TMR checking will be required to be performed because these objects (the subscribers) are in another TMR. The process described here is one of the common causes of a database maintenance performance

Exchanging resources between TMRs is a different matter. When resources are exchanged, the name registry in each TMR server is updated with the information of an existing object in another TMR. This provides a yellow pages kind of capability that allows the TMR to find an object when it has to. The name registry is a single object that needs to be checked during the maintenance process. The registry's check method does not need to track objects down anything across TMR boundaries. Therefore, exchanging objects results in no performance issues when you perform a framework database maintenance operation.

Exchanging endpoint resources across TMR boundaries is not an issue. No objects are created when this exchange is done, and the Hub TMR's database does not grow substantially by the exchange.

The following table identifies all Tivoli framework resources and informs you whether they are exchangeable between TMRs or not.

Table 3. Framework exchanged resources between TMRs

Tivoli Framework resource	Exchangeable
ActiveDesktopList	No
Administrator	Yes
AdministratorCollection	Yes
Classes	No
Distinguished	No
Endpoint	Yes
EndpointManager	Yes
Gateway	Yes
Job	Yes

Tivoli Framework resource	Exchangeable
ManagedNode	Yes
PatchInfo	No
PcManagedNode	Yes
PolicyRegion	Yes
Presentation	No
ProductInfo	No
ProfileManager	Yes
ProfileEndpoint	No
Repeater	Yes
Scheduler	No
TMF_Notice	Yes
TaskLibrary	Yes
TaskRepository	Yes
TopLevelPolicyRegion	Yes

It is important to remember that resources and resources types are created by both the Tivoli Framework and Tivoli applications. Therefore, there are sets of resources that must be exchanged if they are to work across TMR boundaries. Also, every Tivoli application may have specific resource names that are not exchanged and, thus, might exhibit different behaviors when crossing a TMR boundary.

6.3.4 Authorization roles across TMR boundaries

A TMR role enables an administrator to perform operations that may affect resources anywhere in the local TMR. If you assign an administrator any TMR role other than super, the role does map to the same role across the boundaries of connected TMRs. For example, if an administrator has the TMR role admin in the Hub TMR, this administrator will have the admin role in the Spoke TMR. The same is valid when there are two TMRs connected in a one-way connection.

The super role does not map to super across TMRs; it maps to users in connected TMRs. Administrators with the super role can perform tasks that require the super role only within the TMR in which the administrator was created. To assign an administrator the super role in an interconnected TMR environment, you must create separate administrators in each TMR. However, creating separate administrators still does not allow tasks requiring the super role to complete across TMRs. This mapping is a security precaution so that no administrator accidentally gets the super role in all TMRs.

6.3.5 RIM considerations

When preparing a Tivoli Solution Logical Design, it is important to take into consideration not only the applications involved, but also the resources these applications create and work with when being installed.

A very important topic within these considerations is the RIM. The RIM is a Framework service used by certain Tivoli applications to get access to a database.

The RIM is a distributed service implemented in three different parts as described below:

- A specific joint of API's used by the Tivoli applications.
- The RIM object that is stored in the distributed Tivoli object database.
- The RIM daemon that is used by the APIs. The machine where this daemon is running is known as the RIM host.

The RIM daemon may be a heavy process that affects the performance and use of resources of a system. For this reason, the selection of the machine where the RIM is going to be placed is critical for the performance of the Tivoli solution. The RIM host is a managed node that, depending on the application that is going to make use of the RIM service, may have more than one function.

6.3.5.1 Inventory RIM considerations

When planning the profile definition schema for Tivoli Inventory, some attention should be given to the location of the Inventory RIM host.

When an Inventory profile is created, it resolves the object ID of the Inventory RIM host in the TMR in which it is created. When the profile is distributed, it will use that RIM host to pass data back up to the Inventory server. When an Inventory profile is created in the Hub TMR and distributed to endpoints defined as subscribers in the Spoke TMR profile manager, all the inventory traffic will pass up through the Hub TMR's RIM host. This will limit performance by bypassing the RIM hosts that may be defined in the Spoke TMRs.

Basically, there are two types of scan that should be considered. One is the *rolling* inventory scan, where the enterprise is to be scanned over a period of time. The second would be the one off scan where an operator would scan a given machine. For performance reasons, Inventory profiles that are used to support the *rolling* scan requirement should be created in the Spoke TMR. Inventory profile pushes should originate from within these Spoke TMRs using the RIM host in those TMRs to direct the results to a common inventory database pointed to be all the RIM hosts. For special off scans, an Inventory profile can be created in the Hub TMR is distributed directly to the endpoint to be scanned. Figure 35 shows a graphical representation of the Inventory profile distribution schema.

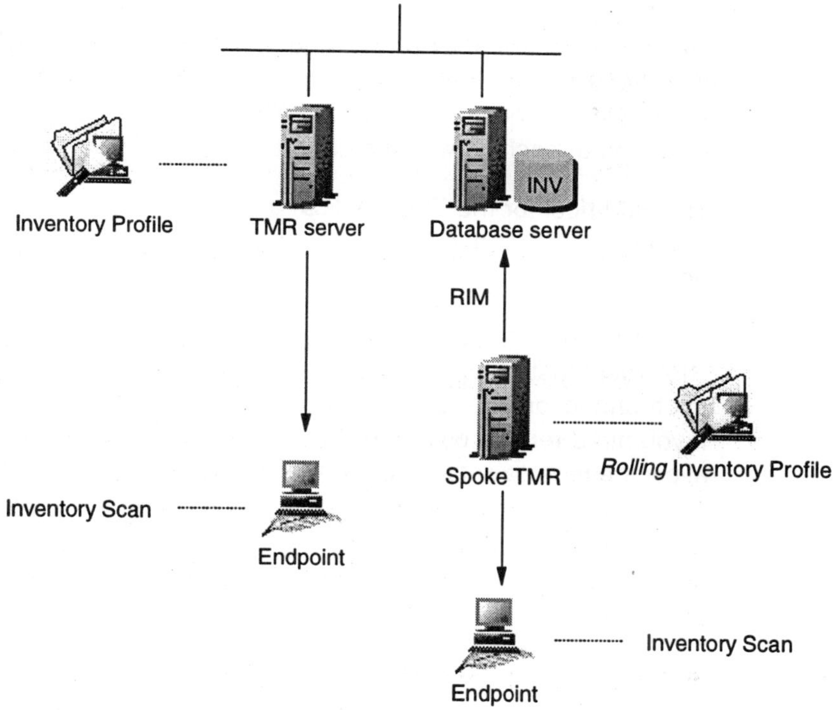

Figure 35. Recommended inventory scan

6.3.5.2 Tivoli Enterprise Console considerations

The configuration of the Event Server, the RIM host, and the Consoles for Tivoli Enterprise Console depends on the locations and the number of administrator consoles you are planning to create, the location of the Event Server, and the amount of information you are calculating.

Since the main functions of the Enterprise Console are to receive, parse, and store events and event information, there is a high rate of information exchange between the Event Console, the Event Server, and the Database. For this reason, you may decide to have all of them on the same box, or decide to have them in separated machines. Either way may present advantages and disadvantages, as we will describe in the following segments.

The installation of the Event Consoles is not such a critic process although you have to take care about the number of consoles and the machines where you create them and their locations. You may change their locations. This does not apply with the Event Server and the RIM host because the installation and configuration of them are the basis of the rest of the TEC logical design.

The Event Server is the place where all the event reception, event filtration, event correlation, rules processing, and console updating takes place. For this reason, it is recommended to select a dedicated machine, and although you could also decide to have the RIM host on the same server, the result would be a machine with a high rate of memory and processor load.

The RIM host for the TEC application, since it is the device the Event Server will retrieve information from and write information to, will require a big deal of network bandwidth as well as a large amount of memory.

For an interconnected TMR design, the location of the Event Server and the RIM host must be on the same region, and, depending on your interconnection needs, you may have only local consoles or remote consoles. If you need remote consoles, there must be a two way connection in order to allow the remote console to connect to the Event.

Chapter 7. Policies

This chapter describes the policy considerations when designing a Tivoli solution and provides technical information required to be applied when designing the policy region, profile manager, and Tivoli administrators' schema.

7.1 What are policies?

A policy is a written rule that you put into effect for a system that Tivoli enforces when management operations are being performed by administrators. Several classes of objects in the Tivoli Framework are policy driven objects. This means that their behavior can be controlled, to some extent, by policies. These policies are themselves objects. A policy driven object will check the policies to which it is submitted when changes and operations are applied to it.

7.1.1 Policy objects and policy methods

Policy objects are objects used to store the policy for a certain type of policy driven objects. It represents a collection of methods that define how the policy is implemented. Policy objects can be for either default or validation policies. Each policy driven object has a basic policy object defined for it and which is used for cloning.

Any number of policy objects can exist in a TME. The policy objects are associated to the policy driven object either through policy regions or to the profiles directly (additional information will be described in 7.2, "Profile policies" on page 118).

Each policy object will have several policy methods. Each method represents how one specific aspect of a policy is implemented. The number and names of the methods is defined by the policy object. A policy object for a specific policy driven object will always have the same policy methods.

7.1.2 Default policies

Default policies are used to determine two types of information: What will be displayed in the GUI interface and when the objects are opened or created. They are also used to set the values for fields not supplied by the user.

Some products, such as Tivoli Remote Control, use the default values as a way of restricting the access to certain machines, operations, and modes of use.

Other resources will use them to define which values should be displayed in the list. This is the case with profile managers. The values listed in the subscriber lists are determined by policies.

7.1.3 Validation policies

Validation policies are used to verify the values supplied by users when changing or creating objects. They are called before the update is done so that they can be used to ensure the values are in accordance to the policy. Note that not all objects have validation policies.

The validation policies are checked when the changes are done by the command line interface (CLI) or by the GUI. When a Tivoli administrator is performing some activities by using the CLI commands, where no defaults values are provided, it can be very important to set validation policies to ensure that the commands are not being used in violation of the policies.

7.2 Profile policies

Some of the framework applications implement policies by associating the policies directly to a given profile. This is the case for Tivoli User Administration and Tivoli Security Management, for example.

The way these products where designed, each profile will represent a specific group of resources under the same policy. If policies were to be defined in the policy regions, and each profile had its own policy, they would have to be in different policy regions. To avoid this, policies are determined per profile, not policy region.

Each profile contains a set of default and validation policies. The profile default record specifies the default values used when a new profile item is added. The default values are profile-specific. The profile validation records specify the validation policies used when a new profile item is added or an existing profile item is modified. An administrator that wants to edit profile default or validation policies must have the senior or super role.

The profiles policies can be set using the command line interface or using the GUI interface. These policies are discussed in the product manuals and on redbooks associated to the product. Refer to them for more information on how to manipulate these policies.

7.3 Profile manager policies

As with other managed resources within the Tivoli architecture, profile managers are also controlled with default and validation policies. The profile manager policies can be modified in order to attend the operational requirements of one particular Tivoli environment. This can be achieved by using the commands depicted in 7.5.2, "Tivoli commands for policies" on page 125.

The default policy defines which managed resources can become subscribers to a profile manager. The following are the default policy methods provided by the Tivoli architecture for profile managers:

pm_def_subscribers This method is called when it's time to retrieve all available potential subscribers to a profile manager.

pm_def_profile_types This method is called when it's time to retrieve all available, indirectly managed profile resource types of the policy region argument for choosing which type of profile to create.

pm_def_profile_managers This method is called when it's time to retrieve all available profile managers to clone a profile to.

The Validation Policies govern profile manager subscriptions. The following are the validation policy methods provided by the Tivoli architecture for profile managers:

pm_val_subscribers This method is called when it's time to validate potential subscribers to a profile manager.

pm_val_subscription This method is called when it's time to validate potential subscribers to a profile manager or a profile endpoint.

pm_val_remove_subscribers This method is called when it's time to validate the removal of a subscriber of a profile manager.

pm_val_remove_subscription This method is called when it's time to validate the removal of a subscriber of a profile manager or profile endpoint.

7.4 Using policies

Policies are an extremely powerful tool that can easily be used to enhance existing logical designs. They can be used to:

- Increase security
- Enforce design rules and characteristics
- Simplify the administrator views

They do not replace proper logical design and can be very difficult to implement if the design is not effective.

Policies, as security elements, should not be seen as a replacement for other security aspects. They should be used when the TMR roles and resource roles have been already used and do not provide the required security.

Also, be aware that policies can have a performance impact. Over elaborated and slow policies will slow down regular operation, potentially leading to failures. Always make them as simple as possible and use them only when other options have been exploited.

7.4.1 Changing Tivoli supplied default

Each resource type that has been designed to work with policies will have a system wide default created by Tivoli. In some cases, customers will want to have their own policy available across all the policies. The easiest way to have this is to change the policies supplied by Tivoli.

This has been widely suggested in educational material but can pose support problems. The best way to have these global policies is to create a policy based on the Tivoli supplied policy and then create all policies using that modified policy as illustrated in Figure 36 on page 121.

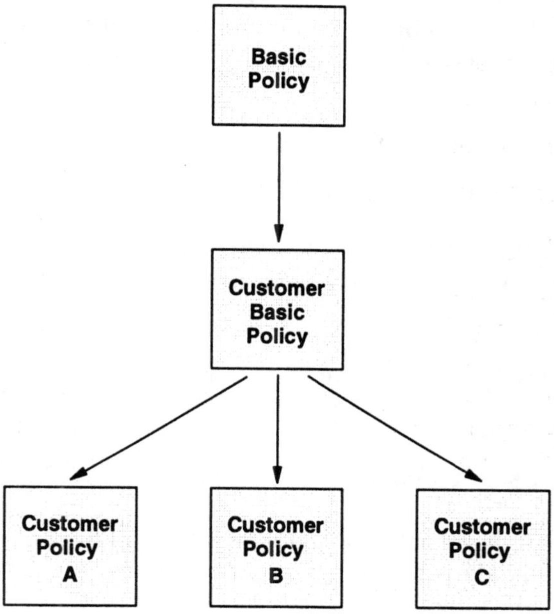

Figure 36. Creating customer basic policies

Before creating the specific policies, the administrator creates a customer basic policy. This policy will be adjusted according to the global policies defined by the enterprise. Once this base policy is created, this customer specific basic policy is used as a model.

Another option is to have a basic policy saved in files and have a script that creates a new policy and applies the values stored in the files to this new policy before editing a given policy.

7.4.2 Policies and policy regions

Some policy driven objects have policies associated directly to them. This is the case of Tivoli User Administration profiles and Tivoli Security Management profiles. In this case, each profile has its own policy, and they can all be grouped in one policy region even if they have different policies.

Most policy driven objects have their policies defined by the policy region they exist in. Each policy region can define one validation and one default policy for a given resource type. Different policies can be used for different resources.

This has a direct impact on the policy region design. If resources of a given type should have different policies, they will have to be created in different policy regions. This is one reason to use policies with caution. If too many different policies are to be enforced, the number of policy regions can increase drastically.

7.4.3 Using default policies

The main use of default policies is to restrict the amount of managed resources visible when working through the desktop. CLI commands allow a much larger visibility of resources. With commands, such as `wlookup`, any administrator can know all the resources available. But, not all administrators have access to the CLI.

Default policies can be used to limit visibility of objects. For example, if within a given region, only endpoints should be subscribers, change the default policies so that only endpoints are displayed. Changes like this can make it much easier to ensure that resources are used correctly.

Default policies are critical for Remote Control security because this product only has default policies, and they can restrict the type of operation being done with Remote Control.

7.4.4 Using validation policies

Validation policies objective is to check the values supplied by the user and see if they are acceptable values. It is the natural place to enforce policies like:

- Naming conventions
- Subscriber restrictions
- Actions restrictions

These restriction may not really be required in all environments but should be used to insure a smooth and effective use of the TME solution.

Another use of validation policies is security enforcement. This allows administrators to be restricted even further than the normal Resource roles and TMR roles would allow.

Remember that validation policies will be in effect in the entire region. This means that no administrator will be immune to them. This will mainly control the actions being performed on the entire region.

One way of using policies to enhance security is to create a freeze policy. This policy will return a FALSE or negative values on all methods that refer to changes. While this policy is in effect, no change will be possible. When an administrator wishes to change something within the region, he or she must first disable the policy. Once changes have been made, they enable the policy.

7.5 Working with policies

The commands and procedures required to create and edit policies are described in the *TME 10 Framework 3.6 Reference Manual*, SC31-8434. This section provides some additional information on how the commands should be used together.

7.5.1 How policies are written

The policies object is a set of policy methods. Each method stores the value for the policy as text or a binary file. This text can contain any number of lines and may represent a constant value or a script file. If the policy method is a text, the value can be edited using any text editor.

Policy methods can have any of these values:

Empty There is no value store on the method. This represent an inexistent or non-implemented policy.

Constant values This is a text constant value. The same value is always used, and it would be equivalent of a script that echoes that value to the standard output and exits with a return code of 0.

Script Is a normal shell script that returns the values through the standard output (just by writing to it) and can exit with several different codes. If the exit code is 0, the policy is assumed to have run correctly. Other values indicate failure when executing the script.

Binary File It is theoretically possible to use a binary program within a policy. If a program is used, be aware that it will not be platform independent, which may lead to problems when running the policies.

The simplest policy after an empty policy is the constant policy. Figure 37 on page 124 shows the value for a constant policy. Independent of the parameters, the policy will always return TRUE and run effectively.

```
TRUE
```

Figure 37. Sample constant policy

Figure 38 shows a script that also returns a constant value. The policies shown in Figure 37 and Figure 38 are equivalent. However, the last one does not perform in the same way. If the policy always returns the same value, it should be a constant value, not a script to avoid unnecessary overhead.

```
#!/bin/sh
echo "TRUE"
exit 0
```

Figure 38. Sample constant script policy

The last sample, shown in Figure 39, represents a script that does some kind of validation. In this example, the first parameter represents the operation being done and the second parameter represents the object to which the operation is being applied.

```
#!/bin/sh

OPER=$1
OBJ=$2

if [ "$OPER" = "DELETE" ]; then
        echo "FALSE"
elif [ "$OPER" = "LOCATE" ]; then
        echo "TRUE"
else
        exit 1
fi
exit 0
```

Figure 39. Sample script policy

This policy returns FALSE if the operation is a DELETE and returns TRUE if the operation is a LOCATE. If the operation is not one of the two, it exits with a return code of 1, which indicates the policy was not invoked with the proper parameters.

This is an example that shows how policies can be used to enforce security on objects.

7.5.2 Tivoli commands for policies

Most of the manipulation of policy region specific policies has to be done using the command line interface. Once the required objects are created and edited, there is a GUI interface to define which policies should be used.

Most action on Policy Region policies must be done using the CLI. There are several commands that should be used to manipulate the policies. Here is a brief explanation on each one:

`wsetpr`	Assigns the policy used in a policy region, enables or disables policy validation, and adds or removes a managed resource in a policy region.
`wchkpol`	Checks policy-region members against policy.
`wcrtpol`	Creates a new policy object for a class. This new object can then be adjusted. It is also possible to create the new object having as a base a pre-existing object.
`wdelpol`	Deletes a policy object. Both validation and default policy objects can be deleted.
`wlspol`	Lists available policy default and validation objects for a given resource type.
`wlspolm`	Lists policy methods for a given resource type.
`wgetpolm`	Lists the body or constant value of a default or validation policy method.
`wputpolm`	Replaces a policy method's body.

7.5.3 How to use the commands

This section provides some information on how the commands listed above should be used in order to create, edit, and apply policies.

7.5.3.1 Listing policy objects and policy methods

In order to change or create policies, the administrator must know which policy already exist and what methods each one contains. This can be done using the `wlspol` and `wlspolm` commands.

The `wlspol` command will list all objects of a certain resource type that are under validation or default policies. An example can be seen in Figure 40 on page 126.

```
# wlspol -d ProfileManager
BasicProfileManager
TestProfileManager
# wlspol -v ProfileManager
BasicProfileManager
TestProfileManager
```

Figure 40. Sample usage of the wlspol command - Resources

The `wlspolm` command will list the methods contained in a default or validation policy object. An example can be seen in Figure 41.

```
# wlspolm -d ProfileManager
pm_def_profile_managers
pm_def_profile_types
pm_def_subscribers
# wlspolm -v ProfileManager
pm_val_remove_subscribers
pm_val_remove_subscription
pm_val_subscribers
pm_val_subscription
```

Figure 41. Sample usage of the wlspol command - Policies

A specific policy method is defined by the resource type, policy object, and policy method. All three values must be known in order to get or set the value of a policy method.

7.5.3.2 Creating and deleting policy objects

You can create a new default policy object using the `wcrtpol` command. The following is an example that creates the default policy *NewDefaultPolicyName*:

```
wcrtpol -d ResourceType NewDefaultPolicyName [ParentDefaultPolicyName]
```

The following is an example that creates a validating policy method called *NewValidationPolicyName*:

```
wcrtpol -v ResourceType NewValidationPolicyName \
[ParentValidationPolicyName]
```

In both examples presented above, a parent policy can be optionally specified. If no parent is specified, the default policy for that type of resource will be used for the copy.

In our next illustration, we will create a profile manager validation policy named *ValProfileManagerPolicy*. It can be done by using the following command:

```
wcrtpol -v ProfileManager ValProfileManagerPolicy
```

Using the validation policy created above as parent, we can create an additional validation policy named *Val2ProfileManagerPolicy* using the following command:

```
wcrtpol -v ProfileManager Val2ProfileManagerPolicy ValProfileManagerPolicy
```

If a policy is no longer needed, the policy object can be deleted. To delete a policy object, use the following command:

```
wdelpol -v ResourceType ValidationPolicyObjectName
```

In our example, to delete the objects created above, use the following commands:

```
wdelpol -v ProfileManager ValProfileManagerPolicy
```

```
wdelpol -v ProfileManager Val2ProfileManagerPolicy
```

7.5.3.3 Editing policy methods

The policy methods are stored within the policy object. Two commands are provided to access the values. The `wgetpolm` command will read the current value and display it in the current output. The `wputpolm` command will read the new policy value from the standard input and store it in the object.

The easiest and safest way to handle these values is to use the `wgetpolm` command and save the output to a file, edit the file, and use `wputpolm` to save the new value to the policy object.

In order to run these commands, the following arguments are needed:

- Resource type name
- Policy object name
- Policy method name

To obtain this information, use the `wlspol` and `wlspolm` commands and record the name of the policy objects and policy method. Once these values are known, issue the following command to get the policy method and store it to a file:

```
wgetpolm -d ResourceType PolicyObjectName PolicyMethodName > /tmp/pol.txt
```

Once you have edited and properly changed the file containing the policy, use the following command to set the policies values:

```
wputpolm -v ResourceType PolicyObjectName PolicyMethodName < /tmp/pol.txt
```

In order to read and set the value for the pm_def_subscribers policy method of the default policy TestProfileManager use the following commands:

```
wgetpolm -v ProfileManager ValProfileManagerPolicy pm_def_subscribers > \
/tmp/pol.txt
```

```
wputpolm -v ProfileManager ValProfileManagerPolicy pm_def_subscribers < \
/tmp/pol.txt
```

Any text editor can be used to edit the files. Be sure to test the policies before applying them, especially in production environments.

7.5.3.4 Defining, enabling, and disabling policies

Policies can be defined and enabled using both the Desktop GUI and the CLI commands.

To set the policies through the GUI, select **Properties -> Managed Resource Policies...** from the menu of the region in question. A dialog window, such as the one shown in Figure 42 on page 129, will appear.

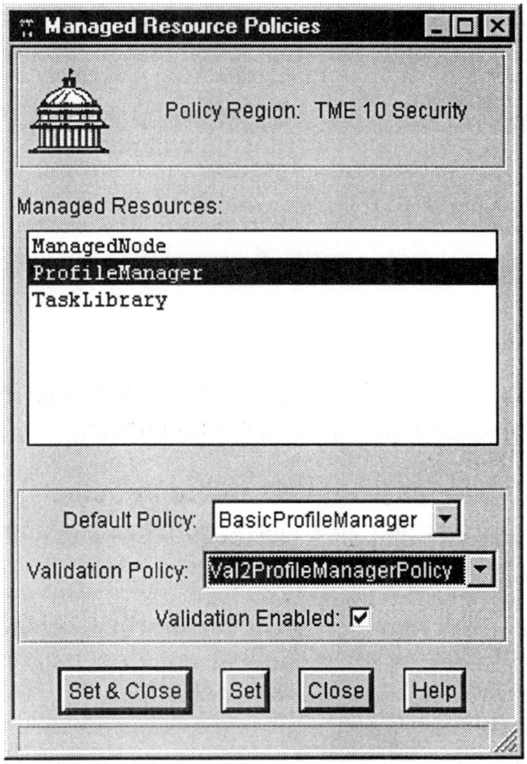

Figure 42. Setting policies for a policy region

Select the resource type and the select the validation and default policies. Check **Validation Enabled** in order to enforce the validation policy. To commit the changes, select the **Set** or **Set & Close** buttons.

The same activity can be done using the CLI commands. In order to define which default or validation policy should be used within a given policy region, use the following commands:

```
wsetpr -d PolicyName ResourceType @PolicyRegion:PolicyRegionName
```

```
wsetpr -v PolicyName ResourceType @PolicyRegion:PolicyRegionName
```

For example, to set the validation policy *Val2ProfileManagerPolicy* for the profile manager defined in the *TME 10 Security* policy region, perform the following command:

```
wsetpr -v Val2ProfileManagerPolicy ProfileManager \
@PolicyRegion:TME 10 Security
```

In order to enable a policy for a given resource type within a policy region, use the following command:

```
wsetpr -e ResourceType @PolicyRegion:PolicyRegionName
```

For example, to set enable the policy for the `ProfileManager` resource in the *security.pr* policy region, use the following command:

```
wsetpr -e ProfileManager @PolicyRegion:security.pr
```

In order to disable the validation policy for a single resource type, use this command:

```
wsetpr -E ResourceType @PolicyRegion:PolicyRegionName
```

For example, to set disable for the policy for the `ProfileManager` resource in the *security.pr policy* region, use the following command:

```
wsetpr -E ProfileManager @PolicyRegion:security.pr
```

It is also possible to set which policy should be used and enable them in a single command as shown here:

```
wsetpr -e -v Val2ProfileManagerPolicy -d TestProfileManager ProfileManager
@PolicyRegion:security.pr
```

7.5.3.5 Checking policies

Enabled validation policies will be in effect for any changes in the policy driven objects after they are enabled. Any objects that already exist will not be validated automatically. To validate these objects, one must manually check the object. The `wchkpol` command does this. The check is done by issuing the following command:

```
wchkpol -r ResourceType PolicyRegionName
```

For example, to validate a policy for *security.pr* policy region from the examples above, use:

```
wchkpol -r ProfileManager @PolicyRegion:security.pr
```

Chapter 8. Bringing it all together

This chapter is aimed to describe the interaction between the elements involved in the Tivoli Logical Design. The previous chapters provided a great deal of information on the elements that should be taken into consideration when building a logical design of Tivoli. The interaction between these elements will now be explained in further detail.

8.1 Policy regions, profile manager, and administrators together

The final relationship between policy regions, profile managers, and administrators will result in the administrators' desktop and in the access control for all the Tivoli Management environments. This access control also dictates what activities Tivoli administrators will perform and how they perform these activities. Thus, it is the corner stone for the entire logical design, and proper choices are fundamental for the effectiveness of such a design.

This section discusses some of the issues that should be taken into consideration when integrating all elements into the logical design.

8.1.1 Policy regions, policies, and resource roles

As described previously, administrators' resource roles are defined by granting the roles to a given policy region. For this reason, the way administrators have their access controlled will affect the way policy regions are created.

One of the best practices regarding policy regions is to have the minimum of them as possible. Considering this, and the policy region relationship with policies, it is advised to create policy regions or subregions if:

- There is a resource role requirement.

  If administrators need to have different accesses on sub-groups of the resources defined in a policy region, subregions should be used.

- Policies must be enforced differently.

  If resources within a region have to be submitted to different policies, then subregions should be created.

As a rule of thumb, policy regions should only be created if there is some benefit to the logical design. Resource grouping alone is not enough to justify the creation of different regions. Grouping can be easily done with collections and profile managers. However, if this grouping reflects different administrative rights and different policies, then policy regions must be created.

8.1.2 Policy regions and profile managers

Profile managers, as with other resources, must be created within a certain policy region. Profile manager hierarchy can be supported by a single policy region. That is, all levels of a profile manager hierarchy are contained in one policy region. The number of policy regions can vary depending on how security and policies must be defined.

Figure 43 shows the simplest scenario possible. All profiles are created within one policy region.

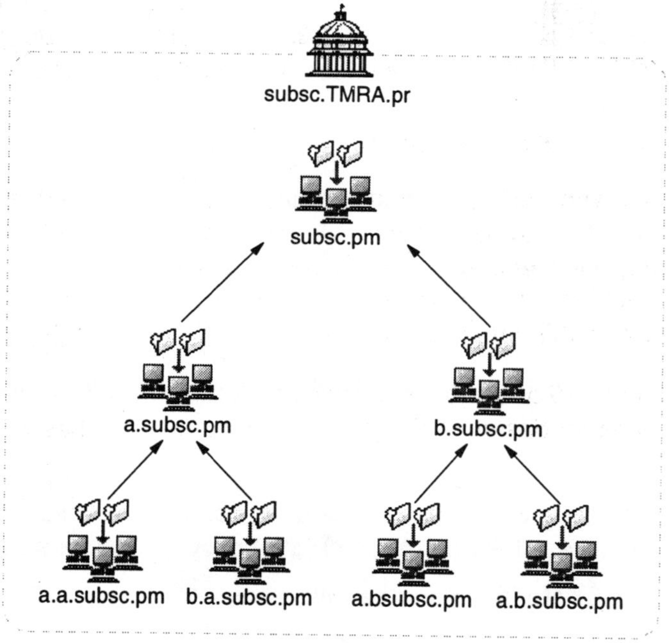

Figure 43. Profile manager hierarchy within policy regions

This simple approach is useful when all profile managers will be accessed by all users, and they are under the effect of the same policy. It keeps the total number of policy regions low.

Figure 44 on page 133 shows an example with profile managers being grouped in policy regions by level.

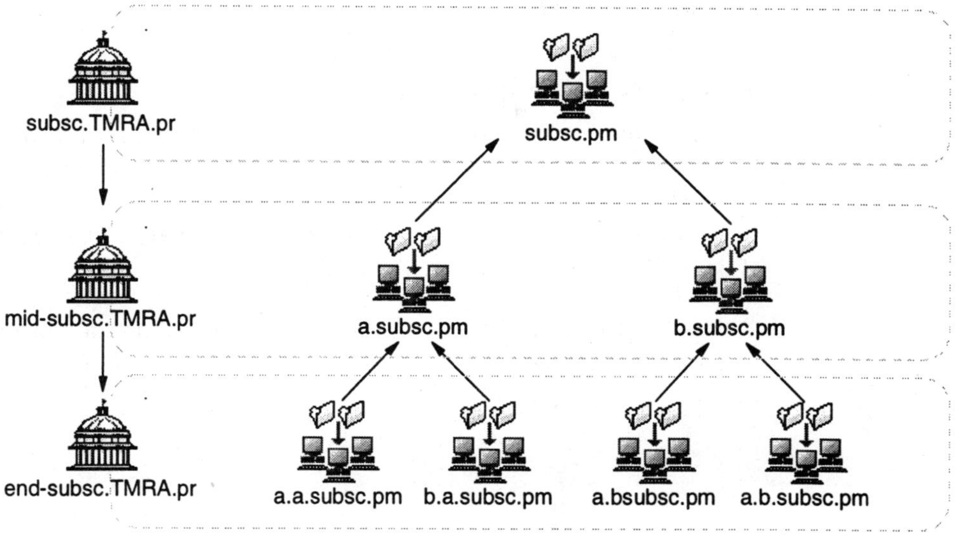

Figure 44. Profile manager grouped by level in policy regions

This approach can be very useful when policies are different from level to level. For example, policies in the end-subsc.TMRA.pr could be designed to only allow endpoints to be subscribers, while in the mid-subsc.TMRA.pr, only profile managers are accepted as subscribers. Policies must be related to the level within the hierarchy for this design to be useful.

Figure 45 on page 134 shows a different partition schema for the same profile manager design. This division is done by branches within the hierarchy.

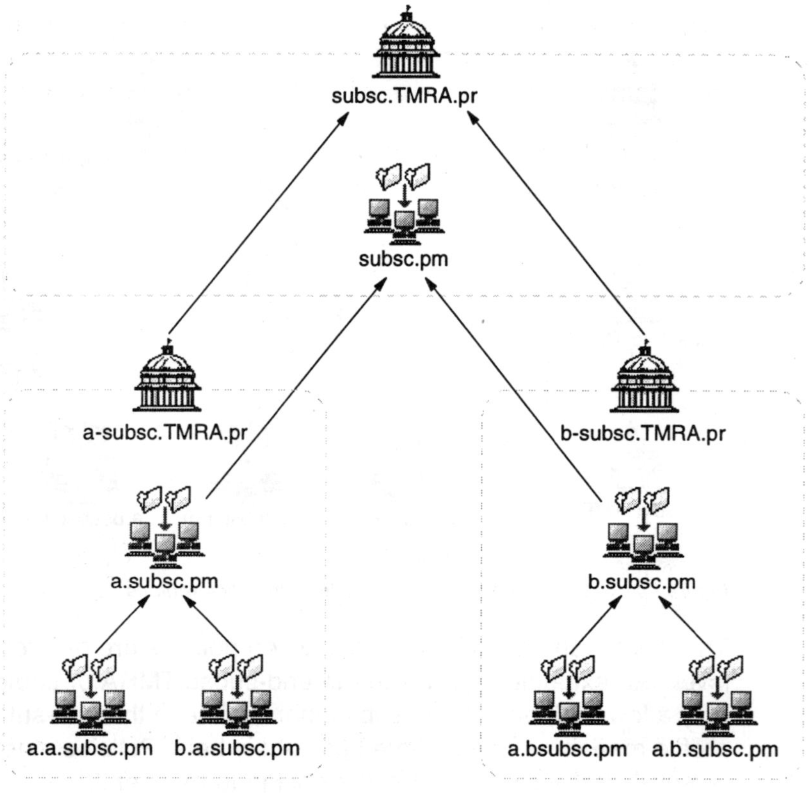

Figure 45. Profile manager branches in policy region

This type of grouping can be used when different administrators will have different access to the profile managers. If an administrator has to distribute in a-subs.TMRA.pm, but not in b-subsc.TMRA.pm, the roles will have to be set in the a-subsc.TMRA.pr policy region. The number of policy regions depends on how the administrators are set up.

Combination of this partitioning can be done, and resources can be grouped by other criteria. The final design should be able to handle both policy and security requirements.

8.1.3 Distributing profiles

Profile based applications all handle the distribution of profiles in the same way. The admin resource role is required in order to distribute a profile. This role is needed on the region where the profile exists and on the region containing the subscribers.

Using the design where subscribers profile managers are stored in a different region means any administrator that is supposed to distribute a profile must have the admin role on both the application and subscriber region. This requirement may give more control than really required for the administrator.

For example, assume the design where we have an application and a subscribers policy region design, as shown in Figure 46.

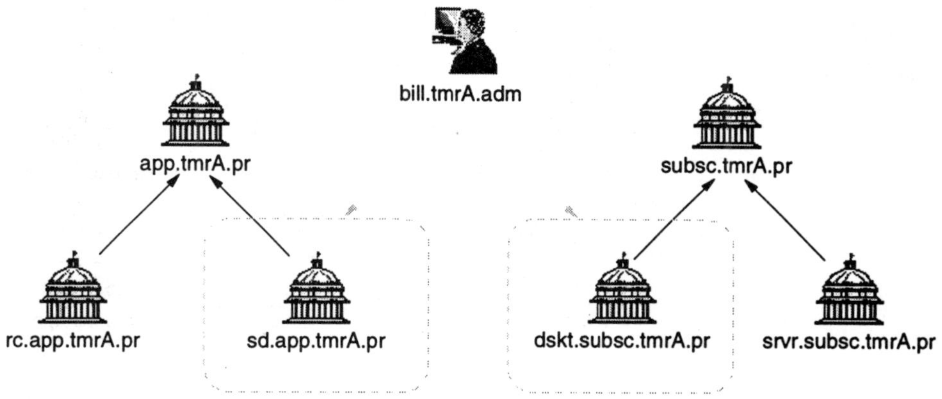

Figure 46. Setting roles for distribution

The administrator bill.tmrA.adm has access to all software distribution packets that contain the sd.app.tmrA.pr policy region and can distribute them to all subscribers in the dskt.subsc.tmrA.pr region.

If this is the only administrative requirement, the policy regions used above are well suited. However, if another administrator has to have access to only a subset of these resource, the ideal way is to subdivide the policy regions so that not all resources are available. Figure 47 on page 136 shows such a division.

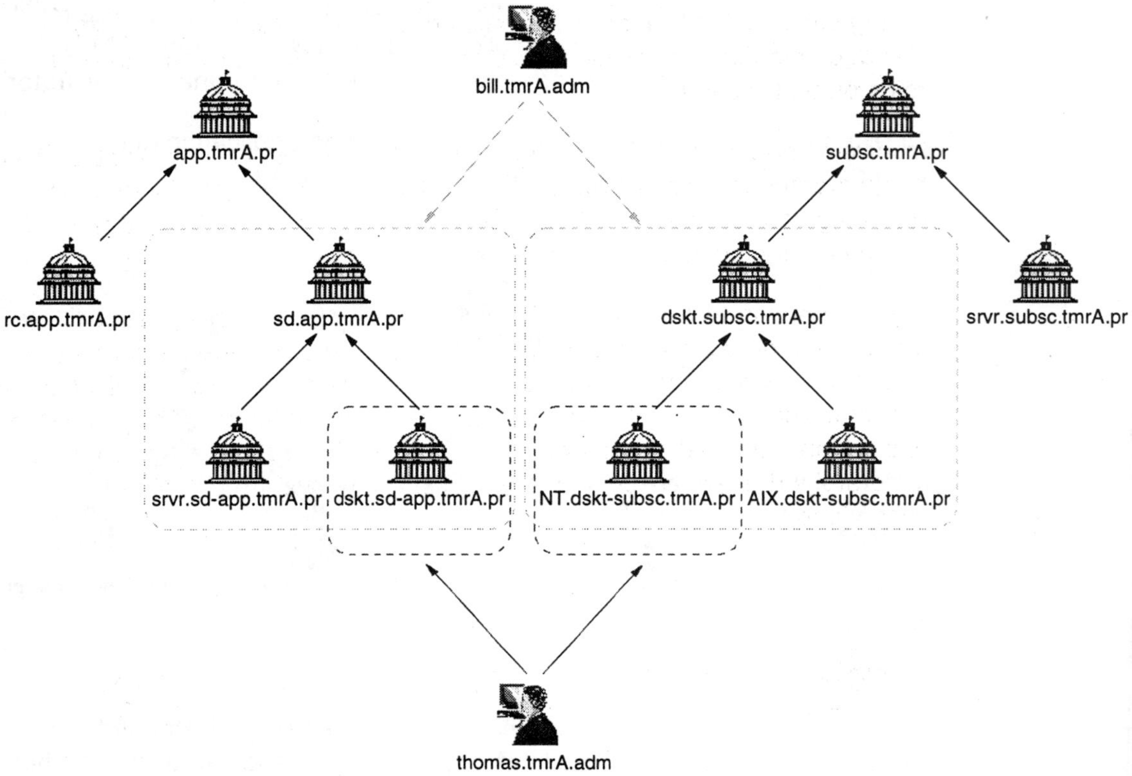

Figure 47. Setting more granular distribution roles

The administrator, thomas.tmrA.adm, is required to distribute software only to Windows NT desktops and can only distribute some file packages of software. In order to accomplish this both regions are divided into subregions. The administrator, bill.tmrA.adm, is granted access to all subregions, and thomas.tmrA.adm is only granted access to the resources needed to perform distribution activities.

Obviously, both administrators could have been granted full access to both subsc.tmrA.pr and sd.app.trmA.pr. However, both administrators would have much more access than required to perform their roles. Since distribution of profiles requires admin role, this could potentially lead to serious security problems in the future.

8.1.4 Roles, distribution, and subscription

As mentioned before in 4.3.4, "Profile manager hierarchy" on page 46, profile distribution is governed by the subscribers in the profile manager hierarchy, and no security checking is done during distribution time. Security is checked during subscription, but once a profile endpoint is subscribed to a profile manager, distribution can be done to it even if the administrator does not have roles on that resource.

Incorrect understanding of this security model can result in undesirable power being granted to administrators. The model is, however, very interesting, providing various ways of controlling and distributing the administration of resources among different administrators.

The distribution of a profile can be initiated in many different ways. Some of the distribution methods have different security requirements and produce different results. Figure 48 shows a typical profile manager and policy region schema. The policy regions are unrelated so that resource roles granted to one region will not affect other regions. The profile managers are organized in a hierarchy (the arrows point to the subscriber where the objects are subscribed to).

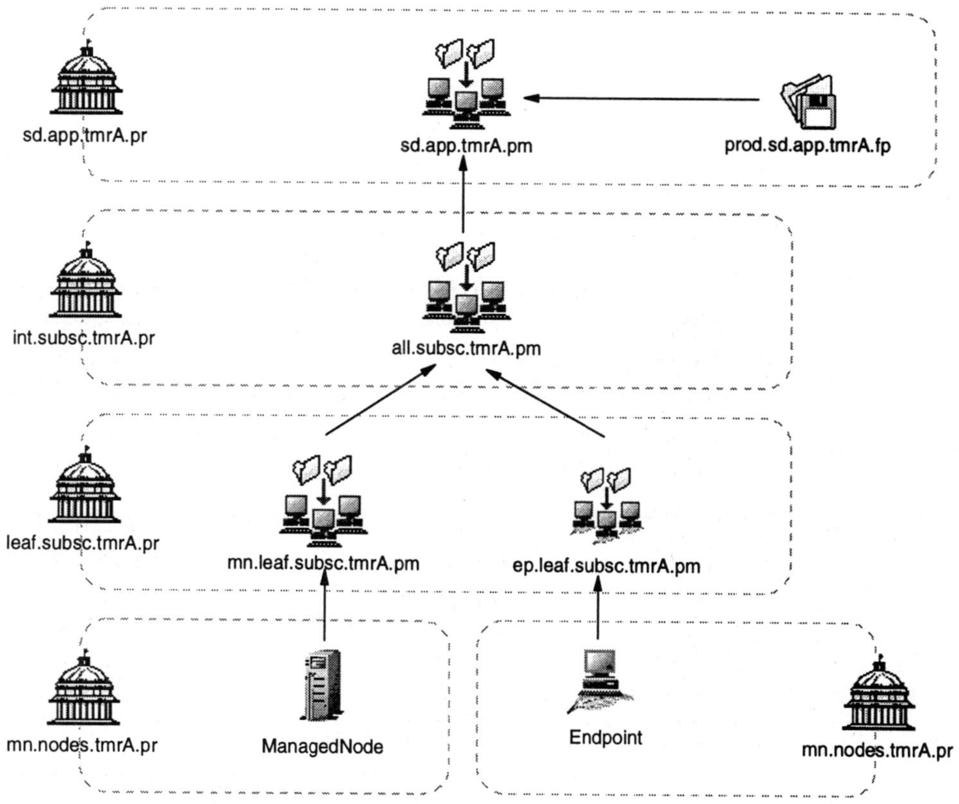

Figure 48. Example profile manager and policy region schema

Using this schema, several combination of roles where granted to an administrator. With each of the combination of resource roles different distribution methods where used. Table 4 shows which distribution worked and which failed due to insufficient authorization.

The table has different cases shown in the *case* column. In each case, the administrator had admin resource role to different policy regions (the regions are shown in Figure 48 on page 137). The table column *Has admin* indicates if the administrator had admin rights to that policy region shown in the *Name* column. The *Distributed Using* column indicates which distributed method was used as follows:

Drag & Drop Using the desktop drag and drop facility, that is, dragging the profile over the target profile endpoint or profile manager.

Prf. Mgr. Menu Using the Profile Manager -> Distribute... menu on the profile manager window.

Profile Menu Using the Distribute... option on profile popup menu or within the profile editing window.

CLI Using the command line interface (`wdistfp` and `wdistrib` commands).

The last column, *Subscribe to Profile Manager,* indicates if the administrator could subscribe a resource in that region to a profile manager.

For this table, the administrator had admin resource role on sd.app.tmrA.pr. Distribution was attempted to any profile manager or profile endpoint within the regions. The X indicates when distribution was successful.

Table 4. Roles, distribution, and subscription

Case	Resources		Distribute Using				Subscribe to Profile Manager
	Name	Has admin	Drag & Drop	Prf. Mgr. Menu	Profile Menu	CLI	
A	int.subsc.tmrA.pr			X	X	X	
	leaf.subsc.tmrA.pr			X	X	X	
	mn.nodes.tmrA.pr			X	X	X	
B	int.subsc.tmrA.pr	X	X	X	X	X	X
	leaf.subsc.tmrA.pr			X	X	X	
	int.subsc.tmrA.pr			X	X	X	

Case	Resources		Distribute Using				Subscribe to Profile Manager
	Name	Has admin	Drag & Drop	Prf. Mgr. Menu	Profile Menu	CLI	
C	int.subsc.tmrA.pr	X	X	X	X	X	X
	leaf.subsc.tmrA.pr	X	X	X	X	X	X
	mn.nodes.tmrA.pr			X	X	X	
D	int.subsc.tmrA.pr	X	X	X	X	X	X
	leaf.subsc.tmrA.pr	X	X	X	X	X	X
	mn.nodes.tmrA.pr	X	X	X	X	X	X
E	int.subsc.tmrA.pr			X	X	X	
	leaf.subsc.tmrA.pr	X	X	X	X	X	X
	mn.nodes.tmrA.pr			X	X	X	
F	int.subsc.tmrA.pr	X	X	X	X	X	X
	leaf.subsc.tmrA.pr			X	X	X	
	mn.nodes.tmrA.pr	X	X	X	X	X	X

Analyzing this table provides interesting information on how profile manager, distribution, and roles work in conjunction. The following consideration can be taken from Table 4 on page 138:

- Drag and drop requires admin on both the region where the profile exists and the target region.
- Using any other distribution method if the endpoint is subscribed to the profile manager directly or indirectly. The distribution can be done independent of having any resource role on the targets.
- Subscription requires admin resource roles on the object being subscribed.

This illustrates the concept that security is checked at subscription time and not a distribution. It also implies that if the resource is "visible" within the profile manager hierarchy, it can be a target for the profile. Thus, only potential targets should be subscribed (directly or indirectly) to a profile manager.

Another important issue shown in Table 4 on page 138 is that an administrator can drag and drop and can subscribe the target to the profile manager. Depending on how administration is done, this behavior may be unwanted. If the administrator responsible for distribution is not responsible for creating and managing the subscriber groups, they should not have admin resource roles to the targets. This effectively eliminates the possibility of using drag and drop, but does allow distribution to be done by other means.

Note

Note that applications that produce local copies of profile only allow distribution to the next level or to all levels. This is also true with the drag and drop interface and the command line interface. Using Figure 48 on page 137 as an example, a Sentry profile can not be dragged from sd.app.tmrA.pm to mn.leaf.subsc.tmrA.pm, ep.leaf.subsc.tmrA.pm, or to a managed node. With software distribution and inventory, this is possible.

8.2 Major design options

Some design options will cause the entire model to be shaped in a specific way. Tivoli has identified two major methods needed to be identified in the beginning of the architecture and design process. After you have identified how resources will be administered, it is time to decide the way resources are to be grouped. These are discussed in the following sections.

8.2.1 Centralized or distributed administration

The location of administrators, be it physical location or place within the organization, has considerable influence in the logical design. Administration of the Tivoli environment may be:

Centralized All administrator are located in one place. Administrator have access to all resources from a central place.

Distributed Administrators are distributed throughout the organization, each administrator having access to a subset of the managed resources.

The difference between centralized and distributed is much more relevant when interconnected TMRs are used. Nevertheless, the design of policy regions will be affected by the way administrators are defined.

Another alternative is to have certain activities distributed and some performed centrally.

The model to be used must be based on the procedures that should be in place after Tivoli is deployed. The existing procedures probably can be streamlined with Tivoli; thus, after Tivoli is in place, local administration can be relocated.

Having a centralized administration can be a good way of maximizing the use of administrators. One administrator can handle several locations. It also reduces the need of trained local administrators, freeing them to be used in other areas.

On the other hand, with centralized administration keeping track of local differences, changes may become much more difficult.

Distributed administration can make local differences easy to account for. Each local administrator is responsible for their area. However, keeping consistent global resource management can be much more difficult.

8.2.2 Grouping resources

The way resources will be grouped will have an effect on the entire design. This will affect the number of policy regions and the number of profile managers that will have to be created.

Resources can be grouped in various ways. Which way should be used depends on how the groups will be used. In general, resource will be grouped to become subscribers of profile managers and of task libraries. When they serve this purpose, the grouping must be made according to the way profiles and tasks will be distributed.

Frequently one grouping schema will not cover all requirements. If this occurs, several groupings should be used. The most common grouping schema are:

Location Physical location of the resources. This is useful when location based distribution are to be made.

Organization Where resources are located within the organization, for example, accounting, marketing, sales, support. This is useful when activities are performed on resources of a given organization.

Resource Type By platform or TMF resource type. This is useful for activities concerning either platform or resource, for example, applying a patch on all Window 95 machines.

Activity	Group resources by which activity they are involved in. For example, database server, mail server, e-business, call center. Very useful for resource monitoring and service specific tasks.

The grouping can be done in as many groups as necessary. This grouping should be made using the profile manager for most of the cases. If a set of profile managers must be involved in some kind of restriction policy, then they must also be placed in different policy regions.

Chapter 9. Creating a logical design

Creating a Tivoli Logical Design is very similar to creating a database logical design. The general process involves the following steps:

1. Gather and consolidate requirements for the design
2. Create a first draft design
3. Validate design and possibly repeat the previous steps until a good and definitive design appears

Information and requirements used in a logical design comes from several sources, such as company policies, project goal, managers, local IT managers, designer's experience, and so forth. The more information, the better.

With as much information as possible the next step is to create an initial design. This design should be able to handle all the requirements determined in the first phase.

The initial design must then be validated. This is done in two steps. First, the design should be tested for the requirements, then the final user of the design should analyze it and validate it. Changes will probably be needed as new requirements and information appear during the validation process.

The final logical design should be the one that satisfies all user' needs within the limits of the TME. During the design process most of the practices and procedures that will be used during the operation will probably have been determined and documented.

Note

Providing a method for logical design is a difficult task. The reader should use whichever method they feel comfortable with. The method used here is just a suggestion and should be adapted to best fit your design methodology. This chapter contains important considerations that should be taken into consideration and are valid even if the method presented here is not entirely used.

9.1 Gathering information and requirements

The entire logical design will be as good as the information available for its creation. Information required for the design comes from several sources, such as:

- Physical design
- Customers' expectations and objectives with the TME environment
- Existing company policies
- Managers
- IT staff
- Designer's experience

Information can only be gathered efficiently if there is a goal for the gathering. In the case of the logical design, the initial, and mostly basic objective, should be gathered to answer questions, such as:

- What will be the Policy Region schema?
- What will be the Profile Manager schema?
- Who will be the Tivoli administrators?
- Which resource and TMR roles will each administrator have?

However, the source for this information will normally not be concerned or knowledgeable about the Tivoli implementation. It is the responsibility of the designer to find the answer to these questions.

The information should be gathered with these question in mind, but not to answer these question directly. Enough information should be available by the end of this gathering to be able to define the schemes. Some consolidation must be done before the actual design is created.

Once enough information has been gathered, the following questions and considerations should be known:

- How will the application be used. The information should be available for each application being deployed. A clear understanding on how each application will be used should be obtained. This is discussed in more detail in 9.1.2.2, "Application usage" on page 150.
- What are the administrators or administrator groups responsibilities. What do they do? On which resources? How do they do it?

- What resources should not be available to certain administrators? What are the restrictions?
- What are the security restrictions applied to the management environment? Is there a security policy to be enforced? How does the security policy influence Tivoli and vice versa? Should changes be applied to the policy?
- Are all customer requirement included in the requirements report? Does the report have enough detailed information?
- Is there a multi-tier TMR structure, and where do humans interact with the design? For example, will all administrators will be defined at the top TMR or enterprise level, or will some operators be working at a regional TMR level?
- Is the physical design adequate and contain enough detailed information?

9.1.1 Information sources

There are normally many different sources for the information required for the logical design. This section explores some of these source and how they can be used to aid in the designing process.

9.1.1.1 Requirement report

Using detailed questionnaires, the professional in charge of the logical design is able to identify complete and accurate requirements for the solution. This activity helps to establish the proper expectations of the amplitude and scope of the Tivoli solution.

It provides information on which Tivoli products or applications should be used. Each product may influence the schema; so, knowing which ones should be considered is very important.

9.1.1.2 Physical design

The logical and physical design are, theoretically, independent. Most information dealt with by the physical design has no impact in the logical design. The actual location of a resource should not affect how it is managed. The one major aspect of the physical design that affects the logical design is the use of interconnected TMRs.

Much in the same manner as databases, TME performance can benefit from taking some aspects of the physical design into consideration when doing the logical design. Part of the physical design can be brought into the logical design in order to make grouping equivalent to the physical locations.

Mapping the physical sites into policy regions can be useful for several reasons:

- If locations are in other cities or countries, they may operate differently. Things, such as different languages, time zones, and working calendars can cause problems to management.
- If WAN is used, especially slow links, it may be necessary to have special distribution procedures to avoid network bottleneck.
- Software distribution is specially affected by the network. In certain environments, it may be necessary to create profiles per site or other highly site specific profiles.

Grouping by location is always an option when designing policy regions and profile managers; however, physical design may not reflect location in the same way a logical design does.

9.1.1.3 Interviews

Most companies where Tivoli is being deployed for the first time will have some kind of IT support structure already in place. This structure should be used as a starting point for the new Tivoli logical design, especially for the administration mode and Tivoli administrators' design.

There are two different important sources of information concerning the existing structure:

- Management
- Workers

The people who handle IT daily have a very good notion of how the IT structure works and where there are problems that must be addressed. On the other hand, management should know where the structure is not working properly and what is the desired final structure.

Interview people that are likely to become Tivoli administrators and discover:

- What do they do?
- How do they do it?
- What do they need to do what they do?
- What do they think would be helpful to have?
- Are there any problems in the current procedures? How do they think it can be addressed or improved?

These questions will provide a good overview of the structure already in place and hints to what the Tivoli administrative structure should be like.

More information should be obtained from other sources. If the existing structure was perfect, or the actual procedures are satisfactory according to the customer's opinion, there would be few or no need for changes. Since changes are occurring, they should be included in the process. The management level staff should be able to provide:

- The policies that should be implemented.
- How peoples' roles should be changed when implementing Tivoli.
- What are the security policies?
- What kind of accountability should be implemented and defined?
- What kind of restrictions should be applied to the users?

These interviews have the final goal of establishing who will be the administrators and their roles in the Tivoli environment. They also affect how policy regions will be created.

9.1.1.4 Security policy

If the organization has a security policy, Tivoli must comply to, or improve it. Some Tivoli products can be used to enforce a security policy, such as Tivoli User Administration and Tivoli Security Management, for instance. More important, however, is that the Tivoli Logical Design does not violate the security policy.

Tivoli allows administrators to have a very large amount of power on their targets. If administrators are not properly defined, they can easily be violating the security policy using Tivoli. For this reason, the logical design must be made to fulfill the security policy requirements of the environment Tivoli is about to be deployed in.

If there is a security policy, and is does not contain enough information so that Tivoli can not be deployed properly, it may be necessary to adapt the policy accordingly.

Even if no policy is in place, the group of Tivoli architects and consultants should prepare to a lesser required one so that the power of the future Tivoli administrators can be granted properly. Most organization will have some kind of informal security policy in place. Tivoli specialists must be able to recognize, collect, improve, and use the information to define how the administrators will be organized within the logical design.

9.1.1.5 Organizational procedure

Another very important source for some of the design information is the organization's procedures. The following questions are only for a few groups of information that should be gathered about the organizational procedures already in place.

- How are machines rolled out?
- How does the help desk department solve problems? Is there any escalation procedure for problems?
- How are the software packages selected for distribution?
- Is there any procedure for software or hardware inventory?
- What are the groups to be involved in the Tivoli deployment, and what are their roles and responsibilities?

All these procedures can provide information on both how the application should be used and how the administrators should be configured.

This information is frequently not readily available or not formally defined. If it is not defined, the informal procedures should be considered. Well defined procedures are critical for a Tivoli deployment. If they are not formally defined, there should be some effort to include the new Tivoli defined procedures in a new definition.

If there is a formal definition of procedures, they can be used in order to define the way Tivoli applications will be used. If the applications cannot be used with the existing procedures, it may be necessary to change them.

9.1.2 Consolidating the information

Information collected from all the different sources must be consolidated before it can be used in the logical design. The way to be used is left to the designer. Each person has a different way of representing knowledge and should use whichever method he or she finds easier.

The information should be used in two different domains:

- Administrator responsibilities

  This covers what are the potential Tivoli administrators and what will be their responsibilities within the general solution and what will each administrator be using and to what extent.

- Application Usage

  How each Tivoli application will be used. How will the profiles be distributed?

The next section provide some examples on what to look for in the data and how to represent it.

9.1.2.1 Administrators responsibilities

The Policy Region design will mainly be a result of the administrators' responsibilities. The number and differences between administrators can also have some impact on the Policy Region schema.

Before the actual Tivoli administrators can be created, it is important to know how auditing will be done and how the administrators will be grouped. This is a complex problem, and one option can influence the other.

One very compact way of storing and displaying the information concerning administrators and their responsibilities is to create a matrix or table containing on one axle the resources, and on the other, the administrators or administrator groups.

Table 5 is an example of an administrator grouping and responsibility matrix. The left most column contains a rough grouping of resources, and the top rows contain administrator grouping. The middle of the table list which activities are to be performed by an administrator on the resource.

Table 5. Administrators responsibilities matrix

Systems		Administration Groups				
		Help Desk	**Develop.**	**App. Mgmt.**	**Net. Mgmt.**	**Decision**
Servers	**UNIX**	TEC read only			DM, SD, TEC	INV
	NT Server	TEC read only			RC, SD, TEC	INV
	Database (subset of UNIX and NT server)	TEC read only		RC, DM, SD (DB fixes), TEC		
Desktop	**NT Workstation**	RC, SD (patching)	SD (home app.)			INV
	Windows 95	RC, SD (patching)	SD (home app.)			INV

This table provides important information on what each administrator does on each resource. The resource provides an initial listing of what policy regions should be created, and the administrator groups inform how Tivoli administrators belonging to that will access the resources.

Table 5 on page 149 for example shows that Help Desk personnel does remote control on desktops, but not on the server. The servers are handled by the Network Management and the Application Management groups (these group should only have access to the database servers). So, for remote control, there should be a policy region for desktops, server, and database server. Network management should be able to access both servers and database servers.

This type of table can also be used to check if the information gathered contains all information required. Once the table is created, the customer can be asked to validate the table.

These tables should not be created with the policy regions in mind at first. They can provide information on how to create the policy regions, but not be considered to do the policy region mapping by themselves.

9.1.2.2 Application usage

While administrators and their responsibilities will define the policy region schema, the way applications will be used will define the profile manager schema. Application usage deals with how profiles will be created and distributed. For non profile based applications, this involves the way resources will be grouped and configured to be used.

For each profile based application, the following information can be seen as a start of what should be put together:

- How should profiles be grouped?
- How should profiles be distributed?
- What are the restrictions to be applied on the grouping and distribution?
- Will different people create, maintain, and distribute profiles?

For non profile based applications, the following information can be seen as a start of what should be consolidated:

- Is there any resource grouping required?
- Who will create, maintain, and use application resources?
- Which restriction should be applied to the resources?

All this information should be consolidated in tables or matrixes. It may be easier to perform the consolidation for each application separately. Doing it all together can result in too much to handle.

The consolidated information on the application usage will provide a clue to what the profile manager schema should be and some hints on possible changes to the policy region schema. Once again, the consolidated information does not have to be expressed in Tivoli terms, but rather in terms that allow the customer and other people involved in the project to analyze if all information required is available.

Software distribution

Most software distribution operations will be defined by the profile manager schema. Policy regions should be used to restrict the access of the administrators to certain profiles.

Since most products are not likely to be distributed to all platform in all location or departments, it is important to determine how each software type is distributed. This allows the designer to determine which profiles should be grouped and to which targets they will be distributed.

The first consolidation necessary is to know the types of software that will be distributed using Tivoli Software Distribution (home grown applications, patches, development tools, anti-virus, and so forth). For each of these types, the potential targets, grouping, and restrictions should be determined. This information will allow the subscriber profile managers to be defined.

Table 6 shows an example of consolidated information for software distribution. For each type of software, and the possible target grouping, the table shows when and how the grouping is used.

Table 6. Software distribution information consolidation

Target Grouping	Type of Software		
	Patches	Home Grown App.	Bought App.
Platform	OS Patches	Yes	Yes, product can be platform specific
Location	Used for traffic control		
Department	Never, all patches applied to all desktops	Some of the applications are specific to some departments	Yes, depending on type: Office goes to all, develop. goes to R&D, and RDBMS part of home grown app.

Target Grouping	Type of Software		
	Patches	**Home Grown App.**	**Bought App.**
Language	Some patches are language dependant		
Application	Some applications have specific patches		Office application are different according to language

These tables work in the same way as that shown in Table 5 on page 149. They provide a simple way to see how the application will be used. There is some integration between these two tables since not all administrator should have access to all software distribution profiles.

Inventory

Inventory distribution is somewhat similar to software distribution, depending on the inventory strategy inventory profiles can be distributed in basically three ways:

- Automatic collection can be done either enumerating all targets or using sub-groups of the profile manager. In the case of enumerated targets, any profile manager schema that contains all the target endpoints is valid. For the other type, sub-groups should be created to fit some type of grouping as for manual group collection.
- Manual initiated group scan, where a administrator will start the collection on a group of endpoints. In this case, the grouping should be made in type of logical or performance grouping.
- Single target scan or blitz inventory collection is used to collect the information for a single endpoint. In this case, profiles should allow the required collection to be done in one step, and subscribers should include all possible targets for this type of collection.

If logical grouping is needed (for example, for the manual scans), it should be established according to the operators' need. For example, an administrator may need to collect the inventory for all the sales departments in the Austin site and the all sales departments in Dallas. In this case, the profile managers should contain a cross of location and department.

Automatic collection is much simpler if all endpoints are subscribed, the scan is possible. Automated inventory scans are normally handled by scripts. If the script breaks the endpoints into groups, there is no need for any grouping at all. If the grouping should be done because of some external restriction (such as different working hours or days in different locations), then the grouping should reflect these restrictions.

The same technique used for software distribution can be used for inventory grouping. The resulting data can be shown in a table. The question and reason for grouping are different, but the result is the same.

Remote control

Since remote control is not a profile based application, the way the application works will be reflected by the policy region schema. There are two bits of information that must be consolidated:

- Which administrators access what resources
- How they are restricted in their access

The restrictions come in two forms:

- Which modes can be used on the resources. These modes can be controlled by policies or resource roles on the targets.
- How the option within the mode can be used. These options are controlled by policies.

The information should be consolidated into a table like Table 7. This table provides hints on how resources should be placed in policy regions an which policies should be created.

Table 7. Sample remote control access table

Resources	Administrator Groups		
	Help Desk	App. Admin	Network Admin
Desktops	All option, with user approval	none	none
DB Servers	none	All option, no confirmation	All modes but reboot, no confirmation
NT Servers	none	none	All option

9.2 Designing process

The process of creating a logical design is part science, part art. There is not really one design process that can solve all cases. Each person doing a design will have his or her own process.

In this section, we propose a process. This process is to be used to illustrate how the design is created and how the information gathered previously can be used during the design process.

Complexity of the design process varies according to the number of administrator groups and the granularity of the resources' grouping. The more administrator groups and resource groups in the environment, the more complex the design.

Resource grouping granularity should be the highest possible, that is, the least groups possible. If too many groups exist the entire design grows in size and complexity. A fine grained design is more likely to be less flexible and difficult to change.

The same applies to administrator groups, the less the better. But, this does not mean they should be avoided. The total number of administrators and groups will influence the complexity of the design. But, use as many as necessary since administrator roles are the most critical design aspect.

Most large environments will require complex design. In a small environment, with a couple of thousand resources and a dozens of administrators that talk to each other regularly, a coarse policy design and resource role will probably work fine. But if hundreds of thousands of resources are managed, and there are thousand of administrators, the security must be much more close-fitting and, thus, the design will have to be much more granular, complete, and complex.

The naming convention is also critical in the design process. As the design evolves and the granularity is know, it is possible to establish or adjust the naming convention. The final naming convention should be determined by the time the design is completed. However, during the initial phases, having a rough naming convention is enough. During early stages of the design, any way of naming resources that allows them to be identified is acceptable.

9.2.1 General design flow

Since the amount of design option involved in the creation of a logical design can easily be overwhelming, it is better to use an incremental approach. A bottom-up design can be easier to handle. Starting from profile manager and policy region design for each application. Each application's policy region and profile manager schema can be handled as independent blocks. Once the small designs are created, they are put together.

When the blocks are added, the resulting design may have some redundant elements or have elements that will make the design unable to satisfy the requirements. Through progressive refinement, the design is fixed until it can handle the requirement. Figure 49 shows the general logical design creation process.

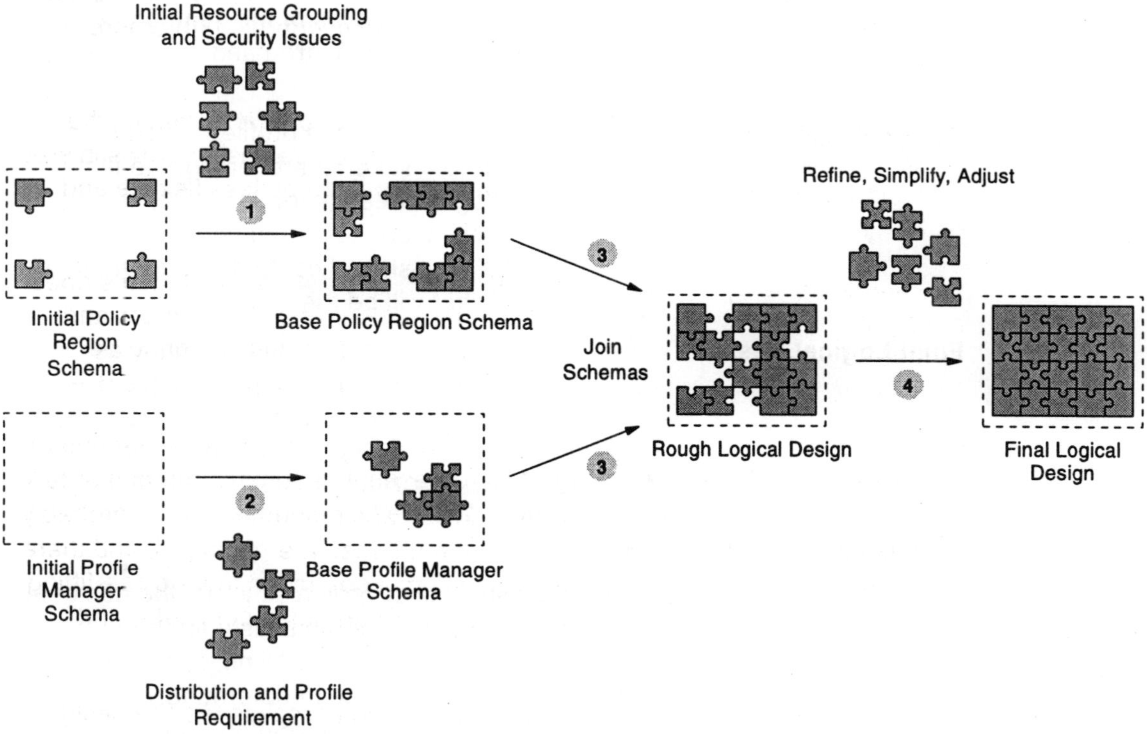

Figure 49. General logical design flow

The dashed boxes represent parts of the design. Each part contains the following:

Initial Policy Region Schema This is the initial policy region design. It represents the basic application, nodes, and subscriber region schema as shown in Figure 50 on page 158.

Base Policy Region Schema This schema is the result of adding the basic resource grouping and security concerns to the initial schema.

Initial Profile Manager Schema This schema is empty at first. Profile manager schema will be completely defined by application and distribution requirements; so, the initial schema is empty.

Base Profile Manager Schema This is the design that should be capable of handling the profile grouping and distribution characteristics of the solution. It can easily be too large and may require simplification.

Rough Logical Design When the base profile manager and policy schema are joined, the first logical design appears. This design still needs to be refined and adjusted. But, it should contain a rough idea of what will be the final design.

Final Logical Design This is the probable design to be implemented. Before it can be used, it should be tested and approved.

The numbers in Figure 49 on page 155 represent the steps of the design. Steps 1 and 2 can be done in any order and are fairly independent. The steps each have the following function:

Step 1 Starting with the initial policy region schema, the designer adds the policy regions required to satisfy each applications' security requirements. All policy region in the basic design should be analyzed to determine which changes are required for each application. Policies and administrator divisions that were collected in the information gathering phase should be added here.

Step 2 This is the equivalent of step 1 for profile managers. Each application should be analyzed to determine how its subscriber profile managers should be created and what application profile managers should be created. It is not necessary to determine where the profile managers will be created. This will be done in step 3.

Step 3 In this step, the profile manager and policy region schemes are united into a rough logical design. In this phase, the profile managers should be associated to policy regions according to the security and policy requirements. It may be necessary to further break down both profile managers and policy regions.

Step 4 The rough logical design will have several flaws and problems. It may require that profile managers and policy regions be created, removed, or modified to meet the requirements gathered previously.

The steps described above do not have to be executed in a strict order. The order proposed is just a suggestion. Steps 1 and 2 can be done in any order. The designer can opt to do step 1 and 2 together. They are shown separately to show that the schemes are reasonably independent and can be approached separately.

The profile manager schema deals mostly with distribution of the application profiles, while the policy region schema handles the security of the applications. Obviously, there are security restrictions to the profile distribution, but this should be left to step 3.

Thinking of each schema separately also reduces the number of design options being handled at one time. A complete set of options will come into play when the two schemes are put together, but then the basic options of each schema are already left behind.

Step 3 is when both schemes are connected. In this step, the profile managers of the profile manager schema must be placed within policy regions. There are two main resources that have to be placed in the policy regions:

- Application profile manager (those containing the profile)
- Subscriber profile manager (those containing the profile endpoints)

For the subscriber profile managers, the simplest approach is to place subscriber in the subscriber policy region without any distinction. This may not be valid due to security restriction. In this case, this must be fixed in step 4.

Application profile managers should be placed in their respective application policy regions. It is very likely that these regions have been divided into subregions. If the profile managers can be easily placed in these subregions, do so. Otherwise, wait until step 4 before adjusting the application policy regions.

The last step is used to make all the changes in the logical design so that it can handle the requirements. This process can be difficult, and many strategies can be used. One way to refine the design is to go through the consolidated information and see that the current design allows that:

- All resources be grouped according to the security requirements
- All administrators to be created according to the security requirements
- Distribution can be handled in the necessary way

Note that the resource roles of the administrators have not been discussed or shown in this diagram. They must, however, be considered. In fact, they will be the guideline for the creation of the policy region and the grouping of resources. Since the policy regions schema can change a lot during the design process, having a complete listing of the resource roles for each administrator can lead to waisted work. However, as the design becomes more stable, the roles to the policy regions should be determined and recorded. One way to do this is by creating tables to store this (see 9.2.4, "Tivoli administrators schema" on page 160).

9.2.2 Policy region schema

The policy region schema should start from a initial policy region design. The schema composed of application, subscriber, and node policy regions is the best starting point (Figure 50 shows such a design).

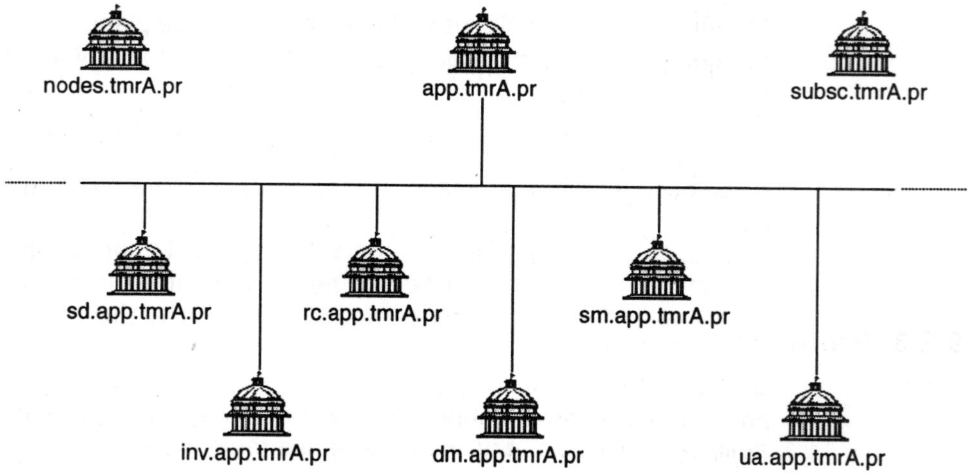

Figure 50. Initial profile manager schema

There are some variations over this basic design, such as:

- Only one top-level policy, and all policies under that policy. For example, a tmrA.pr containing nodes.tmrA.pr, app.tmrA.pr and subsc.tmrA.pr policy regions.
- No top-level application policy regions. All the policy regions under app.tmrA.pr would be at the top level.

These variations and others have little influence on the overall schema. What is critical in this basic policy region schema is that applications, nodes, and subscribers will be placed in different regions.

There is, however, one physical design option that will change the initial policy region schema, the Hub-Spoke architecture. If a Hub spoke is used, the application policy region will stay in the Hub, and the nodes and subscriber policy regions will be on the spokes. So, each spoke would have a policy region subsc.spokeA.pr and nodes.spoke.A.pr, while the Hub would have one region, app.hub.pr.

Once the initial policy region schema has be determined, it must be refined. This should be done for each application being deployed. Using the information on security restriction and the administrator groups, new subregions should be created.

No subregion should be created without a specific region. Whenever a new region is proposed, ask why. Simply to group resource neatly is not a good reason. Good reasons for a subregion include:

- Different policies
- Different administrator resource roles
- Different resource types grouped in them

Creating too many policy regions will make the schema too big and difficult to manage. If a group of resources of the same type is going to be managed by the same administrators and with the same policies, there is no reason to create subregions. Resist the urge to create policy regions for logical grouping. Use profile managers and collections for this.

9.2.3 Profile manager schema

Unlike policy regions, there is not an initial profile manager schema. Since the profile managers are tightly connected to the way the application being deployed will be used, there is no starting schema.

There are two different types of profile managers being created in the schema:

- Application profile managers
- Subscribers profile managers

The application profile manager must be designed taking into consideration security restrictions and profile endpoint grouping. These profiles should only have valid targets as subscribers. If different administrators distribute different profiles, the profile managers should be created for each different access control. Use the same matrixes used for policy regions to determine the need to split profile managers according to administrator roles.

To create the subscriber profile manager, use the information regarding how distribution should be done (such as the information shown in Table 6 on page 151). Consider each distribution type separately. That is, if patches and applications are distributed differently, create different profile manager hierarchies for each one. This will lead to redundancy but makes it much easier to design. On the final refinement steps, these redundant profile managers can be eliminated.

The base profile manager schema should be created without many concerns on the policy region schema. Distribution and profile grouping pose enough problems for the initial design. Once the base profile manager schema is available it should be refined until it can handle all policies and resource role considerations.

9.2.4 Tivoli administrators schema

The administrators schema, or how resources will be grouped, will only be defined in the later steps of the design. It will have influence on both the base profile manager and policy region schema but not be explicitly dealt with. The main reason is that the actual administrators schema depends on the policy region schema, which is bound to change during the creation of both schema.

Once the schemes have been joined into a rough logical design and refined a little, the policy region schema will become more stable. At this point, the administrators' schema should take shape.

This schema is simply the resources granted to each administrator on the resources. The easiest representation of the schema is in a table, such as Table 8 on page 161. This table is just an example of part of such a table.

These tables will normally be very large since there will be hundreds of policy regions and subregions.

Table 8. Administrators schema definitions

Policy Regions	Administrator Groups		
	Help Desk	Network Adm.	Developer
inv.app.tmrA.pr	run_query	admin	
hg.sd.app.tmrA.pr			admin
mn.rc.app.tmrA.pr		admin	
net.dm.app.tmrA.pr		senior, admin	

It may be interesting to have the policy regions ordered according to the hierarchy, for example:

- sd.app.tmrA.pr
- patches.sd.app.tmrA.pr
- hg.sd.app.tmrA.pr
- office.sd.app.tmrA.pr

This is important because granting roles to a policy region gives the same roles to all subregions.

Another option is to break down the tables per applications. Once again, this makes handling the information easier.

9.3 Checking the result

Once a logical design has been created, it should be tested before deployment. Testing can help avoid the deployment of a model that is flawed or does not meet the needs of the organization. Although adjusting or re-creating a logical design is possible, it can be costly to do so.

The toughest test is deployment. This is, however, a very dangerous option. If the model has serious problems, deployment may have to be redone. Even if only minor changes have to be done, they may become difficult if people are using the flawed model.

The easiest testing is done by mentally checking the model. Using the consolidated information, see if the model allows the administrators to do their activities. Ask questions of the model, such as:

- Can an administrator from the help desk group get the inventory for an endpoint they manage?
- Can they control that endpoint?
- Can they control a server?
- Can an administrator in the application support group distribute a home grown application?
- Can he monitor a server?
- Can a member of the server administration group create a new distributed monitoring profile?
- Can they distribute to the appropriate targets?
- Can they adjust the subscriber of a profile?

It is also important to make sure administrators cannot do more than their activities required, especially if security policies dictate so. This testing is partially done during the design.

Whichever testing method is used, it must test the restriction applied to the user, and the distribution of profile. Both must match the requirements established during the gathering phase.

Part 2. Case studies

Chapter 10. First scenario

In previous chapters, we have provided a great deal of information related to the logical design of a Tivoli solution and its various elements. We have also described the facts that should be considered for understanding the environment which Tivoli should be deployed as well as using this information to design your Tivoli logical design.

In this chapter, we provide an example that demonstrates these concepts and processes for designing a logical design of a Tivoli-based solution.

It is very important to keep in mind that there are many ways of accomplishing a successful Tivoli Logical Design. Many of the decisions that need to be made are based on specific environment characteristics.

The scenario we present is based on a fictitious company called BWET Corporation. The symbol BWET was made out by getting the initial letter of the first name of each one of our group members, and it does not represent any real company or organization.

Note

The scenario we are presenting in this chapter is abstract, and many simplifying assumptions have been made. However, you can use this example as a model to understand how the points discussed earlier in this redbook should be applied.

10.1 BWET Corporation overview

The BWET Corporation has decided to implement an effective systems management solution. Its headquarters are located in Texas and consists of four main departments: Support & Systems, Administration, Sales & Marketing, and Production in the main Manufacturing site. The Production department is also composed by ten small factories across the USA. Figure 51 on page 166 shows the BWET organizational structure.

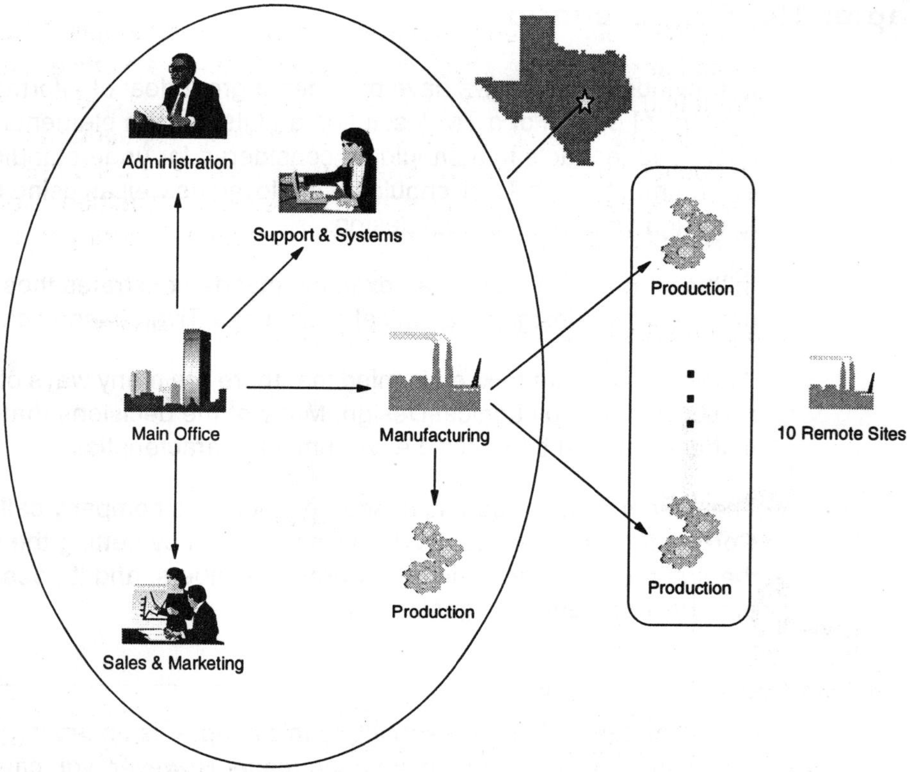

Figure 51. BWET organization structure

10.2 Gathering and consolidating requirements

As we have discussed in Section 1.2, "Tivoli architecture and design considerations" on page 7, when planning a Tivoli solution, careful understanding about the environment where Tivoli is to be deployed is required. We should start our design process by gathering as much information as possible in respect to the physical and logical issues involved in such a design.

As mentioned before, gathering information is not a process that occurs only once, but rather is an iterative process that may recur several times. As requirements are gathered, we structure them to define the management domains. In the following sections, we summarize some of the requirements gathered from BWET.

10.2.1 Physical issues

The BWET departments that are to be considered in this Tivoli solution are spread across twelve physical locations. In the main office are the Sales and Marketing, General Administration, and the Support and Systems departments. The second location is the main manufacturing which has the production line department. Both the main office and the main manufacturing are connected through a T1 speed connection. In addition, there are ten other small factories that are connected to main manufacturing through 64Kbps links.

Figure 52 shows the network topology in use by BWET.

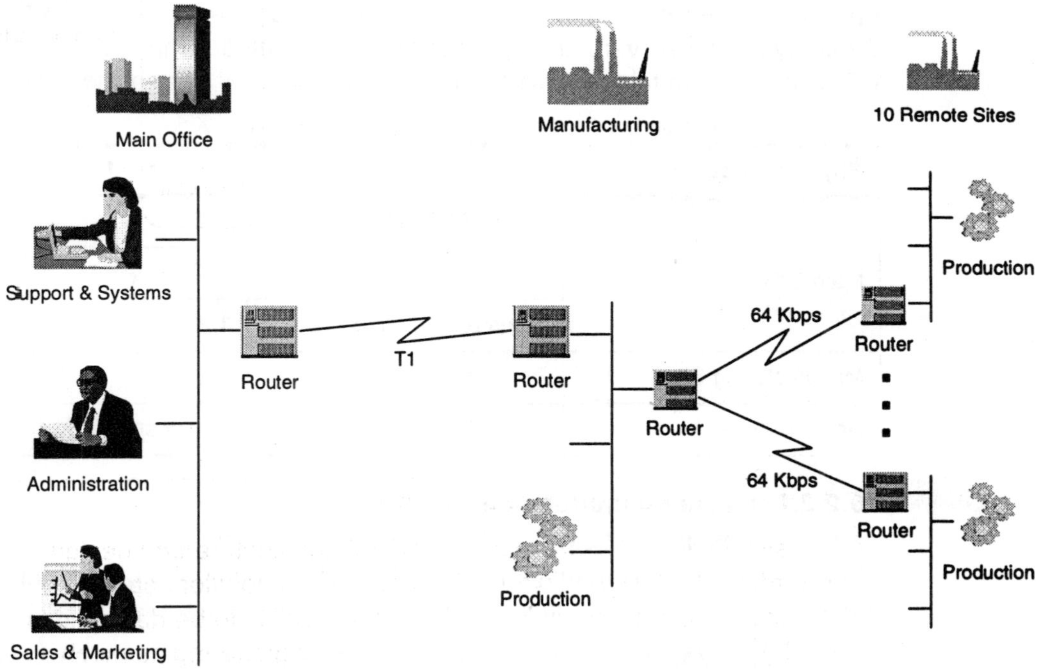

Figure 52. BWET network topology

The standard protocol utilized by BWET is TCP/IP, and all servers and workstation have fixed IP addresses. DNS is used for name resolution for forward and reverse. In addition, there are no firewalls in the network, and there are no performance problems in any segment of the network.

10.2.2 Logical issues

At this time, we should gather all information required to perform an analysis of the logical issues. This includes activities, such as:

- Identify existing systems to be managed by Tivoli.
- Identify the systems management strategy.
- Identify the management disciplines that are to be applied and define the Tivoli applications involved.
- Collect administrative information in order to plan the Tivoli administrators' desktop design.
- Obtain the Tivoli physical design.

10.2.2.1 Systems to be managed

There are approximately 1500 desktops to be managed across the entire organization, and 35 application servers installed organization wide. The operating systems used in the desktops include Unix and Windows 98. Similarly for the servers, the operating systems include Unix and Windows NT. The following table shows the number of desktops per physical location.

Table 9. Number of desktops to be managed

Physical location		**Number of desktops**
Main Office	Support & Systems	100
	Administration	700
	Sales & Marketing	100
Manufacturing Site	Production	500
Remote Sites	Production	10 per site. Total 100

10.2.2.2 Systems management strategy

Any Tivoli design must care for the business objectives of the organization. Therefore, a systems management strategy should be done according to these objectives. For our case study, the objectives are:

- The organization wishes to monitor and control every system change or problem. The managing of system alterations and problems is very important to keep the corporate environment healthy.
- Availability of management environment: The availability of managed servers is essential to keep the production line up and running at all times
- Improve the availability of all the computer resources of the organization. This clearly helps in the business competition.
- Provide remote support for all departments involved in the systems management solution.

- Scalability for future expansion. The organization has plans to deploy Tivoli in the other plants in Europe.
- The organization needs a way of deploying and maintaining a standard configuration of all desktops for each department/job function. It is the organization's target to reduce costs of maintaining different configurations. In addition, an inventory of all computer resources must be part of the solution.

10.2.2.3 Identifying Tivoli applications

Based on the information describe in 10.2.2.2, "Systems management strategy" on page 168, we now need to identify the management disciplines that are involved in this case study and then map the Tivoli applications that best fit the organization's requirements. The following table presents the mapping between the management disciplines and Tivoli applications that are to be deployed in the customer environment.

Table 10. Management disciplines and Tivoli applications

Management discipline	Tivoli applications
Availability Management	Distributed Monitoring
	Tivoli Enterprise Console
Deployment Management	Software Distribution
	Inventory
Operations Management	Remote Control

We now explain how each Tivoli application will be used to meet the organization's requirements.

Tivoli Distributed Monitoring

Tivoli Distributed Monitoring will be used to check the status of a variety of networked resources, such as systems, applications, and processes in the entire enterprise.

Tivoli Enterprise Console

Tivoli Enterprise Console will offer a centralized, global view of the organization computing environment, ensuring the high availability of the organization's application and computing resources. The Tivoli Enterprise Console will act as a central collection point for alarms and events received from the other Tivoli applications and will ensure that all problems will be handled by the appropriate support engineer.

Tivoli Software Distribution

Tivoli Software Distribution will be used by the Support & Systems group to keep the desktops with the most up-to-date and standardized software organization wide.

Tivoli Inventory

Tivoli Inventory will gather the organization's hardware and software inventory to help the Support & Systems department keep on track all the computing resources. It will regularly store hardware and software inventory information, monitor and record changes in software and hardware configurations, manage all enterprise systems from a central point, and examine inventory information to perform system auditing functions.

Tivoli Remote Control

The Support & Systems personnel often need to manage the users' desktops. Tivoli Remote Control will provide a convenient alternative for managing PCs, thus, enabling the Support & Systems personnel to control the keyboard and mouse input and monitor the display output of a remote PC, therefore, being more effective on the solution of reporting problems.

10.2.2.4 Collecting administrative information.

The Support & Systems department is responsible for providing both support and systems administration for their systems in the entire organization. The support personnel are basically divided in three groups:

- Server support

  This group is responsible for installing, upgrading, and maintaining the overall Tivoli management environment. They will define and maintain software packages, inventory of hardware and software, network support, server capacity and performance, backup of the servers, and so on.

- Desktop support

  This group is responsible for supporting users with daily problems, performing routine maintenance, defining the standard software to be used in the desktops organization wide, and keeping the users' desktops in a standard level by installing and/or upgrading software.

- Application specific development and support

  This group is responsible for developing all the *in-house* applications for the organization's needs. They have their own software requirement and their own support personnel in charge of the non-standard requirements.

10.2.2.5 Getting the Tivoli physical design

The IT architects in charge of the physical layout of Tivoli to be used in this solution now have decided on one solution. Note that the physical design presented here represents one of the various possible solution for this case study environment.

The group of IT architects in charge of the Tivoli logical design have now identified, through the physical design provided, the number of Tivoli Management Regions and all the required Tivoli management servers as well as their physical location. Figure 53 outlines the Tivoli physical design for the BWET environment.

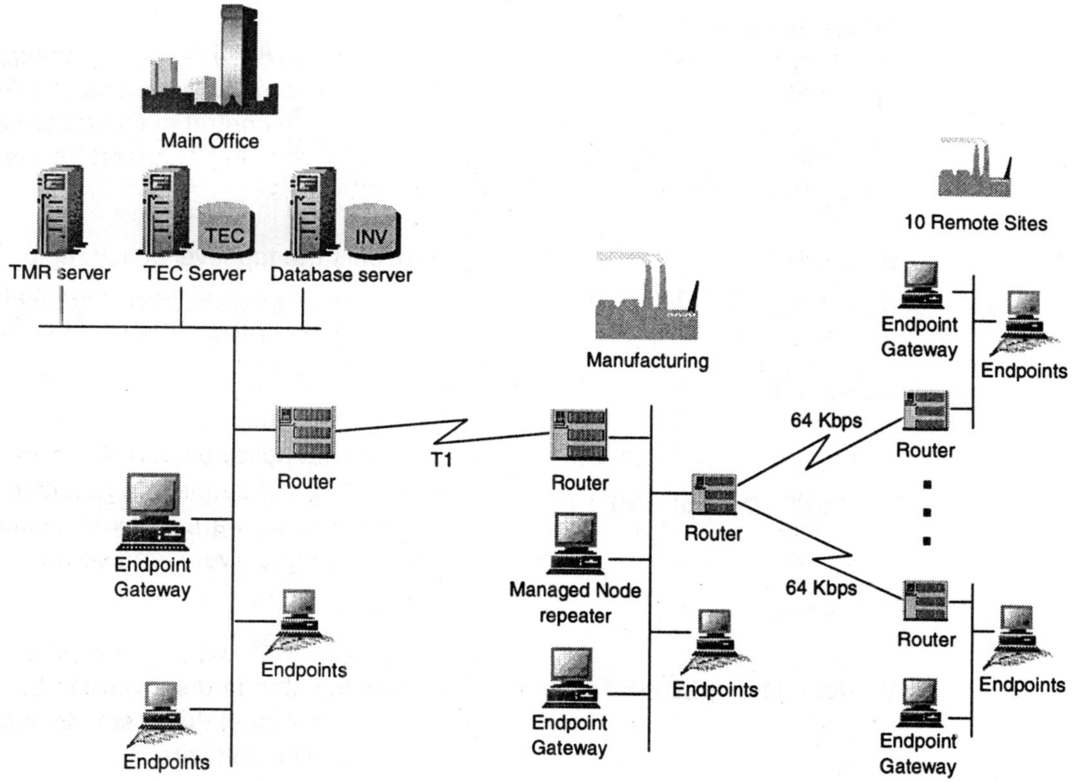

Figure 53. BWET Tivoli physical design

10.3 Logical design

Now that we have a good understanding of the BWET requirements and environment, their existing systems to be managed by Tivoli, the organization's systems management strategy, the management disciplines, that Tivoli applications involved in the Tivoli solution, their administrative organization structure, and have investigated the Tivoli physical design provided, it is time to perform the Tivoli logical design.

This section continues by providing a description of the elements involved in a Tivoli logical design for our case study scenario.

10.3.1 Naming convention

Careful planning should be dedicated to achieve an effective naming convention. All elements of the Tivoli logical architecture will be covered by this naming convention.

The Support & Systems department will be responsible for creating a process to validate the uniformity of names for the newly defined resources after the deployment.

For this case study scenario, we will adopt the naming convention as described in 2.3, "Sample naming convention" on page 23. The following are some examples of resources names to be defined in BWET:

BWET.pr Represents the top level policy region.

Appl.BWET.pr Represents an application policy region. It is defined under BWET.pr policy region.

SD-Appl.BWET.pr Represents a policy region dedicated to Software Distribution. It is defined under Appl.BWET.pr policy region.

Desktop.SD-Appl.BWET.pr Represents a policy region defined under SD-Appl.BWET.pr, which will accommodates the profile manager dedicated to distribute software to the desktop machines.

WinNT.DM-Appl.BWET.pm Represents a profile manager that contains Windows NT Distributed Monitoring monitors. It is defined under the DM-Appl.BWET.pr policy region.

10.3.2 Policy region design

In this section, we will discuss the propositioned policy region hierarchy to be used by the BWET in our case study. This policy region design will follow the recommendations described in Chapter 3, "Policy region design" on page 27.

This policy region hierarchical breakdown provides a mechanism for organizing and managing the BWET systems resources, provides proper access control to Tivoli resources, allows administrators to quickly locate resources within the organization, and allows scalability.

The first level of policy region, as shown in Figure 54, will be partitioned in three levels of the policy region:

- Nodes policy region - Nodes.BWET.pr
- Applications policy region - Appl.BWET.pr
- Subscribers policy region - Subsc.BWET.pr

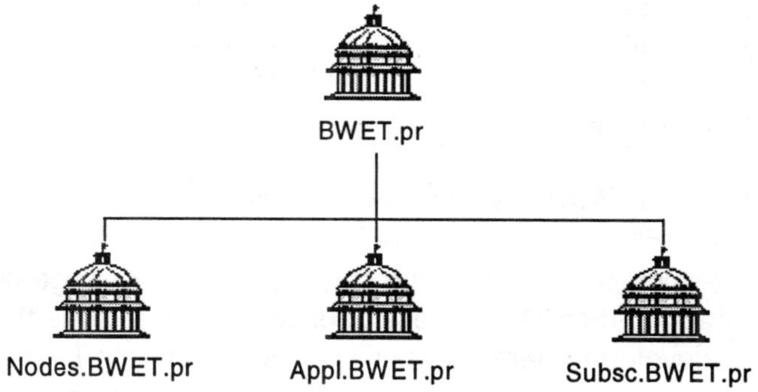

Figure 54. BWET first level policy region hierarchy

10.3.2.1 Nodes policy region

This policy region will provide an organized set of subregions that accommodates all the Tivoli managed systems of BWET organization. The subregions are as follows:

- MN.Nodes.BWET.pr
- desktop-ep.Nodes.BWET.pr
- servers-ep.Nodes.BWET.pr

All managed nodes will be grouped into the MN.Nodes.BWET.pr policy region. The endpoints will be placed into either Desktop-ep.Nodes.BWET.pr or Servers-ep.Nodes.BWET.pr, whether they are desktop machines or server machines. The main intention here is to allow policy regions role security to be enforced for management of these endpoints objects. Without it, TMR wide role would have to be assigned to the administrator. Figure 55 on page 174 shows the nodes policy region hierarchy.

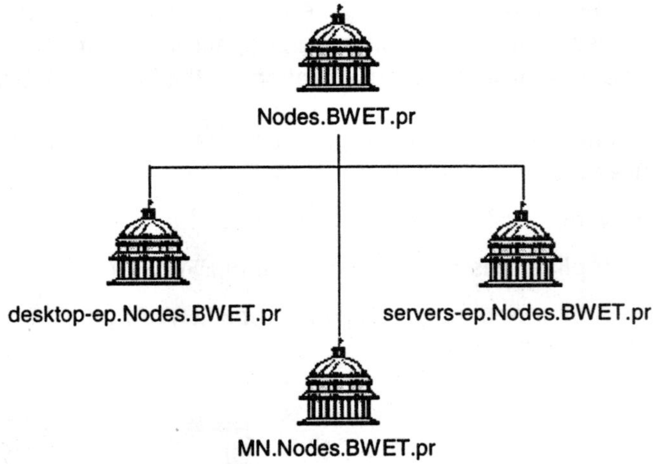

Figure 55. BWET nodes policy region hierarchy

10.3.2.2 Applications policy region

This policy region is the container for all applications' subregions, each of which is devoted to the comprehensive management of each business application. A business application can include third party, internally developed packages, or Tivoli applications. These policy regions will be used to organize and control the access to management operations. Administrators with the authority to perform management operations, such as the distribution of profiles or the execution of tasks, will primarily use this hierarchy. The subregions defined into the application policy region are as follow:

- DM-Appl.BWET.pr
- SD-Appl.BWET.pr
- INV-Appl.BWET.pr
- RC-Appl.BWET.pr
- TEC-Appl.BWET.pr

Figure 56 on page 175 shows the application policy region hierarchy.

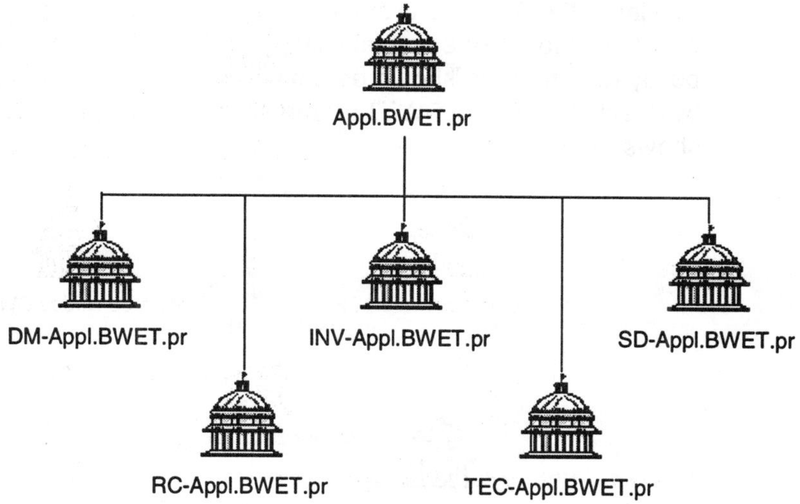

Figure 56. BWET application policy region hierarchy

Tivoli Software Distribution policy region

In the Tivoli Software Distribution policy region, there is the need to define another level of subregions. This level is composed by the desktop.SD-Appl.BWET.pr and servers.SD-Appl.BWET.pr. The reason is that the support personnel responsible for desktops should not be allowed to distribute software to the servers. Therefore, the administrators defined for the desktop support personnel will not have access to the servers policy region. Figure 57 on page 175 shows the Tivoli Software Distribution policy region hierarchy.

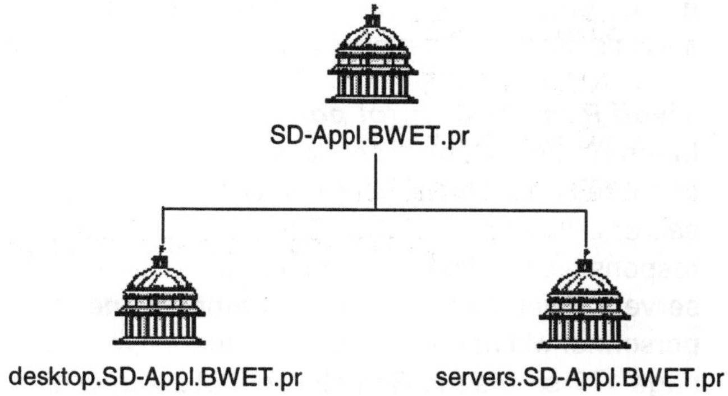

Figure 57. BWET Software Distribution policy region hierarchy

Tivoli Inventory policy region

Similar to the Software Distribution, the desktop support personnel should not be allowed to make eventual scans of the servers. Therefore, in the Inventory policy region, there should be defined another level of subregions composed by desktop.INV-Appl.BWET.pr and servers.INV-Appl.BWET.pr. Figure 58 shows the Inventory policy region hierarchy.

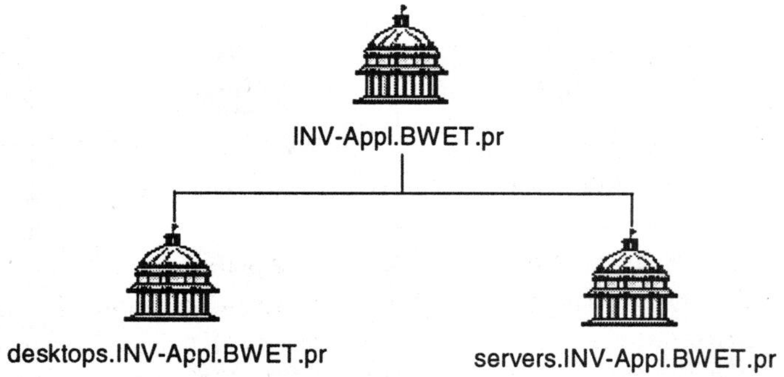

Figure 58. BWET Inventory policy region hierarchy

Tivoli Distributed Monitoring policy region

The approach we have decided to use in this case study is to use a single policy region for Distributed Monitoring. Organizational issues are the most common reason to have multiple subregions. Since that, in our case study scenario, there is no need for the desktop support personnel to monitor the desktops, no policy subregion is required for the Distributed Monitoring policy region, and the administrators defined to the desktop support personnel should not have access to the DM-Appl.BWET.pr policy region. Only the BWET servers and applications running on these servers should be monitored in terms of performance and availability. Therefore, only the server's support personnel will have the required access to this policy region.

Tivoli Remote Control policy region

In the Remote Control policy region there is the need to define another level of subregions. This level is composed by the desktop.RC-Appl.BWET.pr and servers.RC-Appl.BWET.pr. The reason is that the support personnel responsible for desktops should not be allowed to get the control over the servers. Therefore, the administrators defined for the desktop support personnel will not have access to the servers policy region. Figure 59 on page 177 shows the Remote Control policy region hierarchy.

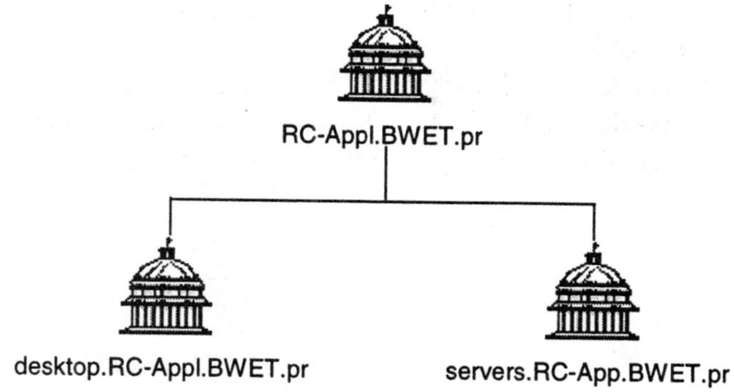

Figure 59. BWET Remote Control policy region hierarchy

10.3.2.3 Subscribers policy region

This policy region will provide an organized set of subregions that accommodate all the subscribers' systems in the organization. These subregions are divided according to the administrative requirements. They are the desktop-Subsc.BWET.pr and servers-subsc.BWET.pr policy regions. A comprehensive tree of profile managers will be created in these subregions. Figure 60 shows the subscribers' policy region hierarchy.

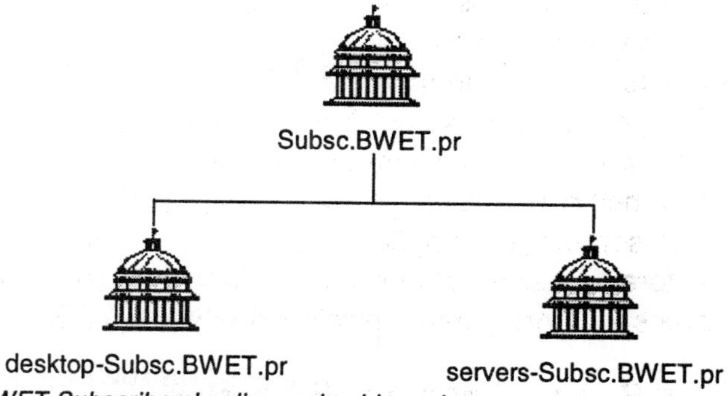

Figure 60. BWET Subscribers' policy region hierarchy

10.3.2.4 Policy region design summary

The following figure, Figure 61 on page 178, provides a summary of our policy region design for BWET.

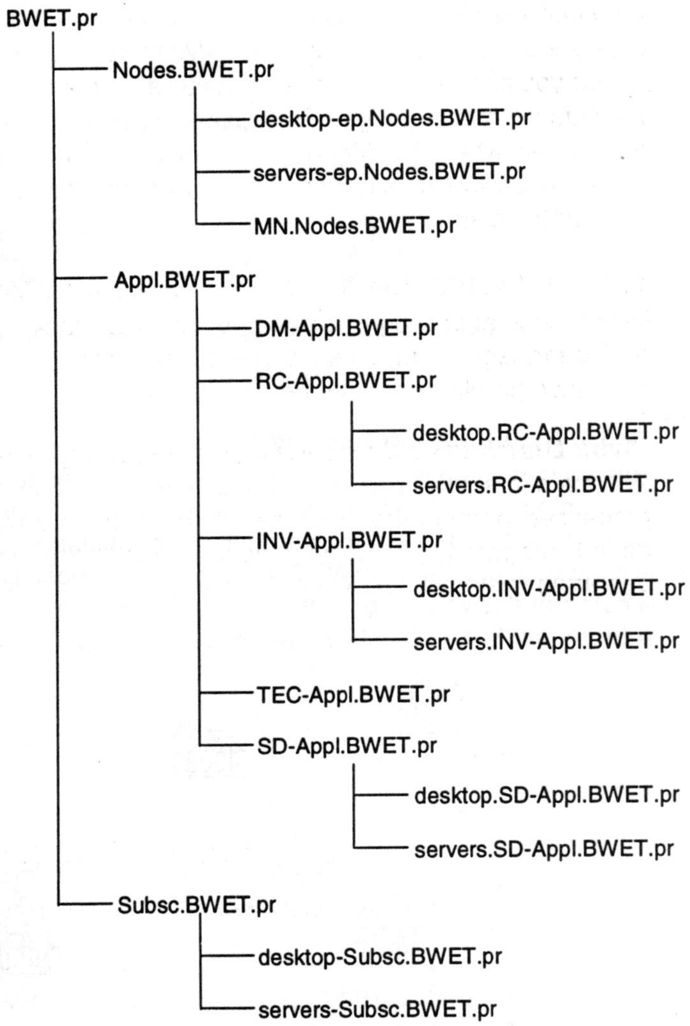

Figure 61. BWET policy region design summary

10.3.3 Profile manager design

In the last section, we provided the policy region design for our fictitious organization. In this section, we provide the profile manager hierarchy design for our case study. Note that it is very important to keep in mind that there are many ways of accomplishing a successful profile manager design, and the design provided here is intended to provide an example.

Based on the fact that there are two profile manager types, we see that all subscriber types, except endpoints, are supported by database mode profile managers. On the other hand, all subscriber types except profile managers, are supported by dataless mode profile managers. Other than operational differences on how the data in a profile is applied, the bulk of this discussion is that you cannot have profile managers and TMA endpoints subscribed to the same profile manager. This lead us to building profile manager hierarchies where the higher level profile managers are running in database mode, and only those profile managers at the lowest level have TMA endpoints as subscribers.

10.3.3.1 Profile manager design for application policy regions

Within each application, specific policy region task libraries and different profile manager hierarchies will be constructed. These profile managers will only have profile managers as subscribers.

Tivoli Distributed Monitoring profile manager design

The main intention is to check the availability of servers, applications and processes in the entire enterprise. In order to do this, the following design is done by separating the profile manager by monitoring purpose and then by operating system as shown in Figure 62 on page 179.

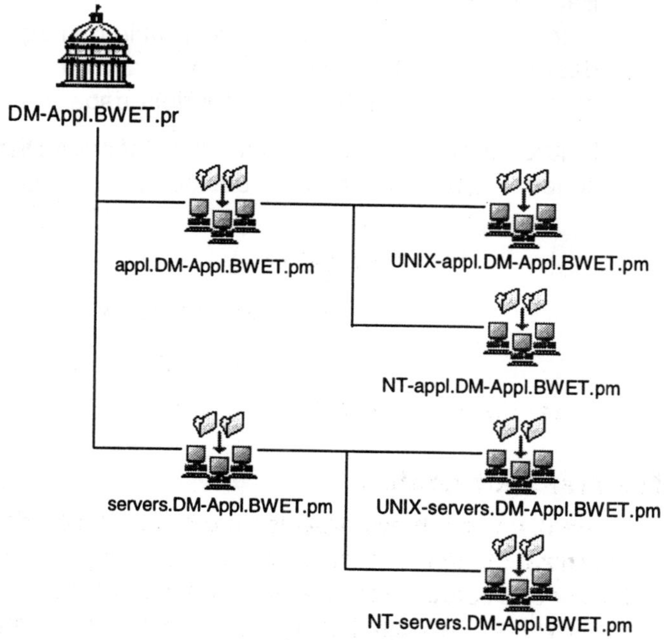

Figure 62. Distributed Monitoring profile manager design

Tivoli Software Distribution profile manager design

The main intention with Software Distribution is to keep the desktops with the most up-to-date and normalized software. In addition, the Support & Systems group will also use it to distribute all applications developed in-house and service packs to servers.

In the desktops' policy region, a hierarchy of profile manager will be created as follows:

- common-desktop.SD-Appl.BWET.pm

  This profile manager holds the file packages that are common to all desktops organization wide. These file packages are part of the normalized software common to all desktops.

- os-desktop.SD-Appl.BWET.pm

  This profile manager holds a second level of profile manager for each of the desktops' operating systems. Inside of these second-level profile managers, the file packages containing the fixes and patches of the desktops' operating systems will be defined.

- dept-desktop.SD-Appl.BWET.pm

  Each department has its own requirements for applications. This profile manager will hold a second-level profile manager, one for each department involved in the solution. Each one of these second-level profile managers will hold the correspondent department's file packages.

  Figure 63 on page 181 outlines the Software Distribution profile manager schema to be defined in the desktop policy region.

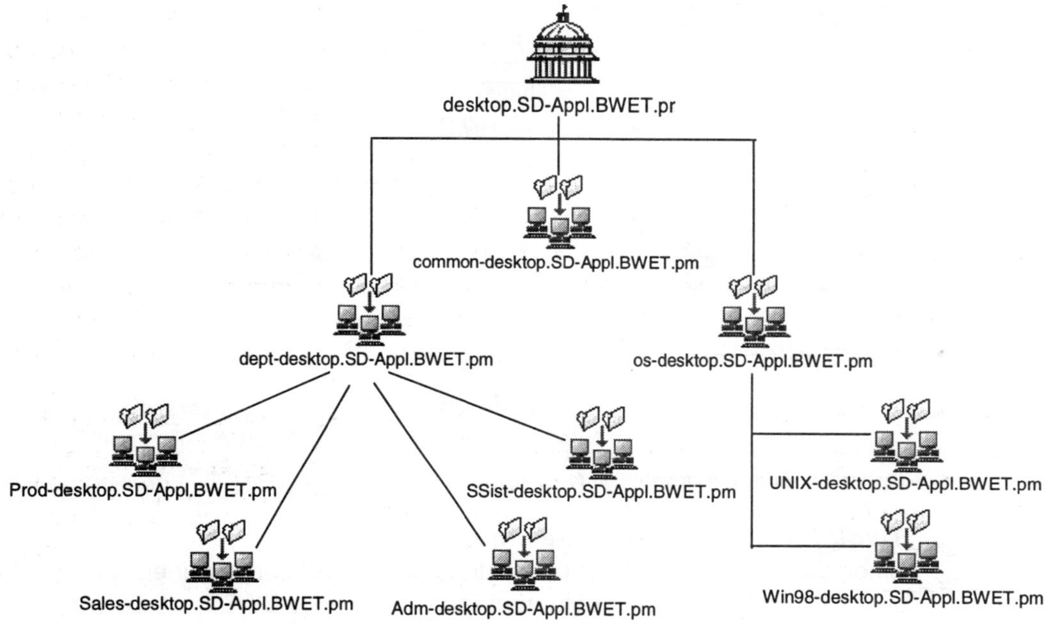

Figure 63. Software distribution for desktops' profile manager design

In the server policy region, the profile manager hierarchy will be as follows:

- appl-servers.SD-Appl.BWET.pm

  This profile manager will hold all file packages for each application used by BWET.

- os-servers.SD-Appl.BWET.pm

  This profile manager holds a second-level profile manager for each of the server's operating systems. Inside of these second level profile managers, the file packages containing the fixes and patches of the server's operating systems will be defined.

  Figure 64 on page 182 outlines the Software Distribution profile manager schema to be defined in the server's policy region.

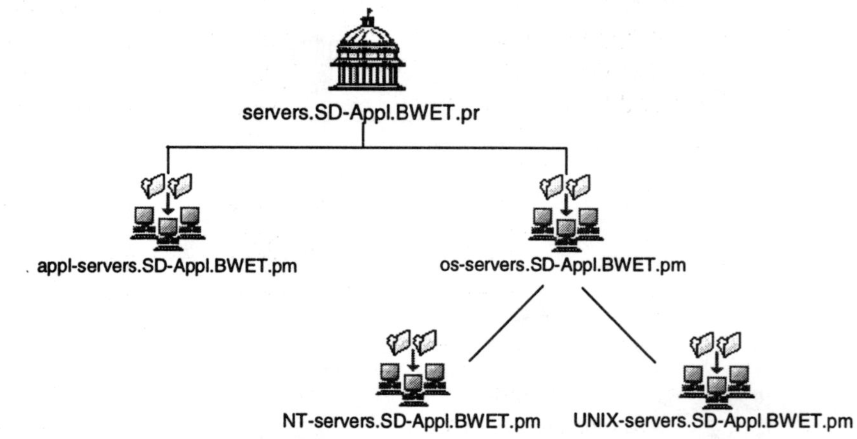

Figure 64. Software distribution for server's profile manager design

Tivoli Inventory profile manager design

Since the authority under the resources that should be scanned is done at the policy region level, the profile manager schema for BWET will be very simple and is shown in Figure 65.

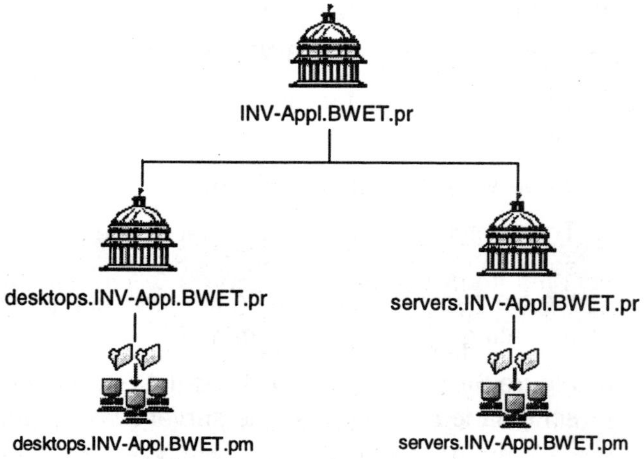

Figure 65. Inventory profile manager design

10.3.3.2 Profile manager design for subscribers' policy region

A comprehensive profile manager hierarchy should be created under the desktop-Subsc.BWET.pr and servers-subsc.BWET.pr subregions in order to provide the required distribution list when the Tivoli administrators for each one of these regions want to distribute profiles.

Figure 66 outlines the desktop subscribers' profile manager schema. In this schema, when creating a desktop, it must be subscribed according to both its operating system and department in the BWET organization. The profile manager desktop-Subsc.BWET.pm will be used, for example, when there is the need to distribute a software package common to all desktops.

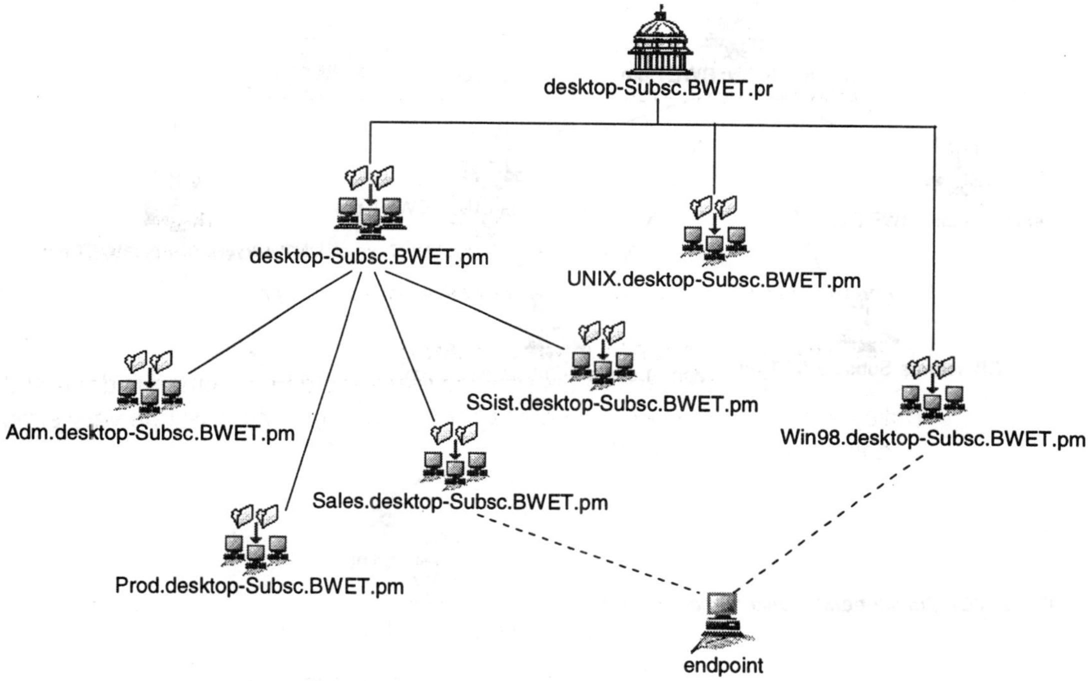

Figure 66. Desktop subscribers' profile manager schema

Figure 67 on page 184 outlines the server's subscriber profile manager schema. In this schema, all servers will be organized according to their operating system and server application. When defining a server in this schema, it must be subscribed to both according to the profile manager of its operating system and according to the application it makes available. The profile manager servers-Subsc.BWET.pm will be used, for example, when there is the need to distribute a software package common to all servers.

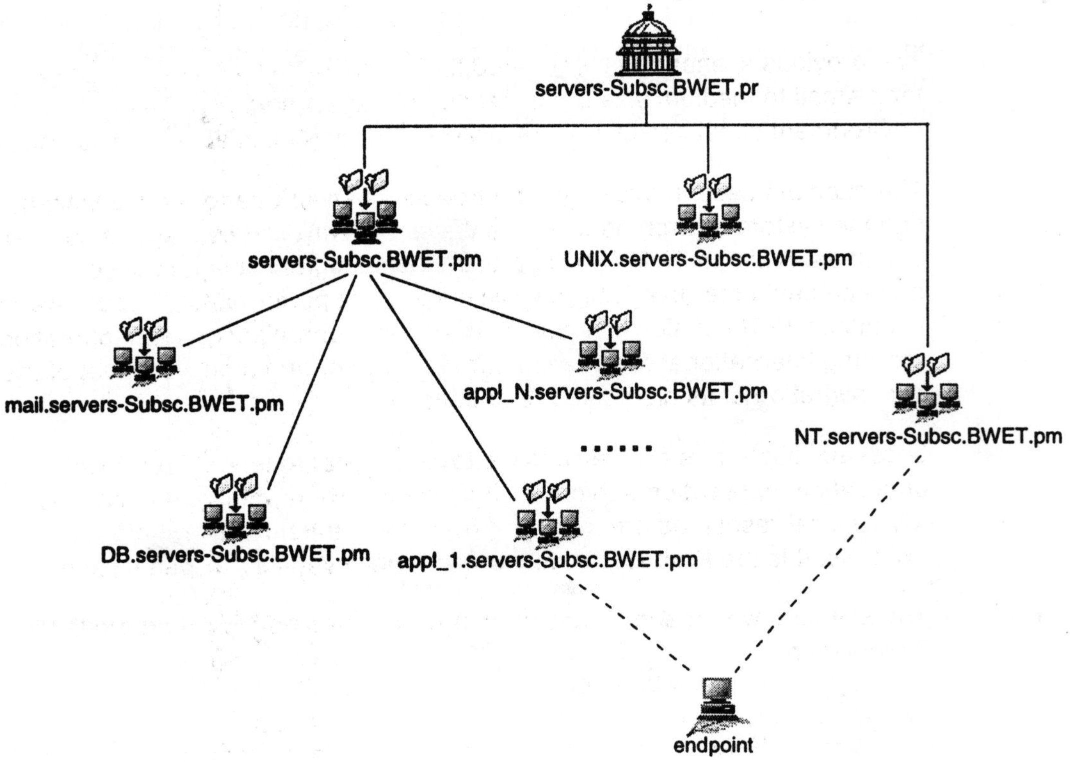

Figure 67. BWET Subscribers' profile manager hierarchy

Chapter 11. Second scenario

The previous scenario demonstrated the logical design and design process for a small to medium size organization. In that scenario, the Tivoli environment consisted of a single TMR server and multiple managed nodes.

The example used in this chapter introduces network performance limitation into the system environment, where the system environment spans several countries. A single TMR server solution is no longer viable for active management of remote resources with adequate performance. In such cases, a multiple-TMR solution is required. In addition, organizations with operations crossing international boundaries introduces another complexity, that of the administration of its distributed resources.

Local administrators are responsible for the management of their local application, application servers, and desktops. There might be instances where local resources are managed from one central location. In our example, it is the Product distribution and Employee payroll departments.

The scenario we present is based on a fictitious company called the BWET Corporation.

Note

The scenario we are presenting in this chapter is abstract and many simplified assumptions have been made. However, you can use this example as a model to understand how the points discussed earlier in this redbook should be applied.

11.1 BWET Corporation overview

BWET Corporation, as a fictitious company, is a major software development company that was initiated from Austin, Texas, USA. BWET Corporation has its own Sales and Marketing department, which is responsible for the marketing of each product that it develops. BWET currently spans its operation in four different countries. The country and their head office location are as follow:

- Austin, Texas, U.S. (Headquarters)
- Mexico City, Mexico
- Brasilia, Brazil

- Sydney, Australia

The structure of the BWET Corporation is such that each country is responsible for all local operations within their respective country. The local operations include Administration, Sales & Marketing, local systems management, and product customization.

Product and patches development are initiated from the Austin headquarter, where new products are developed & tested. Once new products and patches have completed the development and testing phase, they are then distributed to the remaining three countries for local sales distribution.

In the case of newly developed products and patches, once these products and patches are received from the Austin headquarters, local operation will then proceed to customize the product to suit the specification of the local market. Thereafter, the customized product is marketed and distributed to its customers through localized BWET sales offices.

For internal systems upgrade, the Product Distribution division is responsible for distributing the required patches directly to the desktops' workstations and servers from the Austin Headquarters.

The organization structure for BWET Corporation's headquarter at Austin is shown in Figure 68 on page 187. The Product Distribution department is unique to only the Austin operation, where newly developed products, product patches, and all of BWET's systems software are distributed to the remaining three BWET operations located in Sydney, Brasilia, and Mexico City. As seen from the diagram shown in Figure 68, Austin operation has its own Sales & Marketing division to distribute its product across America.

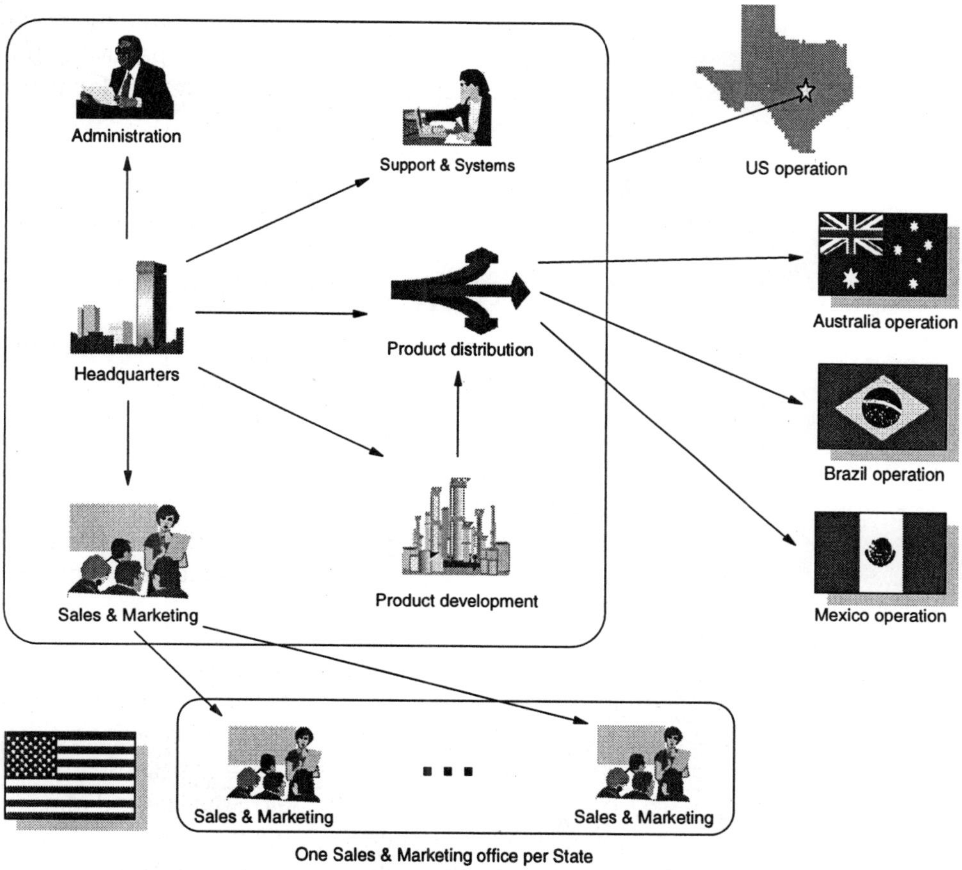

Figure 68. BWET: Austin operation structure

BWET operations are located in Sydney, Mexico City, and Brasilia. Each country's operation has its own Administration, Sales and Marketing, Support & System, and Product Customization divisions. The Product Customization division is responsible for customizing the received product to comply with local standards and specifications. Then, the customized product will be marketed and distributed to its intended customers.

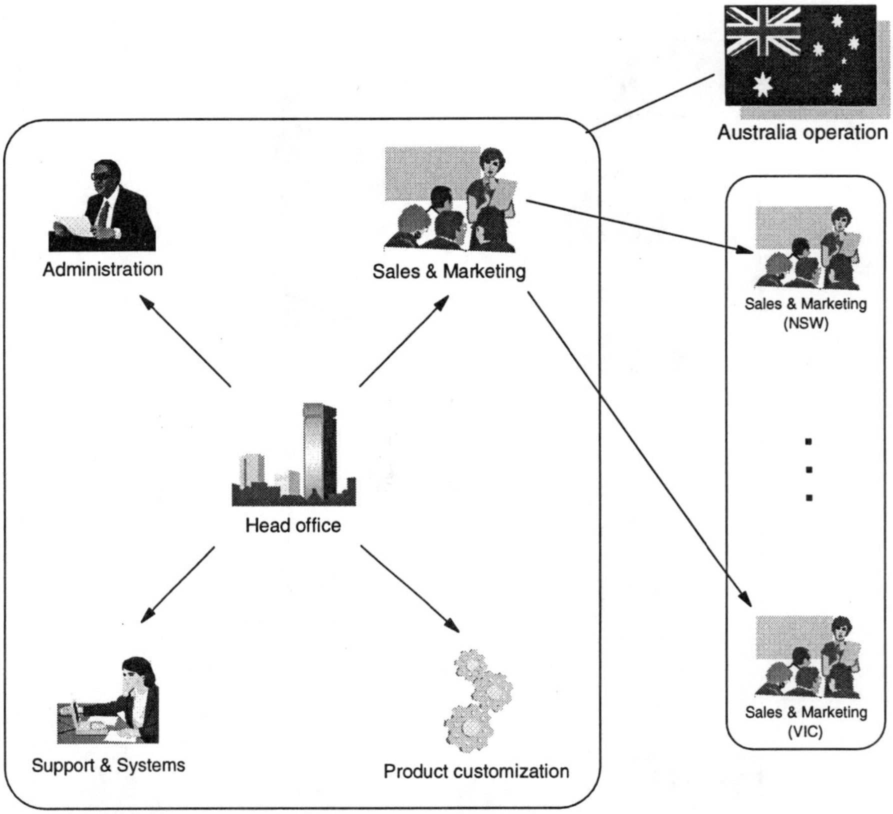

Figure 69. BWET: Sydney operation structure

Figure 69 shows the BWET operation located in Sidney, Australia, as well as the remote Sales & Marketing across Australia.

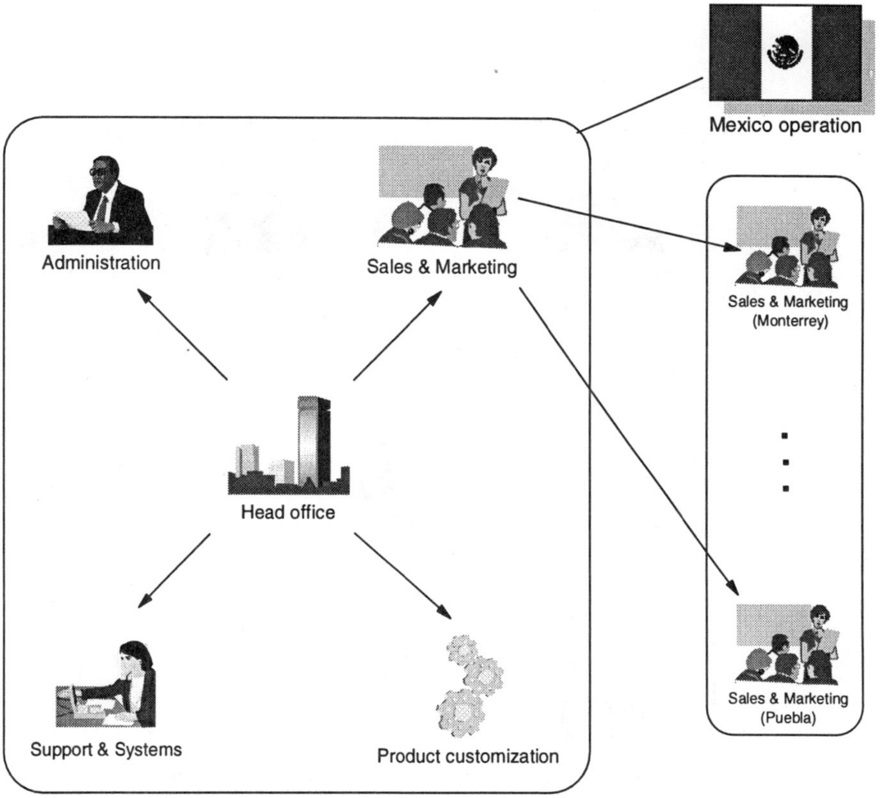

Figure 70. BWET: Mexico City operation

Figure 70 shows the BWET operation located in Mexico City, Mexico, as well as the remote Sales & Marketing across Mexico.

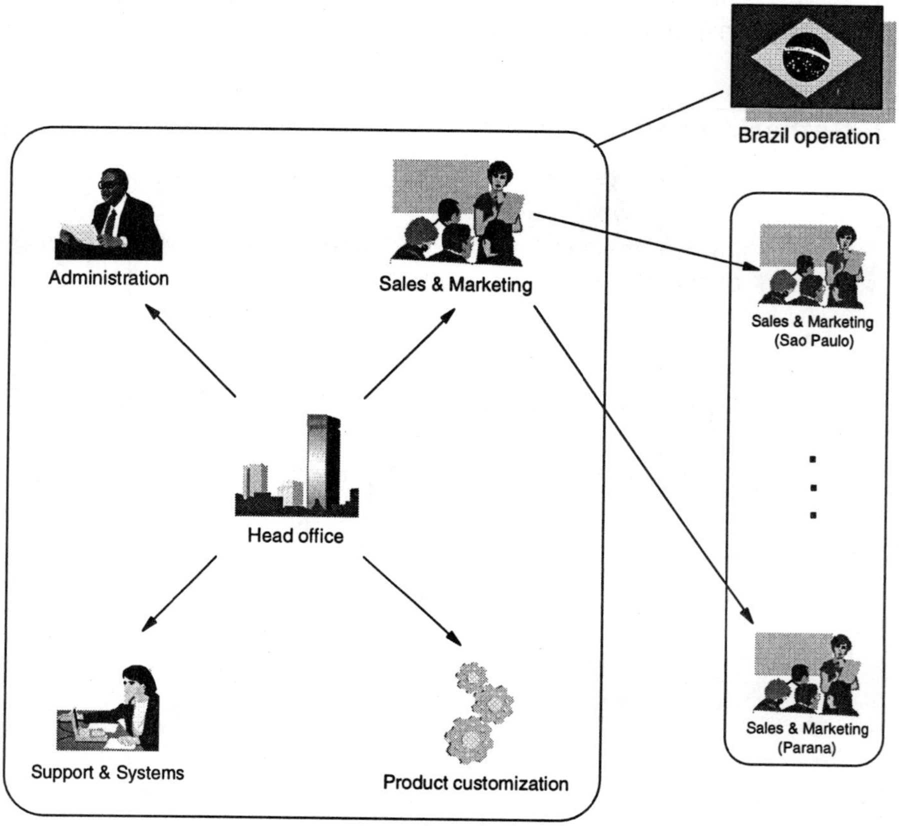

Figure 71. BWET: Brasilia operation

Figure 70 shows the BWET operation located in Brasilia, Brazil, as well as the remote Sales & Marketing across Brazil.

Newly developed products are distributed from the Austin operation down to the remaining three operations. As such, the distribution chain is managed by the Austin operation. That is, all product distribution applications and application servers within the distribution chain are managed from the Austin headquarter.

For consolidation purposes, the Austin headquarter requires access to information concerning sales, payroll, and human resources from all four BWET operations.

Administrators are localized in the head office for each operation. The scope of work for these administrators are performed locally. Access to servers, distributions of desktop software, server monitoring, and inventory are the responsibilities of the local administrators.

11.2 Gathering and consolidating requirements

Similar to the first scenario, careful understanding about the environment is required when designing a Tivoli solution. Thus the design process should always begin with the gathering of information essential for the overall Tivoli design process, both physical and logical.

Selective information gathering can dramatically reduce the amount of time and effort required during the information gathering process. This is especially important when collecting information from an organization that is relatively large in size. In the sections that follow, some of the requirements that are essential for the logical design of a Tivoli solution will be discussed.

Note

The processes demonstrated in this chapter may not apply to some customers under different situations. However, the idea is to demonstrate to readers the concept that is being employed when developing a logical design for Tivoli solutions.

11.2.1 Physical issues

From the highest level, the BWET Corporation has operations that span four countries. Since some operations are currently being managed from the Austin headquarter, the final Tivoli solution must allow administration of remote resources to be performed from Austin. Thus, the network topology between each BWET operations must be considered. The high-level network topology diagram for the BWET Corporation is shown in Figure 72 on page 192.

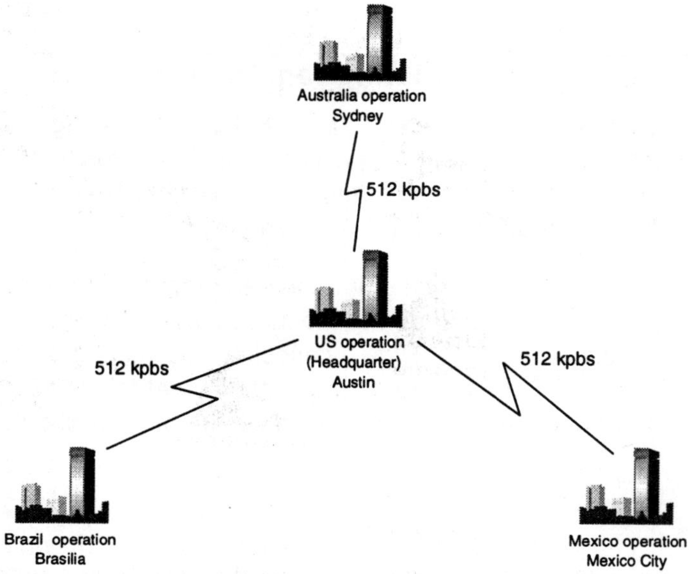

Figure 72. BWET Corporation top-level network topology diagram

On the local operation level, the topology diagrams are shown further. As each country is responsible for its own operation, the BWET Corporation does not have direct connection between Sydney in Australia, Brasilia in Brazil, and Mexico City in Mexico.

Figure 73 on page 193 shows the high level topology diagram of the BWET office headquarters.

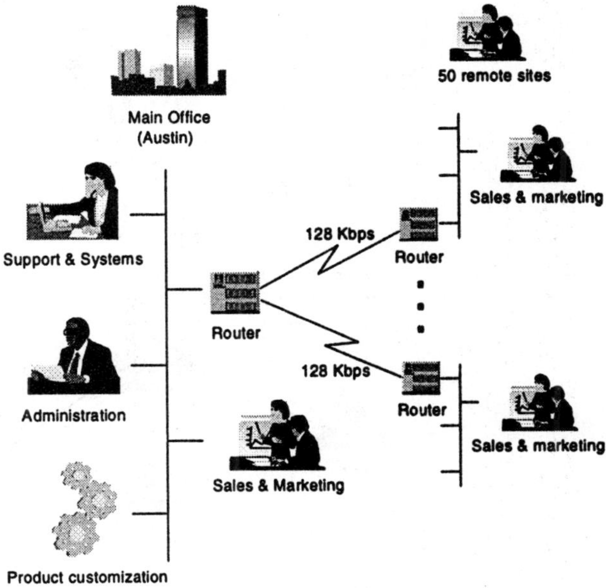

Figure 73. Topology diagram for U.S. operation, head office at Austin

Figure 74 shows the high-level topology diagram of the BWET head office in Sydney, Australia.

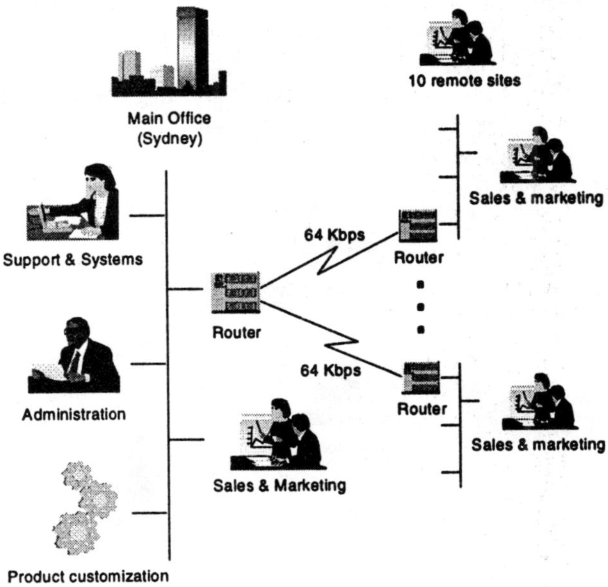

Figure 74. Topology diagram for Australia, head office at Sydney

Figure 75 shows the high-level topology diagram of the BWET head office in Mexico City, Mexico.

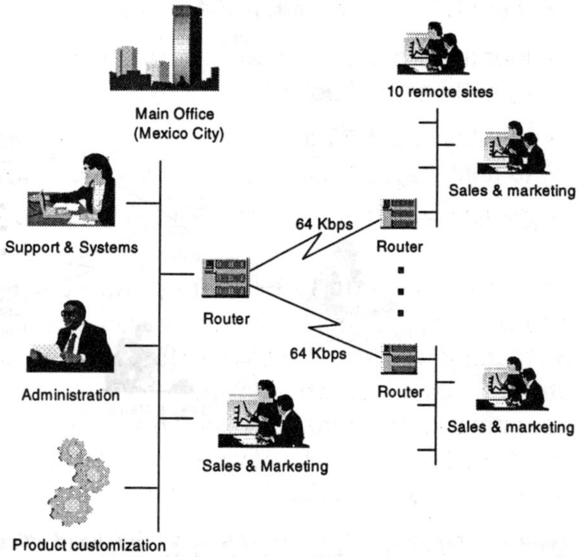

Figure 75. Topology diagram for Mexico, head office at Mexico City

Figure 76 shows the high-level topology diagram of the BWET head office in Brasilia, Brazil.

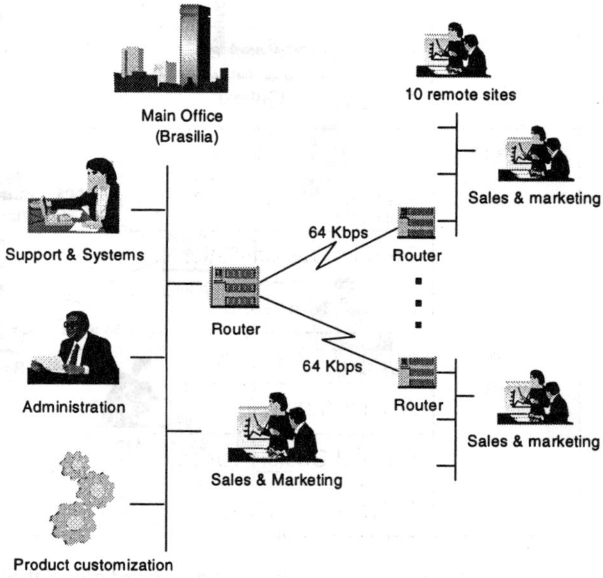

Figure 76. Topology diagram for Brazil, head office at Brasilia

11.2.2 Logical issues

In order to develop a logical design for BWET, the following information is required:

- Identify existing systems to be managed by Tivoli
- Identify system management strategy in accordance to business operations and policies
- Identify appropriate Tivoli application required for the environment in order to fulfil the business requirement and policies
- Collect BWET administrators' structure information

11.2.2.1 Systems to be managed

There are approximately 4,500 desktops and servers of various platforms to be managed across the BWET Corporation. Operating systems that are utilized on desktop workstations consists of Windows 98 and Unix. The operating systems installed on the servers consists of OS/390, UNIX, and Windows NT. Table 11 shows the number of workstations per location and department used in the BWET corporation.

Table 11. BWET desktop workstations location distribution

Location	Local division	Number of workstations
USA	Support & Systems	100
	Administration	500
	Distribution	100
	Product Development	1000
	Sales & marketing	300
Australia	Support & Systems	30
	Administration	200
	Product Customization	370
	Sales & Marketing	100
Mexico	Support & Systems	50
	Administration	300
	Product Customization	400
	Sales & Marketing	200

Location	Local division	Number of workstations
Brazil	Support & Systems	50
	Administration	300
	Product Customization	450
	Sales & Marketing	200

Table 12 shows the number of servers per location and department in use by the BWET corporation.

Table 12. BWET servers location distribution

Location	Local Division	Number of Servers
U.S.	Support & Systems	30
	Administration	6
	Distribution	6
	Product Development	100
	Sales & marketing	50
Australia	Support & Systems	20
	Administration	3
	Distribution[1]	6
	Product customization	40
	Sales & marketing	10
Mexico	Support & Systems	20
	Administration	5
	Distribution[1]	6
	Product customization	50
	Sales & marketing	15

Location	Local Division	Number of Servers
Brazil	Support & Systems	20
	Administration	5
	Distribution[1]	6
	Product customization	60
	Sales & marketing	15
1These servers are managed from the Austin headquarter, but servers are located in local offices.		

11.2.2.2 Systems management strategy

Currently in BWET, no formal system management software and strategy has been deployed. Although some in-house systems management packages have been created for monitoring specific sets of mission critical applications and application servers, traditional methods of support are still being used to provide desktop support within all BWET operations, that is, over the telephone and/or in-person visits to users desktops.

By implementing Tivoli, a system management strategy will be developed in accordance to BWET's business objectives. The objectives of the system strategy for BWET are as follow:

- Servers security and information access

  No one in BWET operations can assess information or systems of another operation. With the exception of the Austin headquarters, which periodically download payroll and sales information from each operation for consolidation purposes.

- Availability of management environment

  The availability of managed servers and applications is essential for continuous uninterrupted operation for all operations.

- Desktop availability

  Provide fast and effective support for all desktop users to reduce desktop down time.

- Standard configuration for desktops

  The organization needs a way of deploying an ad maintaining a standard configuration of all desktops for each division, thereby, reducing the cost of maintaining the desktop environment.

11.2.2.3 Identifying Tivoli applications

Based on the information in 11.2.2.2, “Systems management strategy” on page 197, a set of Tivoli management applications are then identified to fulfil the requirement of the business organization.

Table 13. Tivoli management application for BWET

Business requirement	Corresponding Tivoli management application
Systems and Application management	Tivoli Distributed Monitoring
	Tivoli Enterprise Console (TEC)
Server and Desktop systems support	Tivoli Remote Control
Desktop management	Tivoli Software Distribution
	Tivoli Inventory

Tivoli Distributed Monitoring

Tivoli Distributed Monitoring will be used to monitor the status of a variety of networked resources, such as systems, applications, and processes in the entire enterprise. Monitoring thresholds can be configured to triggered alerts when potential resource outrage is detected, for example, disk space running low.

Tivoli Enterprise Console

The Tivoli Enterprise Console will offer a centralized, global view of the organization computing environment, ensuring the high availability of the organization’s application and computing resources. The Tivoli Enterprise Console will act as a central collection point for alerts and events received from the other Tivoli applications and ensure that all problems will be handled by the appropriate support engineer.

Tivoli Software Distribution

Tivoli Software Distribution will be used by the Support & Systems group to keep the desktops with most up-to-date and standardized software organization wide.

Tivoli Inventory

Tivoli Inventory will gather the organization’s hardware and software inventory to assist the Support & Systems department in detecting unauthorized hardware/software on desktop systems. Inventory will regularly store hardware and software inventory information, monitor and record changes in software and hardware configurations, manage all enterprise systems from a central point, and examine inventory information to perform system auditing functions.

Tivoli Remote Control

The Support & Systems personnel often need to manage the users' desktops. Tivoli Remote Control will provide a convenient alternative for managing PCs, enabling the Support & Systems personnel to take control the user's keyboard and mouse input, monitor the display output of a remote PC, thus, being more effective on the solution of reporting problems.

11.2.2.4 Collecting administrator information

According to Chapter 5., "Administrators' considerations" on page 67, this part of the logical design consists of the following tasks:

- Interview the workers

  This will allow logical design architects to understand actual administrative tasks that administrators are performing in order to determine the actual level of access required by system administrators managing the environment.

- Consult management policy

  This will allow architects to determine the maximum level of access that should be assigned to a specific administrators.

- Compromise policy and responsibility

  This allow architects to determine the appropriate level of access an administrator should have to perform his/her administrative tasks.

According to the organization structure obtained from 11.1, "BWET Corporation overview" on page 185, the BWET system environment is made up of three technology divisions that require access to internal systems in order to perform their administrative tasks. There should be at least three different groups of administrators across the BWET Corporation.

After interviewing the appropriate system administrators and consulting the appropriate management and security policy document, the following administrator groups were identified across BWET Corporation.

Global Product Development group

This group is responsible for the development and testing of new marketable products that are being offered by the BWET Corporation. Once a new product or application has completed its development and product testing phases, the product code is placed on global repository servers located in the Austin headquarters.

This group is also responsible for developing internal server/desktop systems applications and upgrades patches across the BWET Corporation. Applications and upgrade patches that are being developed by this group are mainly in-house applications that do not require any local customization.

In a summary, the responsibilities of the Global Product Development group are:

- Development of new BWET offered products.
- Perform product testing on newly developed products.
- Place product code on repository servers located in Austin.
- Development of applications and upgrade patches for server/desktop systems across the BWET Corporation.
- Perform testing on applications and upgrade patches.
- Requires access to global repository servers.

Global Distribution group

This group of administrators are responsible for distributing new applications and upgrade patches down to all server and desktop systems that are located at each local operation (Austin, Sydney, Brasilia, and Mexico City). Applications that will be distributed by this group require no local customizations. In-house applications fall into this category.

In a summary, the responsibilities of the Global Distribution group are:

- Directly distribute software to any servers or desktops across all BWET operations.
- Requires access to all servers and desktops for distribution of file packages.

Local Product Development group

This group is responsible for the development and testing of software applications and upgrade patches for all server and desktop systems within their local BWET operation. Once these upgrades and patches are developed and tested, they are then placed on repository servers located in their local operation.

This group is also responsible for customizing all new BWET offered products for local distribution. This ensures that all new products comply with all required local standards and specifications.

In a summary, the responsibilities of the Local Product Development group are:

- Development and testing of upgrade patches for server/workstation systems within their local operation.
- Place upgrade patches on local repository servers.
- Customization of new BWET offered products according to local standards and specifications.
- Place customized BWET offered products on local repository servers.
- Requires access to local repository servers.

Local Help desk Support group

This group is responsible for the support of all desktop workstations and workstation applications within their local BWET operation. They provide telephone support to desktop end users at their local BWET operations.

In a summary, the responsibilities of the Local Help desk Support group is:

- Provide desktop and desktop application support to local end users over the telephone.

Local Server Support group

This group is responsible for the health of all server systems and server applications within their local BWET operation.

This group is also responsible for distributing upgrade patches that have been developed by the Local Product development group to all servers within their local operation.

In a summary, the responsibilities of the Local Server Support group are:

- Responsible for general health of all server systems and server applications within their local BWET operation.
- Responsible for redistribution of upgrade patches to all server systems within their BWET local operation.
- Requires access to all server systems across the BWET Corporation within their local operation.

Local Desktop Support group

This group is responsible for the health of all desktop systems and desktop applications within their BWET operation. They are the next level of support after the Local Help desk support group.

This group is also responsible for the distribution of upgrade patches that have been developed by the Local development group to all desktop systems within their local operation.

In a summary, the responsibilities of the Local Desktop Support group are:

- Next level of support for desktop systems after the Support & Systems division (Help desk) group.
- Responsible for the distribution of upgrade patches to all desktop systems within their local BWET operation.
- Requires access to all desktop systems across BWET within their local operation.

Global/local Tivoli management group

This group is created specifically for the management of the overall Tivoli environment within the BWET environment. This includes the monitoring and support of all the TMR servers, TEC servers, endpoint gateways, and other application server managed nodes that have been installed as part of the Tivoli infrastructure as well as creating and configuring Tivoli objects within the BWET Tivoli environment.

On the local level, this group of administrators will be responsible for the creation of policy regions and Tivoli administrators in the local operation TMR as well as the setting of subscriptions to specific profile managers. On the global level, this group will be responsible for the health of all servers that make up the Tivoli infrastructure. This includes the TMR servers, TEC servers, endpoint gateways, and other Tivoli application servers.

In a summary, the responsibilities of the Global/local Tivoli management group are:

- Responsible for overall health of Tivoli infrastructure.
- Responsible for creating and configuring all Tivoli objects within local operations.
- Requires access to all servers that are part of the Tivoli infrastructure

11.2.2.5 Getting the Tivoli physical design

A physical design of the Tivoli solution has been developed by the Tivoli physical architect. The setup of the Tivoli physical design is presented in Figure 77 on page 203. The physical layout for Sydney and Mexico City is not shown in this figure; however, they resemble the physical design for Brasilia.

Note

The physical design presented in Figure 77 for this case study is one of many viable physical designs that can be used for the BWET corporation. However, the physical design should take into consideration factors that may effect the performance of the Tivoli solution, for example, network bandwidth, firewalls, etc.

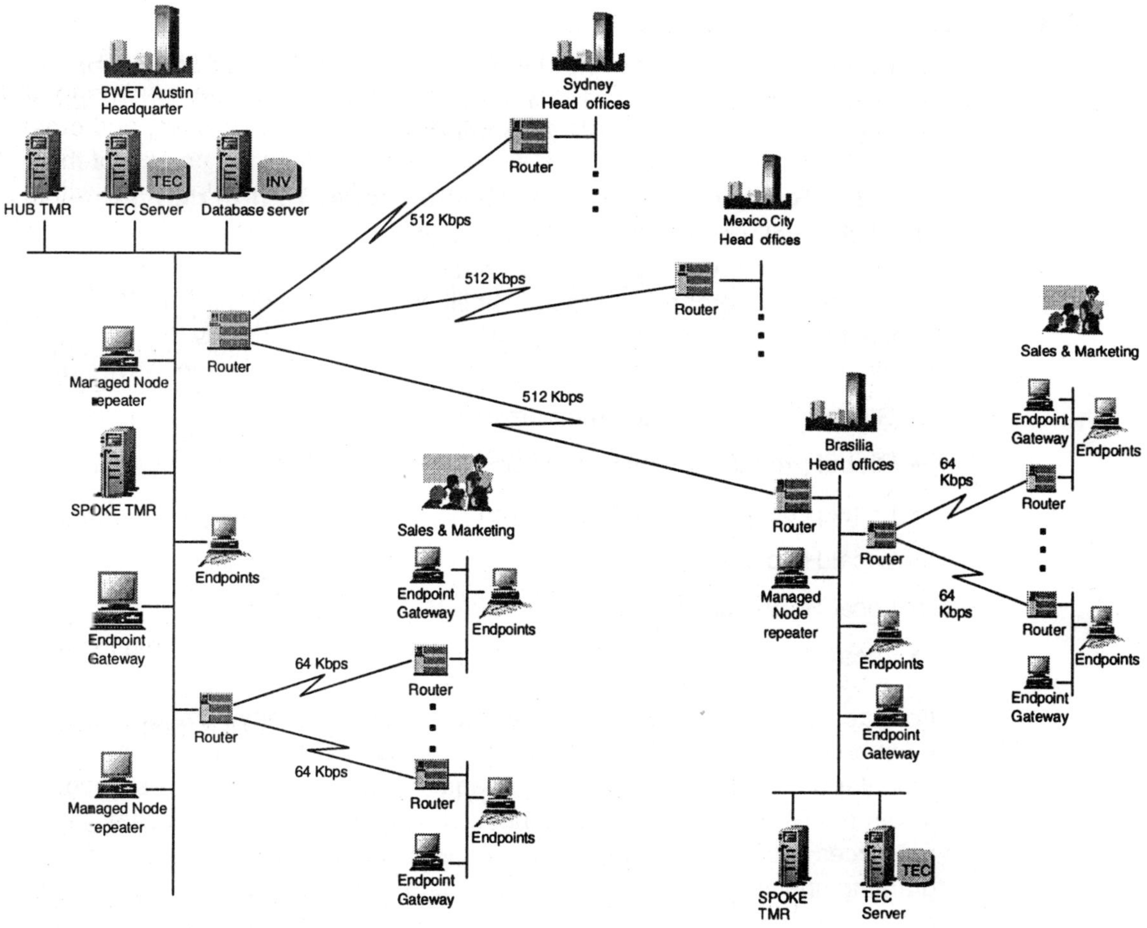

Figure 77. BWET Tivoli physical design

A *spoke* TMR server will be placed at each operation's head office. Other TME clients (managed nodes, TEC Event servers, endpoint gateways, and endpoints) are then placed in their appropriate locations to maximize the performance of the Tivoli infrastructure.

Managed nodes acting as repeaters will be placed at both ends of WAN links to allow tuning capability in accordance to the properties of the specific link. One TEC event server, one Inventory server, and their database servers will be installed on each spoke TMR for these applications.

A *Hub* TMR server will be installed in the Austin head office. The Hub TMR can be used to manage the Tivoli infrastructure within the BWET Tivoli environment.

11.2.3 Consolidating information

In this section, we use the knowledge acquired in 9.1, "Gathering information and requirements" on page 144 in order to proceed with the construction of the logical design for the BWET Corporation.

11.2.3.1 Resource responsibilities for policy region design

Using the methods that were introduced in 9.1.2, "Consolidating the information" on page 148, a matrix should be created containing the mapping of administrator groups and responsibilities. As discussed in 11.2.2.4, "Collecting administrator information" on page 199, the following administrator groups have been identified in the BWET system environment:

- Global product development group
- Global product distribution group
- Local product development group
- Local Help desk group
- Local Server support
- Local Desktop group

For each group of administrators, the resources that they have access to must be consolidated. This will give the logical architect an idea on how granular the overall logical design needs to be when grouping resources within the BWET system environment. Using policy regions, system resources within the environment can be logically grouped together. By granting specific administrators appropriate Tivoli resource roles to these policy regions, system administrators' access can be restricted to specific groups of resources. This information was discussed in Chapter 3, "Policy region design" on page 27 and Chapter 5, "Administrators' considerations" on page 67.

The resource responsibility matrix is provided in Table 14 on page 205. This matrix is generated using the information gathered from several information sources, which were discussed in earlier sections of this chapter.

The information retrieved from these sources should give logical architects the required information to start developing an initial Tivoli Logical Design. Sections that follow will describe some of the many processes that can be used in developing schemes that form the overall logical design. These schemes are:

- Policy region schema
- Profile manager & profile schema
- Subscription schema
- Administrator schema

The following table shows the resource responsibility matrix for this case study.

Table 14. Resource responsibility matrix for administrator groups

Systems		**Administrator groups**					
Machine class	**BWET Divisions**	**Global Product Development group**	**Global Product Distribution group**	**Local Product Development group**	**Local Help desk Support group**	**Local Server Support group**	**Local Desktop Support group**
Server **Operating Systems (UNIX, NT, OS/2)**	**Administration**	-	SD, INV	-	-	SD, INV, DM, TEC, RC	-
	Sales & Marketing	-	SD, INV	-	-	SD, INV, DM, TEC, RC	-
	Support & Systems	-	SD, INV	-	-	SD, INV, DM, TEC, RC	-
	Product Development/ Local Customization[1]	-	SD, INV	-	-	SD, INV, DM, TEC, RC	-
	Product Distribution (Austin only)	-	SD, INV	-	-	SD, INV, DM, TEC, RC	-

Systems		Administrator groups					
Machine class	**BWET Divisions**	**Global Product Development group**	**Global Product Distribution group**	**Local Product Development group**	**Local Help desk Support group**	**Local Server Support group**	**Local Desktop Support group**
Desktop	**Austin, U.S.**	-	SD, INV	-	RC, INV	-	SD, INV, RC
Operating systems	**Sydney, Australia**	-	SD, INV	-	RC, INV	-	SD, INV, RC
(NT, Win95, OS/2)	**Brasilia, Brazil**	-	SD, INV	-	RC, INV	-	SD, INV, RC
	Mexico City, Mexico	-	SD, INV	-	RC, INV	-	SD, INV, RC
		-	SD, INV		RC, INV		SD, INV, RC

[1] Local Customization Division is similar to the Product development division in Austin in the sense that these groups are effectively performing the same type of activities except on a global and local level.

11.2.3.2 Application usage for profile manager and profile design

This section explains how the Tivoli applications involved will be used so that we can consolidate this information to perform the profile manager schema.

Tivoli Inventory

Inventory will be done by automated scripts and by flash scan on resources by the administrators. When administrators do manual scans, they will do so one machine at a time. Only local administrators collect inventory information, and they only do so for the resources they support. For this reason, targets are grouped into server and desktop. Each location has one of these groups. There is no need for further grouping within these groups.

Tivoli Software Distribution

Software distribution will be done by both local and global administrators. The global administrator will distribute to both servers and desktop, while the local administrator will distribute only to the group they support (desktop or servers). Table 15 list the grouping per software type.

Table 15. Software distribution characteristics

Software Type	**Distribution Grouping**			
	Location	**Department**	**Platform/OS**	**Function**
Inhouse App.		Always Used	Always Used	
Global Tools	Used for performance	Always Used	Always Used	
Local Tools	Used, but not relevant since distribution is done locally	Always used	Always used	Desktop/ Server separation for administrators
OS Patching	Used, but ignore because distribution is local		Always used	Desktop/ Server separation for administrators

Note that the function separation has some influence in the security model. Therefore, this is a strong candidate for a top-level profile manager. Local tools and OS patches are handled locally, thus, location is not relevant.

Tivoli Distributed Monitoring

Only servers are monitored, and this is done per location. Naming conventions are the same throughout the local administrations. There is some global monitoring of resources in use to maintain the Tivoli infrastructure. This is done at the Hubs using subscribers in the spokes.

Tivoli Remote Control

Local administrator will control their local machines; however, global administrator may also control the machines that are used to support the Tivoli environment.

Tivoli Enterprise Console (TEC)

TEC will be used in both local and global levels. The global TEC server will consolidate events in the Tivoli infrastructure servers, while local TEC servers will handle the events at the local level. Only one group of administrators has access to the TEC events.

11.3 Logical design

In this section, a logical design will be developed for the BWET Corporation. Information that was gathered and consolidated in 11.1, "BWET Corporation overview" on page 185 and 11.2, "Gathering and consolidating requirements" on page 191 will be used in developing the appropriate schemes for policy region, profile manager, profiles, and subscriber within the BWET Tivoli environment.

In designing the Hub-Spoke Tivoli configuration for BWET, the design will initially be focused on the spoke TMRs. Hub design will then be discussed once all spoke TMR designs are completed. For illustration purposes, the logical design for the U.S. (Austin) operations and Brazil (Brasilia) operations will be discussed for the spoke TMRs. The logical design for the remaining two operations (Mexico and Sydney) will resemble that of the Brazil design.

11.3.1 Initial and base policy region schema

This section describes the policy region schema to be used by the BWET Corporation. All recommendations provided in Chapter 3, "Policy region design" on page 27 were taken into consideration.

11.3.1.1 Spoke TMRs policy region schema

According to 9.2.1, "General design flow" on page 154, the logical design process is initialized with an initial policy region design. Thereafter, a base policy region design should be developed after taking consideration of information and issues that were gathered during the information gathering phase. This section will first discuss the initial policy region design process, then demonstrate how to use the information that has been gathered to develop a base policy region for the BWET Corporation.

The initial design for BWET will be the same for each remote location. Figure 78 on page 209 shows the policy region schema of the spoke TMR to be defined in each BWET remote location. The initial design shown in this figure base the overall Tivoli logical design by function. That is, the policy region schema is grouped in such a way that grouping of resources are based on Tivoli application management functions. This proves to be the most effective way to group system resources in an environment where administrators are distinguished by their work function. For example, an administrator can be granted the right to use Tivoli Remote Control for active controlling of remote desktops by being assigned resource rights to the policy region containing the remote control object.

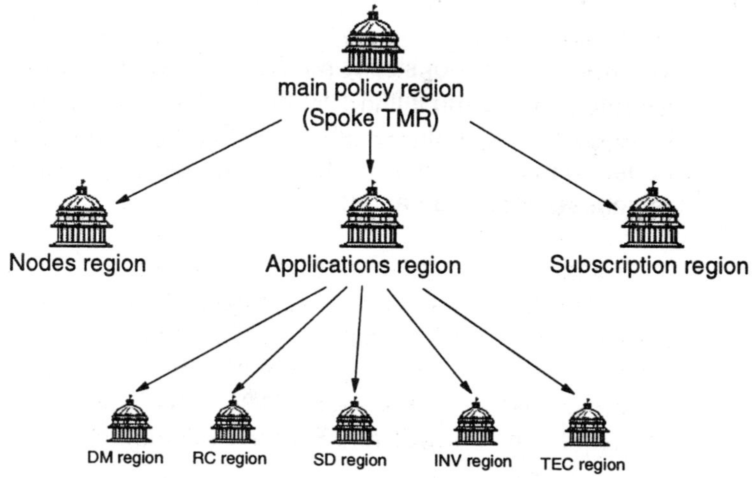

Figure 78. Initial Spoke policy region design for BWET

Note that the name for the policy region has not been given at this stage of the logical design. A naming convention for the policy region schema should be given only when a majority of the policy region that will be implemented in the environment has been declared in the design schema. It is only then that the required granularity of the schema is known. However, a meaningful temporary name has been given to illustrate the purpose of each policy regions that has been created in the design.

In the initial policy region schema, the following policy region were created:

Nodes region This policy region contains only TME clients (TMR server, managed nodes, endpoint gateways, PC managed nodes, and endpoints). This allow the grouping of system resources and the setting of policies to resources by group/policy region.

Applications region This policy region contains the third level of policy regions for each Tivoli management application as shown in Figure 78. Only profile managers, application profiles (file package, autopack, sentry profile, inventory profile, ACP), and remote control objects will be defined into these policy regions. Again this allow easy access control to application by means of profile manager subscriptions.

Subscription region This policy region contains a profile manager with only system resources as subscribers. This determines the ultimate receivers of profiles from different management applications.

The resource responsibility matrix from Table 14 on page 205 can then be used to develop the initial design as shown in Figure 78 on page 209, to the base policy region design shown in Figure 79. Four policy regions have been added to the initial policy schema: The managed node region, endpoint region, server region and the desktop region.

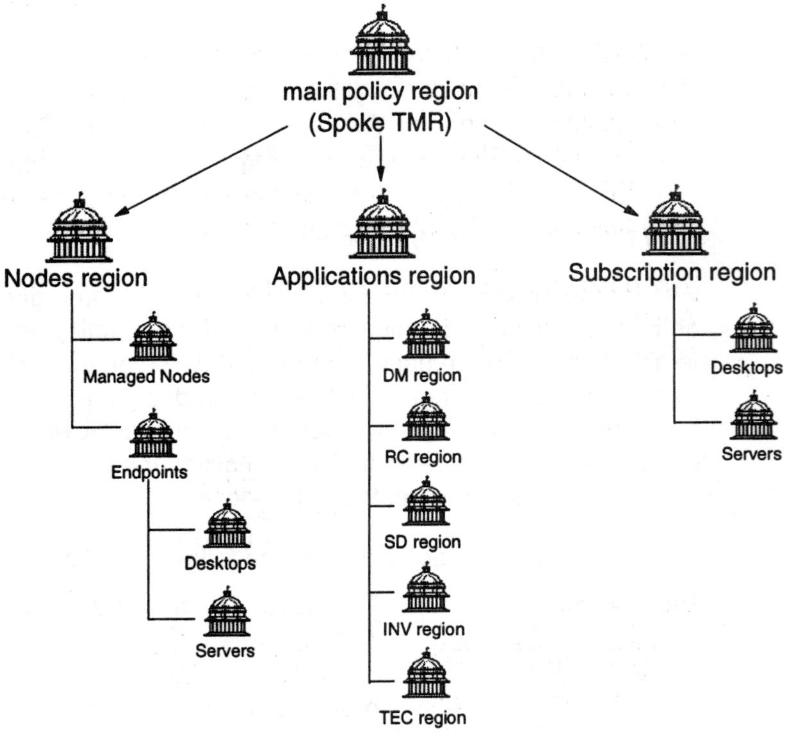

Figure 79. Base policy region design for a generic Spoke level

Under the Nodes policy region, the managed nodes and the endpoints' policy regions were created in order to group all Tivoli clients into either Tivoli Framework clients (TMR, TEC, INV server, endpoints gateways) or Light Client framework (endpoints). Since there will be no more than 30 TME10 Framework clients, there is no need to create subregions under the Managed Node policy region. On the other hand, two subregions were created under the endpoints policy region. The Server and Desktop subregions were created to separate the endpoints into severs and desktop workstations. This was done because of the large number of endpoints in the BWET environment. As administrators' responsibility is not bound by system operating platforms, no further policy subregion is created within the Server and Desktop policy region. Logical architects may wish to use Tivoli Generic Collection to group severs and endpoints by business units, if required.

The Subscription region is further broken down into Server and Desktop subregions. This enables default policy to be set on subscription profile managers to only display server endpoints to the Server support group and workstation endpoints to the Local Desktop Support group. A hierarchy of the profile manager will be created under these subregions.

11.3.1.2 Hub TMR policy region schema

The purpose of the Hub TMR is to manage the Tivoli infrastructure that has been installed onto the BWET system environment. The Tivoli infrastructure includes all TMR servers, all Tivoli management application servers (TEC, INV, SD, RC), and endpoint gateways that have been used to manage system resources within the BWET environment.

The policy region schema for the Hub TMR is shown in Figure 80. The Australia operation will be used as the representative model for other operations (Brazil, Mexico, and USA) of BWET.

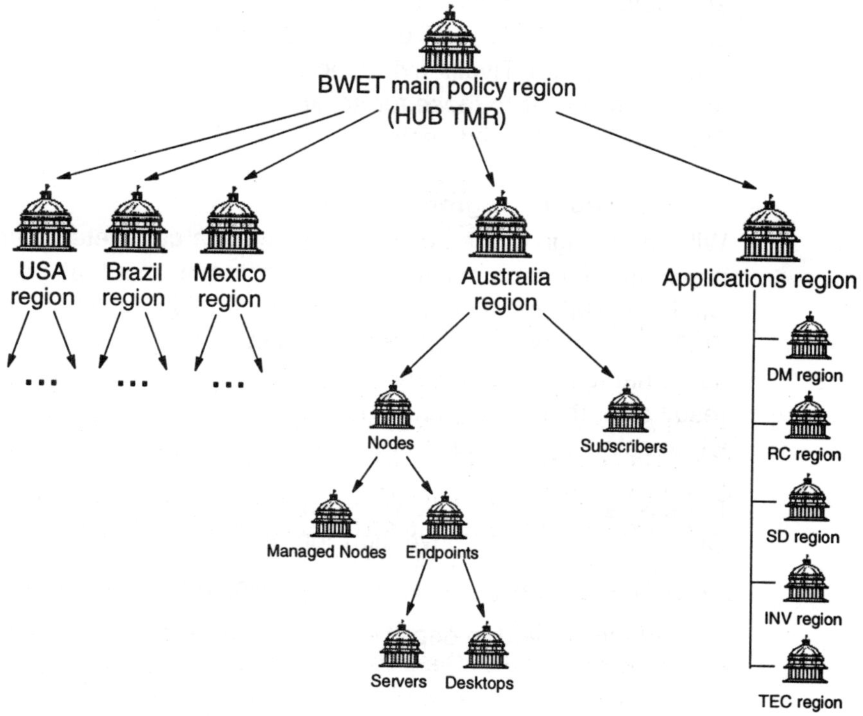

Figure 80. Hub TMR policy region schema for BWET Corporation (Hub level)

The *Hub* TMR for the BWET Corporation can be created by establishing a TMR inter-connection between the designated Hub TMR server to each overseas TMR server (*Spoke* TMRs). TMR servers can be inter-connected by either establishing a one-way connection from one managing TMR server (*Hub* TMR server) to other TMR servers, or by establishing a two-way inter-connection between two or more TMR servers. Since a *Hub-Spoke* configuration entails the management of one or more TMR servers from one single TMR server, a one-way connection is required to be established from the managing Hub TMR server to any TMR servers that it will manage. In the case of the BWET Corporation, a one-way inter-connection should be initiated from the designated *Hub* TMR server to the Austin TMR server, Sydney TMR server, Brasilia TMR server, and to the Mexico City TMR server.

Once these TMR servers are interconnected, the resources within each spoke TMR will be accessible from the Hub TMR server. This is shown in Figure 80. After the TMR servers are interconnected, all the resources within the spoke TMR will be updated to the Hub TMR server database. Thus, the logical structure for each overseas operation (sections NOT highlighted in Figure 80) will be implemented by default to the overall *Hub* TMR logical structure upon inter-connection.

To manage the Tivoli infrastructure using Tivoli management applications, an application policy region is created within the *Hub* TMR. This policy region will contain profiles and Tivoli objects that will be used to manage all TME servers within the BWET Tivoli environment. The logical design for the application regions is similar to those for spoke TMRs, and its structure is depicted in Figure 80 (highlighted section).

11.3.1.3 Policy region names

With the design of the policy region schema completed, names can be nominated for each policy region. As a requirement, all policy region names within an TMR must be unique. This restriction applies to inter-connected TMRs also. If two or more policy regions from two or more TMRs have the same name before they are interconnected, unpredictable properties might result after these TMRs are interconnected. Therefore, care must be taken when selecting a naming standard.

For scenario two, the following standards, in addition to those described in Chapter 2, “Naming convention” on page 19, will be applied:

- Only lower case will be used on policy region names.
- Each field used to depict different groupings will be separated by a “.”.

- Country code used are shown in Table 16.

Table 16. Country code U.S.

Country	Country code
Hub	hub
U.S.	us
Australia	au
Mexico	mx
Brazil	br

- From left to right, fields will start from generic groups to more specific groupings.

Following these standards, in addition to those discussed in Chapter 2, "Naming convention" on page 19, policy region names for each Spoke TMR and for the Hub TMR are as follow:

Spoke TMR (U.S. operation)

Table 17. Policy region names for U.S. operation logical design

Policy region purpose	Policy region name
Top policy region	us.pr
Nodes region	us.node.pr
Managed node region	us.node.mn.pr
Endpoints region	us.node.ep.pr
Desktop endpoint region	us.node.ep.dsk.pr
Server endpoint region	us.node.ep.srv.pr
Subscription region	us.sub.pr
Severs subscription region	us.sub.svr.pr
Desktops subscription region	us.sub.dsk.pr
Profiles region	us.app.pr
TEC region	us.app.tec.pr
Inventory region	us.app.inv.pr
Software Distribution region	us.app.sd.pr
Remote Control region	us.app.rc.pr

Policy region purpose	Policy region name
Remote Control region (desktop)	us.app.rc.dsk.pr
Remote Control region (server)	us.app.rc.srv.pr
Distributed Monitoring region	us.app.dm.pr

Spoke TMR (Brazil operation)

Table 18. Policy region names for Brazil operation logical design

Policy region purpose	Policy region name
Top policy region	br.pr
Nodes region	br.node.pr
Managed node region	br.node.mn.pr
Endpoints region	br.node.ep.pr
Desktop endpoint region	br.node.ep.dsk.pr
Server endpoint region	br.node.ep.srv.pr
Subscription region	br.sub.pr
Servers subscription region	br.sub.srv.pr
Desktops subscription region	br.sub.dsk.pr
Profiles region	br.app.pr
TEC region	br.app.tec.pr
Inventory region	br.app.inv.pr
Software Distribution region	br.app.sd.pr
Remote Control region	br.app.rc.pr
Remote Control region (desktop)	br.app.rc.dsk.pr
Remote Control region (server)	br.app.rc.srv.pr
Distributed Monitoring region	br.app.dm.pr

Spoke TMR (Mexico operation)

Table 19. Policy region names for Mexico operation logical design

Policy region purpose	Policy region name
Top policy region	mx.pr

Policy region purpose	Policy region name
Nodes region	mx.node.pr
Managed node region	mx.node.mn.pr
Endpoints region	mx.node.ep.pr
Desktop endpoint region	mx.node.ep.dsk.pr
Server endpoint region	mx.node.ep.srv.pr
Subscription region	mx.sub.pr
Servers subscription region	mx.sub.srv.pr
Desktops subscription region	mx.sub.dsk.pr
Profiles region	mx.app.pr
TEC region	mx.app.tec.pr
Inventory region	mx.app.inv.pr
Software Distribution region	mx.app.sd.pr
Remote Control region	mx.app.rc.pr
Remote Control region (desktop)	mx.app.rc.dsk.pr
Remote Control region (server)	mx.app.rc.srv.pr
Distributed Monitoring region	mx.app.dm.pr

Spoke TMR (Australia operation)

Table 20. Policy region names for Australia operation logical design

Policy region purpose	Policy region name
Top policy region	au.pr
Nodes region	au.node.pr
Managed node region	au.node.mn.pr
Endpoints region	au.node.ep.pr
Desktop endpoint region	au.node.ep.dsk.pr
Server endpoint region	au.node.ep.srv.pr
Subscription region	au.sub.pr
Servers subscription region	au.sub.srv.pr

Policy region purpose	Policy region name
Desktops subscription region	au.sub.dsk.pr
Profiles region	au.app.pr
TEC region	au.app.tec.pr
Inventory region	au.app.inv.pr
Software Distribution region	au.app.sd.pr
Remote Control region	au.app.rc.pr
Remote Control region (desktop)	au.app.rc.dsk.pr
Remote Control region (server)	au.app.rc.srv.pr
Distributed Monitoring region	au.app.dm.pr

Hub TMR (BWET Corporation)

Table 21. Policy region names for Hub TMR logical design

Policy region purpose	Policy region name
Top policy region	hub.pr
Profiles region	hub.app.pr
TEC region	hub.app.tec.pr
Inventory region	hub.app.inv.pr
Software Distribution region	hub.app.sd.pr
Remote Control region	hub.app.rc.pr
Remote Control region (TME server)	hub.app.rc.tmesrv.pr
Distributed Monitoring region	hub.app.dm.pr

11.3.2 Profile manager schema

In this section, we provide the profile manager hierarchy design for our case study. Note that it is very important to keep in mind that there are many ways of accomplishing a successful profile manager design, and the design provided here is intended to provide an example.

11.3.2.1 Profile manager design for application policy region

Within each application specific policy region, task libraries and different profile manager hierarchy will be constructed. These profile managers will have profile managers only as subscribers.

Tivoli Software Distribution profile manager design

In order to handle software distribution resource grouping, the subscriber profile manager for software distribution are divided into three levels:

Hub level These are database profile managers that group resources from Hub initiated software distribution.

Local Mid-level These are database profile managers that group resources from the local leaf level. They serve for both local distribution and for Hub level distribution.

Local Leaf level These are dataless profile managers that contain the endpoints. They are local and very granular.

Each profile manager in the local leaf level will contain resources that have the same:

- Platform (operating system)
- Department
- Function (desktop or server)
- Location (in this case identified by the TMR)

These names will identify which resources should be in each, for example:

- nt.sales.dsk.subsc.us.pm
- w95.sales.dsk.subsc.us.pm
- nt.sales.srv.subsc.us.pm
- nt.sales.dsk.subsc.br.pm
- w95.sales.dsk.subsc.br.pm
- nt.sales.srv.subsc.br.pm

The mid-level will group resources from the leaf level for both local and global distributions. Groups will be like:

- nt.dsk.subsc.us.pm (all NT desktops in the U.S. Spoke)
- nt.sales.subsc.us.pm (all NT server and subscriber of the sales department in the U.S. Spoke)
- nt.subsc.us.pm (all NT server and desktop in the U.S. Spoke)

At the Hub level, resources will be grouped without the spoke identification. The Hub TMR identification will be used to indicate all profile mangers from all TMRs. For example:

- nt.dsk.subsc.hub.pm (all NT desktop from all locations)
- nt.sales.subsc.hub.pm (all NT from the sales department of all locations)

Figure 81 illustrates how these resources are used together.

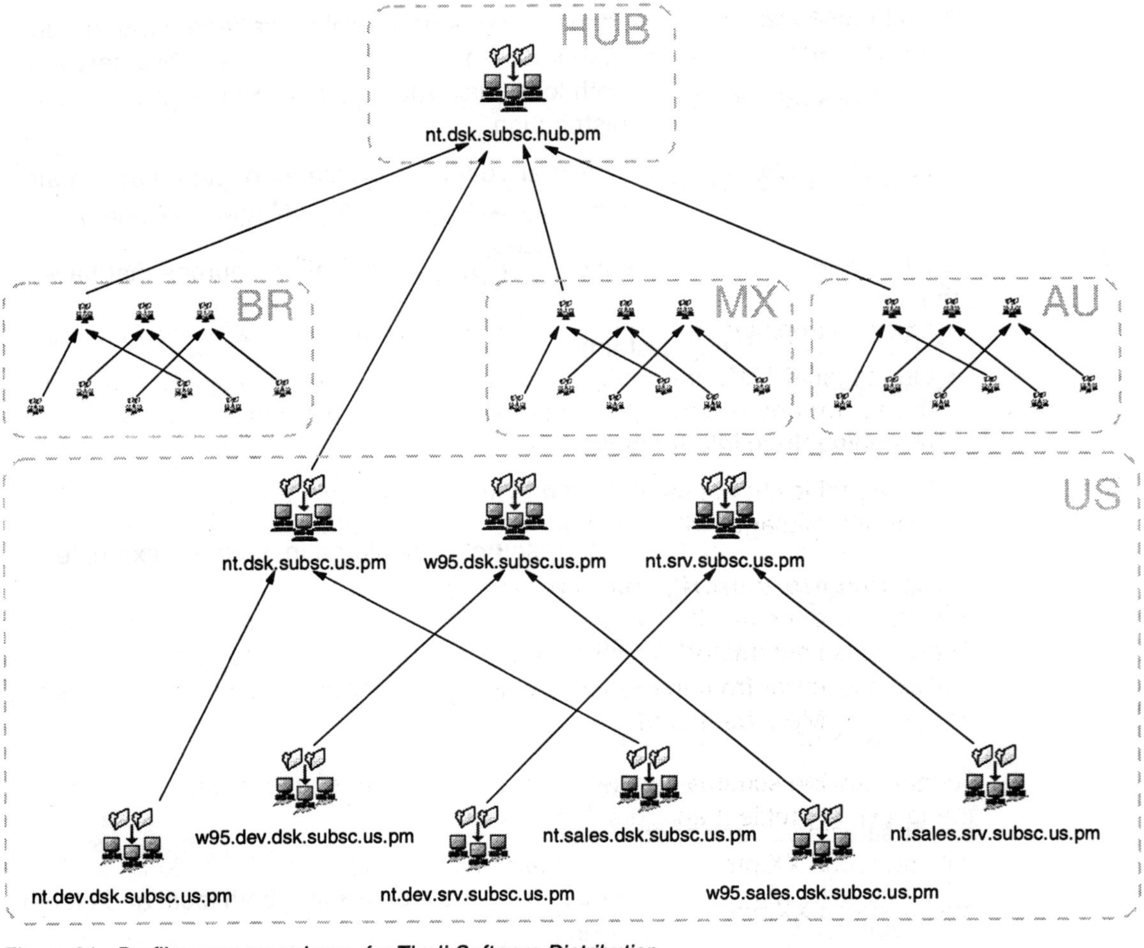

Figure 81. Profile manager schema for Tivoli Software Distribution

Not all profile managers are shown on the figure. It represents a part of the schema, and many different profile managers will be created.

The application profile managers for Tivoli Software Distribution are different on the Hub and the spokes. On the Hub, there is no need to distinguish desktops from servers. This may be necessary for specific software. However, on the spokes, security concerns require that application profiles be separated between the server and desktop.

Since most of the software will be distributed using file packages, the actual operating system does not need to be used to distinguish profiles. The profiles include scripts that determine if the target is valid or not. The actual profile managers will only be created as profiles require them. However, they will follow a general naming and grouping schema:

- The names will be as broad as possible and will be similar to those of the subscribers, for example:

sales.dsk.sd.app.us.pm	For software distributed to sales desktops in the U.S. location.
nt.sales.srv.sd.app.us.pm	This is very granular, but if the profile cannot make the distinction between the servers, then granular profile managers may be needed.
sales.sd.app.hub.pm	Hub application for all machines in sales.

- On the local TMR, the profile managers must always distinguish between the server and desktop (have the dsk and srv in the name). This will help assigning them into the policy regions.
- If the profile cannot be distributed to all targets, then it should be placed in a profile manager with only the acceptable targets.

Tivoli Inventory profile manager design

Inventory is done by different groups of administrators on different resources. There is also automated inventory scanning. Each location does its own scan, and administrator from the Hub can collect data about the machines that take part in the TME infrastructure.

To maintain the schema simple, the subscribers are stored in each location in the following profile managers:

dsk.inv.subsc.XX.pm	Contains all desktops of that location.
srv.inv.subsc.XX.pm	Contains all server of that location.
tmf.inv.subsc.XX.pm	Contains all TME managed nodes that contain any Tivoli application (such as TEC server, endpoint gateways, repeaters).

Theoretically, all the endpoints in the software distribution profile manager could be used for the inventory. But, it is simpler to have different profile managers, especially because there are not that many resources that are acceptable.

The application profile manager has similar names, such as:

dsk.inv.app.XX.pm	Contains profiles to scan endpoints in dsk.inv.subsc.XX.pm.
srv.inv.app.XX.pm	Contains profiles to scan endpoints in srv.inv.subsc.XX.pm.
tmf.inv.app.hub.pm	Contains profiles for scan endpoints in the tmf.inv.subsc.XX.pm profile managers.

Tivoli Distributed Monitoring profile manager design

Most of the monitoring is done by local administrators on local resources. There is no initial proposed profile manager schema for the distributed monitoring of the local resources. However, there is some monitoring done from the Hub. These monitors will be used to survey the Tivoli infrastructure.

For the TME monitors, each spoke will have the following subscriber profile managers:

mn.tmf.subsc.XX.pm	Tivoli managed nodes on the spoke.
gw.tmf.subsc.XX.pm	Tivoli endpoint gateways on the spoke.
srv.tmf.subsc.XX.pm	The TMR server of the spoke.
tec.tmf.subsc.XX.pm	TEC server on the spoke.

The actual application profile managers are not described here. They will be created by administrators, respecting the naming conventions.

11.3.2.2 Profile manager design for subscribers' policy region

A comprehensive profile manager hierarchy should be created under the subscribers' policy region defined in each one of the spokes' TMR servers in order to provide the required distribution list when the Tivoli administrators for each one of these regions wants to distribute profiles.

Figure 82 on page 221 outlines the desktop subscribers' profile manager schema. In this schema, when creating a desktop, it must be subscribed according to both its operating system and department in the BWET organization.

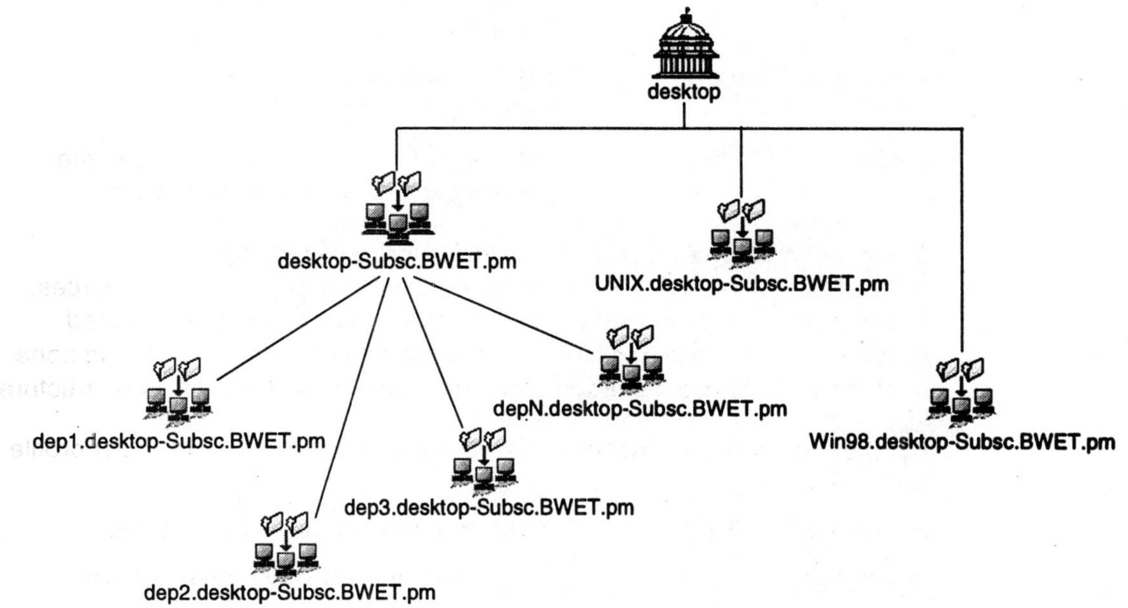

Figure 82. Desktop subscribers profile manager schema

Figure 83 on page 222 outlines the servers' subscribers profile manager schema. In this schema, all servers will be organized according to their operating system and server application. When defining a server in this schema, it must be subscribed to both according to the profile manager of its operating system and according to the application it makes available.

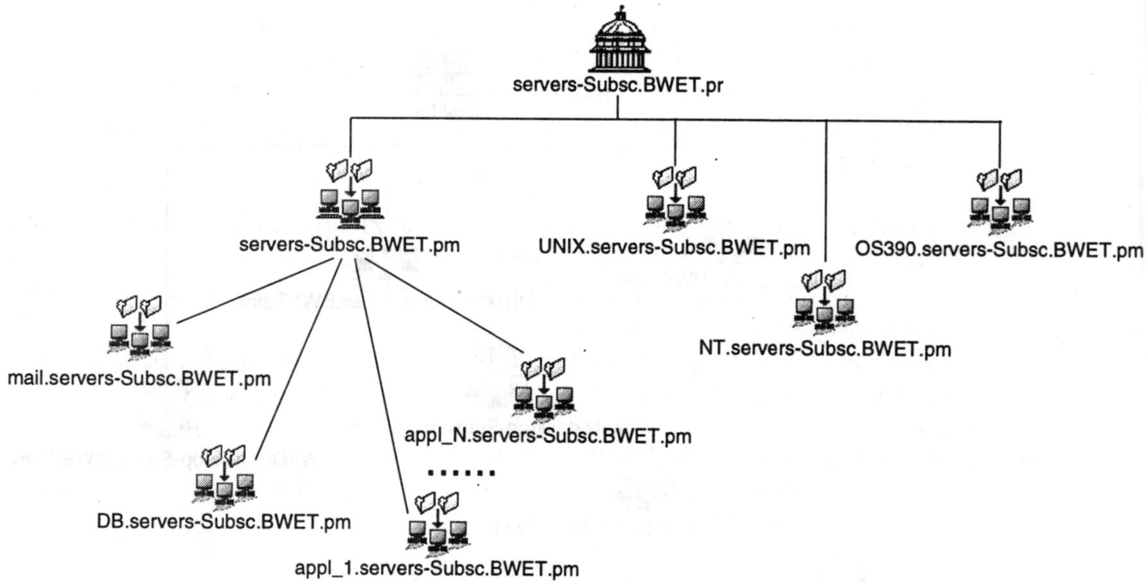

Figure 83. BWET subscribers profile manager hierarchy

11.3.3 Administrators' schema and administrators, desktop design

In all, there are sever groups of system administrators that exist in BWET. The considerations described in 5.2, "Critical considerations" on page 77 have been taken into account while designing the administrator and administrator desktop strategy for BWET.

11.3.3.1 Administrator schema design strategy

Since there are sever groups of administrators within BWET corporation, there will be seven different templates of administrators. These templates are derived directly from the seven administrator groups in 11.2.2.4, "Collecting administrator information" on page 199. The design schema for each of these seven groups is described in the sections that follow.

Global Product Development group (GPD)

This group's primary function is the development of BWET flagship products and the development of in-house server and desktop applications. Once the flagship product and in-house applications are developed, they are transferred to a central software repository where the Global Distribution group retrieves the software for distribution. They are not involved in any of the software packaging and/or distribution process within BWET. Thus, they do not require access to the BWET Tivoli environment.

Global Distribution group (GD)

This group's primary function is the retrieval of software from the central software repository and the distribution of these software to remote local operations. The process relevant to the management of BWET's system resources is the distribution of in-house applications to all servers and desktops within the BWET system environment.

In order to perform this function, the Global Distribution group will required the use of management applications, such as Tivoli Software Distribution and Inventory. Software Distribution is used for the distribution of software to the required server and/or desktop target endpoints. Inventory is used in determining whether an application had been installed on a specific server or desktop workstation through the use of Tivoli's query utilities.

In order for the Global Distribution group to perform its software distribution function within the BWET system environment, it will require the TMR roles and resource roles shown in Table 22.

Table 22. Required roles: Global distribution group

Policy region	**super**	**senior**	**admin**	**user**
Tivoli desktop	TR			
us.node.ep.pr			RR	
us.sub.pr			RR	
br.node.ep.pr			RR	
br.sub.pr			RR	
au.node.ep.pr			RR	
au.sub.pr			RR	
mx.node.ep.pr			RR	
mx.sub.pr			RR	
hub.sd.pr		RR		
scheduler			RR	
TR - TMR role RR - resource role				

The required TMR roles and resource roles are retrieved from, Appendix A, A.3, "Tivoli Software Distribution" on page 245. Since the Global Distribution group is responsible for the creation of file packages and/or autopack packages, they require the senior resource role in the hub.sd.pr where all global packages reside. And, as for the other policy regions in Table 22, this group of administrator requires the admin resource role in policy regions where the subscribers (endpoints or profile managers) reside. This group of administrators were given the admin role to the Scheduler, enabling them the ability to schedule a Tivoli task through the Scheduler.

A task library should be created for this group of administrators, enabling them to create and configure Tivoli tasks and jobs that will be used while scheduling software distribution to be run at specific times.

Local Product Development group (LPD)

This group's primary responsibility is the development and testing of in-house applications and services packs for in-house server systems and desktop PCs. Once these applications and/or upgrades are developed and tested, they will be placed on a local repository server.

In addition, any modification on the BWET flagship software products will be performed by this group for the product's compliance with local standards. Once these modifications are completed, the flagship product is placed on a local repository server.

As the tasks that are being performed by this group do not require access to system resources in the BWET system environment, no Tivoli access is given to this group of administrators.

Local Help desk Support group (LHS)

BWET desktop users who have experienced problems with their desktops and their desktop applications would contact their local help desk support personnel. These personnel will then attempt to resolve these problems in the shortest amount of time over the telephone. With the use of Tivoli Remote Control, help desk support personnel can resolve users' desktop problems directly by assuming the user's keyboard and mouse control.

In addition, help desk support personnel should be able to run an inventory query and display inventory information on an specific desktop PC endpoint in the local operation. This allows help desk personnel to determine whether the particular problem is caused by the absence/presence of a software package on an endpoint.

The schema for the Local Help desk support group is shown in Table 23.

Table 23. Required Roles: Local Help desk group

Policy region	senior	admin	user	query_view	remote_control
desktop			TR		
xx.app.rc.dsk.pr[1]		RR			RR
xx.node.ep.dsk.pr[2]		RR			
xx.app.inv.pr[3]				RR	
[1,2,3] xx - local operation code (us, br, au, mx)					

Note that personnel in this group are granted the admin resource role to the xx.app.rc.dsk.pr policy region. This is to enable the remote control policy that requires user permission before this group can actively remote control a specific endpoint desktop.

Note that a customized query library and inventory query has to created on the Help desk support desktop to allow desktop support personnel to display inventory information on a specific endpoint.

Local Server Support group (LSS)

This group of administrators is responsible for the general health of all BWET internal servers and sever applications. They would require the use of Tivoli Distributed Monitoring, Inventory, Remote Control, and TEC. The schema for this group of administrators is shown in Table 24.

Table 24. Required roles: Local server support group

Policy region	senior	admin	user	remote_control	remote_monitor	remote_reboot	query_view	query_execute
Tivoli desktop			TR					
xx.node.ep.srv.pr		RR						

Policy region	senior	admin	user	remote_control	remote_monitor	remote_reboot	query_view	query_execute
xx.sub.srv.pr		RR						
Event Server		RR[1]	#					
xx.app.sd.pr		RR						
xx.app.inv.pr		RR					#	#
xx.app.dm.pr		RR						
xx.app.rc.srv.pr		RR		RR	RR	RR		
Scheduler		RR						

TR - TMR role
RR - Resource role
xx - Location code (us, au, br, mx)
[1] This role refers to the administration role within the Event Console.

The Local Server Support group are given the remote_control, remote_monitor, remote_reboot access to allow them the ability to monitor, reboot, and actively control a specific BWET server. They are granted the `admin` role in xx.node.ep.srv.pr policy region so that they can only have the specified remote access to the BWET server class machines. In addition, they are granted the admin role to the xx.app.rc.srv.pr policy region, which allows them to remotely access a specific server without remote user permission.

Local Desktop Support group (LDS)

This group is the next level of support for the Local Help desk Support group. If the help desk support is not able to resolve a specific problem within a reasonable amount of time, the call is raised to this administrator group. The required TMR roles and resource roles are shown in Table 33.

Table 25. Required roles: Local desktop support group

Policy region	senior	admin	user	remote _control	remote_reboot	remote_monitor	query_view
Tivoli desktop			TR				
xx.node.ep.dsk.pr		RR					
xx.app.sd.pr		RR					
xx.app.rc.dsk.pr		RR		RR	RR	RR	
xx.app.inv.pr		RR					RR
xx.sub.dsk.pr		RR					
Scheduler		RR					
TR - TMR roles RR - Resource roles							

Local Tivoli Management group (LTM)

This group is responsible for the creation of all Tivoli objects within their local operation (spoke TMR). This includes policy regions, profile managers, profiles, Tivoli administrators, remote control objects, etc., as well as the setting of policies and subscribers to specific profile managers. They should have full Tivoli access except for the interconnection of TMRs. Their required roles are shown in Table 26.

Table 26. Required roles: Local Tivoli Management group

Policy region	super	senior	admin	user	install_product	install_client	backup	restore	rim_view	rim_updte	query_edit	qurey_view
Local TMR management		TR	TR	TR	TR	TR	TR	TR	TR	TR		
xx.app.inv.pr											RR	RR

Policy region	super	senior	admin	user	install_product	install_client	backup	restore	rim_view	rim_updte	query_edit	qurey_view
xx - Location code (br, us, au, mx) TR - TMR role RR - Resource role												

The super TMR role is not granted to this group of administrators because it will enable them to interconnect TMRs. However, they will be able to perform all other required tasks within their local Tivoli environment with the assigned roles to each individual resources.

Global Tivoli Management group (GTM)

This group is responsible for the management of all Tivoli management servers within the BWET system environment. This includes all TMR servers, TEC servers, endpoint gateways, managed nodes, and other Tivoli application management servers. Therefore, this group of administrators will require access to Remote Control, TEC, Software Distribution, and Distributed Monitoring on all Tivoli infrastructure servers.

On its local TMR (Hub level), this group of administrator will be required to create all Tivoli objects that are required for the management of the overall Tivoli infrastructure within the BWET Corporation. This includes the creation of profile managers, file packages, inventory profiles, policy region, remote control objects, Tivoli administrators, profile manager subscriptions, etc. The required roles for this group of administrators are shown in Table 27.

Table 27. Required roles: Global Tivoli Management group

Policy region	super	senior	admin	user	restore	backup	rim_view	rim_update	query_edit	query_execute	install_client	install_product	remote_control	remote_monitor	remote_reboot
TMR - interconnection	TR														
Hub TMR management		TR	TR	TR	TR	TR	TR	TR			TR	TR			

Policy region	super	senior	admin	user	restore	backup	rim_view	rim_update	query_edit	query_execute	install_client	install_product	remote_control	remote_monitor	remote_reboot
hub.app.rc.pr		RR											RR	RR	R R
hub.app.dm.pr		RR													
hub.app.sd.pr		RR													
hub.app.tec.pr		RR													
hub.app.inv.pr		RR							RR	R R					
Event Server (hub)		RR	RR												
Scheduler (hub)			RR												
Administrator Collection (Hub)		RR													
us.node.mn.pr			RR												
br.node.mn.pr			RR												
mx.node.mn.pr			RR												
au.node.mn.pr			RR												
TR - TMR roles RR - Resource roles															

Since there are eight groups of administrators, there should be a minimum of eight templates of administrators for the BWET Corporation. In order to simplify the administration of administrators in an BWET Tivoli environment, only one administrator will be created initially for each administrator group. These initially-created administrators will serve as templates for each administrator group and will be used as reference for each successive administrator created for that particular administrator group.

Eight administrators will initially be created. These are as follow:

- Global Product Development group (GPD)
- Global Distribution group (GD)
- Global Tivoli Management group (GTM)
- Local Product Development group (LPD)
- Local Help desk Support group (LHS)
- Local Server Support group (LSS)
- Local Desktop Support group (LDS)
- Local Tivoli Management group (LTM)

For each local administrator group, four administrator groups will be created for each locality operation as depicted in Table 28.

Table 28. Local administrator group

LPD	LHS	LSS	LDS	LTM
US_LPD	US_LHS	US_LSS	US_LDS	US_LTM
AU_LPD	AU_LHS	AU_LSS	AU_LDS	AU_LTM
MX_LPD	MX_LHS	MX_LSS	MX_LDS	MX_LTM
BR_LPD	BR_LHS	BR_LSS	BR_LDS	BR_LTM

The administrative roles for each administrative group has been discussed in 11.3.3.1, "Administrator schema design strategy" on page 222. From that discussion, two administrator groups are not required access to the Tivoli desktop (Global Product Development group & Local Product Development group). Thus, six administrators are created. For the process and a detailed description of creating administrators, please refer to 5.1.1, "Single administrator" on page 68.

Once these administrators are created, appropriate roles should be assigned to each administrator template. Roles that are required by each administrator template are already discussed in 11.3.3.1, "Administrator schema design strategy" on page 222.

11.3.3.2 Administrator desktop design strategy

This section provides information about the Tivoli administrator desktop strategy to be applied by initially the BWET Corporation.

Tivoli objects on administrator desktop

Given the roles that each representative administrator group are assigned to in accordance to their responsibilities, this process is straight forward. If considerations in 5.2.16, “Desktops icons: What to place on an administrator’s desktop” on page 90 were utilized, administrators should only be able to see and, therefore, be able to access Tivoli objects to which they have access to.

Table 29 through Table 34 contain a list of Tivoli objects that each representative administrator group should have on their Tivoli desktop.

Table 29. Desktop item for Global Distribution group

Global Distribution group (GD)
Event server console
Parent subscription profile manager for all operations to all desktops and servers
hub.app.sd.pr

Table 30. Desktop items for global Tivoli Management group

Global Tivoli Management group (GTM)
Event server (Hub)
Event Server Console (Hub)
Top Level policy region for Hub TMR
Top level policy region for all spoke TMRs
Scheduler (Hub)

Table 31. Desktop items for local Tivoli Management group

Local Tivoli Management group (LTM)
Top level policy region for local TMR
Event Server (Local)
Event Server Console (Local)
Scheduler (Local)

Table 32. Desktop items for local Help desk support group

Local Desktop Support group
Remote Control object specifically for desktop systems with policies governing configuration
Appropriate Inventory query for desktop systems

Table 33. Desktop items for local server support group

Local Server Support group
Local Remote Control object specifically for server systems with policies governing configuration
Event Server Console
Scheduler
Parent subscription profile manager containing all server subscription
Profile managers containing software packages specifically for servers
Inventory query for server systems

Table 34. Desktop items for local desktop support group

Local Desktop Support group
Local Remote Control object specifically for desktop systems with policies governing configuration
Parent profile manager containing all desktop subscription
Profile managers containing all software packages specifically for desktop systems
Scheduler
Inventory query for desktop systems

Tivoli desktop security

One feature of the Tivoli desktop is the ability of users being able to browse through all Tivoli resources using the Tivoli navigator. This might allow administrators to locate specific Tivoli resources more effectively. However, it poses a problem for senior administrators who required strict access on his/her resources from other administrators within the environment. Since only the user TMR role is required for any user to randomly browse through any resources that have been represented as an Tivoli object. For example: policy region, endpoints, managed nodes, profile managers, profiles, etc.

In 5.3.2.1, "Adding security to Tivoli built-in navigator" on page 93 and 5.3.2.2, "Removing all menu items from administrator desktops" on page 95, different methods have been illustrated to add extra security to the existing desktop. These added security measures will be utilized in the BWET Tivoli desktop.

The added TMR roles of navigator for use of the Tivoli navigator, as described in "Adding security to Tivoli built-in navigator" on page 93, will be used in the BWET Tivoli environment. Only administrators from the Global and Local Tivoli Management group will be assigned the navigator TMR role to use the navigator function since only these two groups would require the use of the Tivoli navigator to locate a specific Tivoli objects amongst other objects.

As for the removal of extra menu items from a specific administrator's desktop, as described in 5.3.2.2, "Removing all menu items from administrator desktops" on page 95, this security measure can be used on all non-Tivoli management groups. This will restrict them the ability to create, remove, or delete any objects to the Tivoli environment.

Managing administrators

The management of administrator could be straight forward if there is a small number of administrators within the environment. However, if there is a large number of administrator in the environment, locating an administrator could becoming time consuming. Where there are large discrepancies between administrators from different administrator groups (as for BWET Corporation), administrators can be managed more effectively if administrators are logically grouped by the administrator group that they belong to.

In BWET Corporation's case, there are four local groups within each local operation. Thus, four logical groups would need to be created to separate four groups of administrators. The names for these groups are:

- XX_LTM
- XX_LHS
- XX_LSS
- XX_LDS

where XX denotes the country code for each local operation. Country codes are used for these groups to distinguish between groups from different operations since all local operations will be inter-connected through the Hub TMR.

Tivoli administrators can only reside in administrator collections from each spoke TMR's top-level policy region. Therefore, Tivoli generic collections are utilized in creating logical separation for different administrator groups within each operation. This is demonstrated in Figure 84. Note that in Figure 84, XX denotes the country code of the local operation

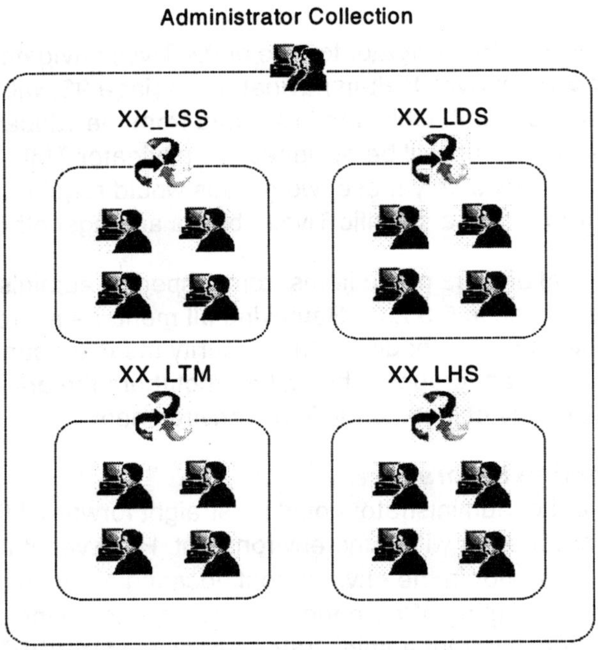

Figure 84. Local administrator logical arrangement

The same approach can be used for Hub level administrator administration. This is depicted in Figure 85 on page 235.

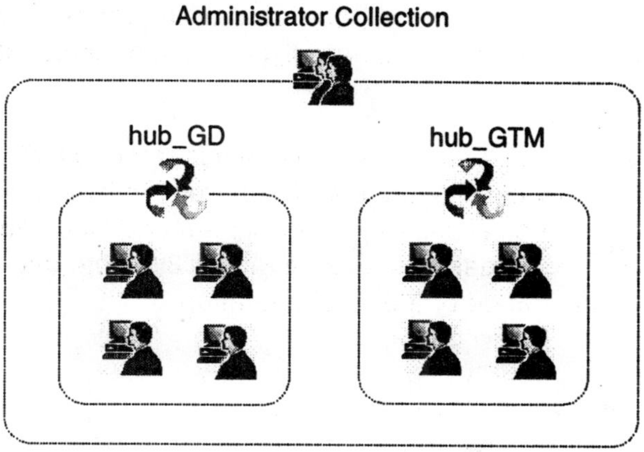

Figure 85. Hub level administrator arrangement

Part 3. Appendices

Appendix A. Tivoli administrators roles

This appendix contains the administrative roles (TMR or resource level) required when performing certain administrative tasks with Tivoli. These roles have a decisive impact when designing the Tivoli administrators' desktop. The sequence of tables presented here are related to 5.3, "Administrators' desktop design" on page 91.

The following Tivoli management applications will be covered:

- Tivoli Framework
- Tivoli Remote Control
- Tivoli Software Distribution
- Tivoli Enterprise Console
- Tivoli Distributed Monitoring
- Tivoli Inventory
- Tivoli Security Management
- Tivoli User Administration

Note

Tivoli has enhanced the number of roles for Tivoli User Administration and Tivoli Security Management by introducing a number of fine-grained roles to the respective products. Please refer to *TME 10 User Administration 3.6 User's Guide*, GC32-0291 and *Security Management User's Guide 3.6*, GC31-8475 for a complete list of the fine-grained roles.

In distinguishing between TMR roles and resource roles, the following convention will be used:

RR Resource roles

TR TMR roles

A.1 Tivoli Framework

Table 35 shows the administrative tasks and relates to the required administrative role to perform the task for Tivoli Framework.

Table 35. Tivoli Framework

Tasks	super	senior	admin	user	backup	install_client	install_product
Create policy sub region		RR					
Delete policy region		RR					
List a default policy object	RR	RR					
Change the name of a policy region (senior, policy region)		RR					
Moves resources from one policy region to another (senior source and destination policy region)		RR					
Open a policy region (user, policy region)				RR			
Set default policy for a class	RR	RR					
List available default and validation object policy for a class	RR	RR					
Specific which default or validation policies will be used for the specified resource in a policy region. Add/remove managed resources, enable/disable policy validations in a policy region.	RR	RR					
Create a top-level policy region	TR	TR					
Create generic collections (user, TMR)				TR			
Read notices from notice board				TR			
Forward notices via e-mail (user TMR)				TR			
Mark notices as read or unread (user, TMR)				TR			
Save notices (user, TMR)				TR			
Create/delete a new administrator		RR					
List administrator's name, logins, roles, and notice group[1]			RR				

Tasks	super	senior	admin	user	backup	install_client	install_product
Changes administrative resource roles, login information, and notice group subscription of an administrator	RR	RR					
Changes administrator TMR roles (senior TMR roles)		TR					
Drag and drop resources to an administrator's desktop (user, TMR)				TR			
Create/delete a profile manager in a policy region	RR	RR					
Create/delete a profile or clone/copy an existing profile within profile managers	RR	RR					
List Tivoli resources that subscribe to the specific profile manager	RR	RR	RR	RR			
Change mode of an profile manager (data or dataless mode)	RR	RR					
Subscribe Tivoli resources to specific profile managers[2]	RR	RR	RR				
Unsubscribe Tivoli resources from specific profile managers[3]	RR	RR	RR				
Show subscription for a profile manager	RR	RR	RR	RR			
Distribute profiles from one profile manager (drag & drop)[4]	RR	RR	RR				
Distribute profiles from one profile manager (through select menu)[4b]							
Move a profile manager between policy regions.[5]	RR	RR					
Move a profile between profile managers.[6]	RR	RR					
Install/remove TME client (managed node).[7]	RR					RR	
Install TME 10 products/patches[8]	TR						TR
List all current TMR connections information including remote TMR server, remote region, connection mode, and exchanged resource properties.[9]	TR	TR					
Establish connection (insecure or secure connection) between the TMR servers in two TMRs.[10]	TR						

Tasks	super	senior	admin	user	backup	install_client	install_product
Disconnect the connection (one-way or two-way) between two TMRs.[11]	TR						
Exchange resources in the local name registry from one or more remote TMRs.[12]	TR	TR					
Drag and drop top-level policy regions from remote TMR to an administrator's desktop in the local TMR (admin, TMR).			TR				
View a list of available endpoint gateways	TR	TR	TR				
Creates an endpoint gateway through the endpoint manager		TR					
Deletes an endpoint gateway through the endpoint manager		TR					
Delete an endpoint through the endpoint manager		TR					
Refresh gateway view	TR	TR	TR				
Refresh endpoint view	TR	TR					
Returns the properties of an managed node, PC managed node, or endpoints	RR	RR	RR	RR			
Create a PC managed node						RR	
Display or change properties of a PC managed node			RR				
Edit properties of an managed node or PC managed node	RR	RR	RR				
Open a manage node window				RR			
Open an X terminal on an UNIX managed node				RR			
Back up Tivoli database					TR		
Browse for list of installed products				TR			
Schedule a job in the task library.[13]	RR	RR	RR				
Remove a job from the schedule.[14]	RR	RR	RR				
Disable/Enable a job in the schedule.[15]	RR	RR	RR				
Edit the properties of an scheduled job.[16]	RR	RR	RR				

Tasks	super	senior	admin	user	backup	install_client	install_product
Browse a list of scheduled jobs.[17]				RR			
Change the display format of the schedule.[18]				RR			
Find/Sort scheduled jobs in the scheduler.[19]				RR			
Create/delete a task library		RR					
Create/delete a task in a task library	RR	RR	RR				
Create/delete a job in a task library	RR	RR	RR				
Edit a job/task in a task library	RR	RR	RR				
Move a task library between policy regions[20]	RR	RR					
Set the default/validation policy for a task library	RR	RR					
Execute a job[21]	-	-	-	-	-	-	-
Execute a task[22]	-	-	-	-	-	-	-

[1] Must have at lease admin role in administrators group to list information about another administrator. Otherwise, can only list information on current principal administrator.
[2,3] Must have these administrator roles in policy regions where the subscribing profile managers are located and in policy regions where the subscribed resources are located.
[4,5,6,7] Must have these roles in the source and designation policy region.
[4b] Must have these roles only in policy regions where profiles are located.
[8] Must have these administrator roles as TMR role.
[9] Having admin role can not list TMR connection as documented in the Framework Reference Manual. Must have these role as TMR role.
[10,11,12] Must have these administrator roles as TMR role.
[13,14,15,16,17,18,19] Must have these roles in the scheduler.
[20] Require roles in source and designated policy region.
[21,22] Requires role as specified by the job.

A.2 Tivoli Remote Control

Table 36 shows the administrative tasks and relates to the required administrative role to perform the task for Tivoli Remote Control.

Table 36. Tivoli Remote Control

Tasks	super	senior	admin	user	remote_control	remote_monitor	remote_reboot	remote_probe	remote_receive	remote_send	remote _chat
Create Remote Control object in a Policy Region	TR	TR	TR								
Open the Remote Control Managed Resource	RR	RR	RR								
Active remote control a remote target workstation[1]					RR						
Monitor the actions on a remote target workstation[2]						RR					
Restart a remote target workstation[3]							RR				
Perform file transfers from the controller to the remote target workstation[4]										RR	
Perform file transfers from the remote target workstation to the controller[5]									RR		
Exchange written information with the remote target workstation's user[6]											RR
[1,2,3,4,5,6] Must have these access in the policy regions where the remote control object and endpoints are located. Endpoints must be linked to policy regions if resource roles are to be given. [4,5,6] These features are only available on Remote Control Version 3.6.5											

A.3 Tivoli Software Distribution

Table 37 shows the administrative tasks and relates to the required administrative role to perform the task for Tivoli Software Distribution.

Table 37. Tivoli Software Distribution

Tasks	super	senior	admin	user	SWDist_end_user
Create/delete file packages in a profile manager[1]	RR	RR			
Edit properties of a file package[2]	RR	RR	RR		
View file package properties[3]	RR	RR	RR	RR	
Distribute file packages to an endpoint (drag & drop file packages)[4]	RR	RR	RR		
Distribute file packages to an endpoint (through menu dialog)[5]	RR	RR	RR		
Remove file packages from an endpoint[6]	RR	RR	RR		
Import file package definition[7]	RR	RR	RR		
Export file package definition[8]	RR	RR	RR	RR	
Calculate size of file package[9]	RR	RR			
Create/Delete autopack in a profile manager[10]	RR	RR			
Edit properties of an autopack[11]	RR	RR	RR		
View properties of an autopack[12]	RR	RR	RR		
Distribute autopacks to an endpoint[13]	RR	RR	RR		
Remove autopacks from an endpoint[14]	RR	RR	RR		
Calculate size of an autopack pack[15]	RR	RR	RR		
Clone a file package/autopack profile[16]	RR	RR			
Schedule a distribution	TR	TR	TR		
User request software distribution through Software Distribution Userlink[17]					TR

Tasks	super	senior	admin	user	SWDist_end_user

[1,2,3,5,6,7,8,9,10,11,12,13,14,15,16] Must have these roles in the profile policy regions.
[4] Must have these roles in the profiles policy region and endpoints policy regions.
[17] This task is initiated from the subscriber to the autopack or file package profile. User must enter the administrator's login account name and password to initiate a distribution through the Web interface.

Note

In testing file package distribution under the lab environment, the team had found that administrator authorization requirements are different from what the manual had suggested.

When drag-and-drop methods (drag file package to subscribers) are used to distribution file packages, the administrators performing the distribution must have at least admin resource role in the policy region where the profile resides and the policy region where the subscribers reside. This is different from the suggested authorization roles specified in the product manual.

When file packages are distributed via the dialog-select method (right click on file package and select **Distribute...**), or the dialog method (select file package and subscribers, select **Profile manager -> Distribute -> Distribute Now**), administrators only require admin role on the profiles policy region. In addition, administrators with the admin role within the profile policy region can distribute file packages to subscribers that subscribed (directly or indirectly through profile managers) to the principle profile manager where the profile are created. As an illustration, four profile managers were created under lab conditions. Each of these profile manager were created in four different policy regions as follows:

tmrA.swd.app.pm Profile manager containing the file package tmrA.swd.test.fp. This profile manager is in policy region tmrA.swd.test.pr.

tmrA.test.link01.pm Profile manager subscribed to tmrA.swd.app.pm. This profile is in the tmrA.swd.test01.pr policy region.

tmrA.test.link02.pm Profile manager subscribed to tmrA.test.link01.pm. This profile is in the tmrA.swd.test02.pr policy region.

tmrA.test.link03.pm Profile manager subscribed to tmrA.test.link02.pm. This profile manager is in the tmrA.swd.test03.pr policy region. Endpoint shark is subscribed to this profile manager.

The hierarchical structure of these profile managers is shown in Figure 86 on page 248. The findings from our lab work is that if the select-dialog-method or the dialog-method were used, Administrators only require admin resource role in order to distribute file package profiles to any subscribers that are directly or indirectly subscribed to the principal profile manager, tmrA.swd.app.pm, for the example in Figure 86 on page 248.

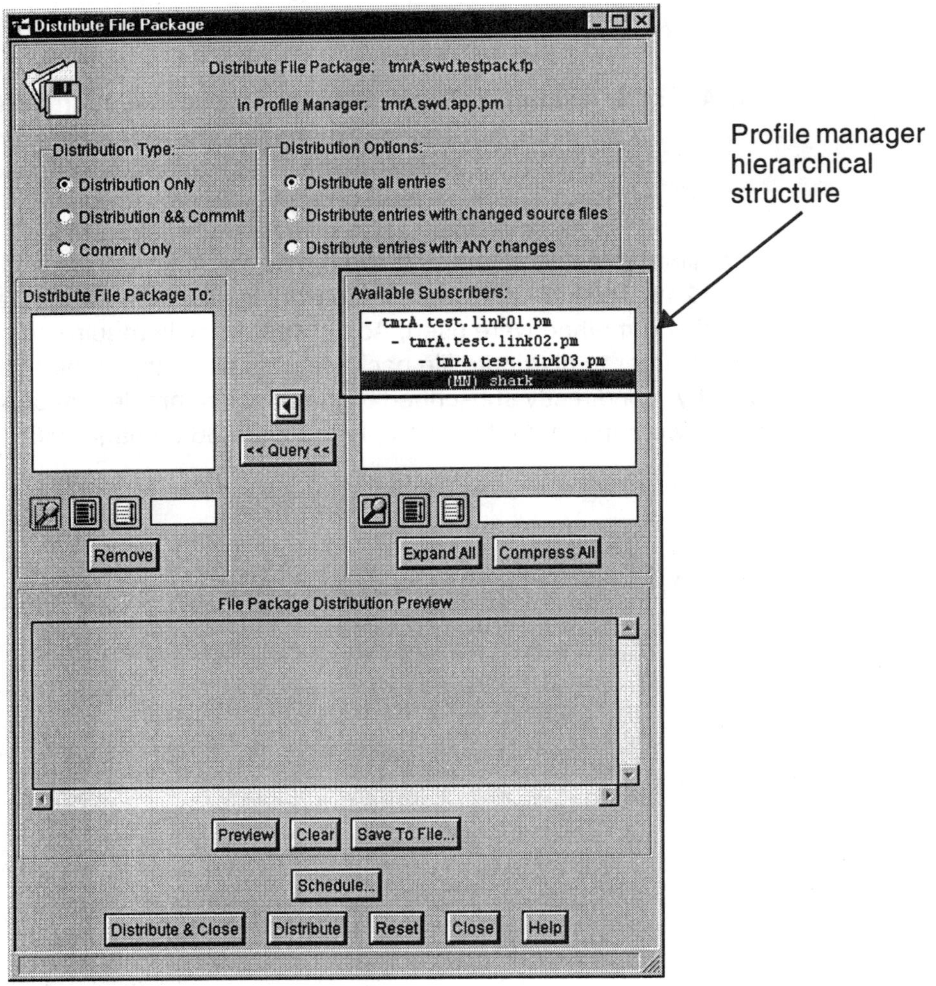

Figure 86. File packages distribution example

A.4 Tivoli Enterprise Console

Table 38 shows the administrative tasks and relates to the required administrative role to perform the task for Tivoli Enterprise Console.

Table 38. Tivoli Enterprise Console

Tasks	super	senior	admin	user	none*
Start Tivoli Event Server	RR	RR			

Tasks	super	senior	admin	user	none*
Stop Tivoli Event Server	RR	RR			
View/Edit Tivoli Event Server configuration parameters	RR	RR			
View/List existing event source properties	RR	RR	RR	RR	
Edit existing sources at the event serve	RR	RR			
Resets event source attributes to previous saved version	RR	RR			
List/View existing event group and event group filter properties	RR	RR	RR	RR	
Create/Delete an event group	RR	RR			
Edit an event group properties	RR	RR			
Reset event group attributes to previous saved version	RR	RR			
Add/Delete event group filters	RR	RR			
Edit event group filter properties for an existing event group	RR	RR			
Clone (copy) an event group	RR	RR			
List rule bases on the event server	RR	RR			
Create/Delete rule base	RR	RR			
Copy a rule base	RR	RR			
Edit rule base properties (Label and rule base location)	RR	RR			
Compile rule base	RR	RR			
Load rule base	RR	RR			
List rule base classes/rule set	RR	RR			
Import rule base classes/rule set	RR	RR			
Create rule set in a rule base	RR	RR			
Delete rule set in a rule base	RR	RR			
Edit rule set in a rule base (create/delete/edit rules in a rule set)	RR	RR			
Configure event console to appropriate event server	RR	RR			
Assign event groups	RR	RR			
Open Tivoli Enterprise console	RR	RR	RR	RR	

Tasks	super	senior	admin	user	none*
Editing Event console viewing options (Severity Display, Event Group Display, Rearrange Group, Message Time limits)[1]	RR	RR	RR	RR	RR
View messages body[2]	RR	RR	RR	RR	RR
Sort messages[3]	RR	RR	RR	RR	RR
Edit message display field[4]	RR	RR	RR	RR	RR
Create an automated tasks within an event console[5]	RR	RR	RR		
Delete an automated tasks within an event console[6]	RR	RR	RR		
Open an automated tasks within an event console[7]	RR	RR	RR		
Execute task from within an event console[8]	RR	RR	RR	RR	
Acknowledge an event[9]			RR		
Close an event[10]			RR		
Create/Delete an Adapter Configuration Profile (ACP)[11]		RR			
Cloning an ACP[12]		RR			
View ACP settings					
Editing the properties of an ACP[13]			RR		
Setting ACP distribution default settings[14]			RR		
Editing Default and validation policies for an ACP[15]		RR			
Add an ACP record within an ACP[16]		RR			
Edit ACP records within an ACP[17]			RR		
Copy an ACP record[18]			RR		
Move an ACP record[19]			RR		
Locking/Unlocking an ACP record[20]			RR		
Delete ACP records within an ACP[21]			RR		
Distributing an ACP (Drag & Drop)[22]			RR		
Distributing an ACP (Highlight ACP and subscribers, **Profile Manager -> Distribute**)[23]			RR		

Tasks	super	senior	admin	user	none*
All roles are defined as resource roles in resource "EventServer" unless stated otherwise. * The role *none* derived from the event console administration roles and can only be assigned and used within the event console. 1,2,3,4 The *none administration role* will over-ride all other administration roles declared for the specific administrator in that enterprise console. 1,2,3,4,9,10 The roles defined here are defined as administration roles and are assigned to administrators from within the Tivoli Enterprise Console **-> Assign event Groups** 5,7 This task required senior or super role for resource "EventServer" and admin roles from within Event Console. 6 This task required admin, senior or super role for resource "EventServer" and admin roles from within Event Console. 8 Roles required for this task depend on the "roles required" configuration of the selected task. 9,10 These roles are event dependent. Administration roles required are defined in the **acl** slot for each event. Administrators without the exact administration roles can view the event but cannot acknowledge or close the event.**The default acl for events is admin.** 11 - 21 These tasks required administrator to have the specified roles in policy regions containing the ACP. 22 This task required the specified roles in policy regions containing the ACP and its target subscribers. 23 This task required the specified roles in policy region containing the ACP.					

A.5 Tivoli Distributed Monitoring

Table 39 shows the administrative tasks and relates to the required administrative role to perform the task for Tivoli Distributed Monitoring.

Table 39. Tivoli Distributed Monitoring

Tasks	super	senior	admin	user
Read notices from the different Sentry notice boards				RR
Create Sentry Profiles[1]		RR		
Clone Sentry Profiles1		RR		
Delete Sentry Profiles 1		RR		
Populate Sentry Profiles			RR	
Copy monitors between Sentry Profiles			RR	
Distribute Sentry Profiles			RR	
Move monitors from one Sentry Profile to another			RR	

Tasks	super	senior	admin	user
Add monitors to a Sentry Profile			RR	
Edit a monitor from a Sentry Profile			RR	
Specify the T/EC Server of a monitor within the Sentry Profile			RR	
Set the message styles of a monitor within the Sentry Profile			RR	
Set the monitoring schedule of a monitor within the Sentry Profile			RR	
Enable or disable monitors within a Sentry Profile			RR	
Delete monitors in a Sentry Profile			RR	
Sort entries of monitors within a Sentry Profile				RR
Sort and display monitor attributes within a Sentry Profile				RR
Find a monitor within a Sentry Profile				RR
Set default Policy values of a Sentry Profile		RR		
Set basic default policies			RR	
Set default policies for responses			RR	
Set the distribution actions of a Sentry Profile			RR	
Lock or unlock a monitor			RR	
Navigate between Profile copies				RR
Create an indicator collection		RR		
Associate a Sentry Profile with an indicator collection		RR		
View the icons in an indicator collection			RR	
View the indicator log of a Sentry Profile icon within an indicator collection			RR	
Clear the indicator log of a Sentry Profile icon within an indicator collection			RR	
Save a Sentry Profile indicator log to a file			RR	
Mail a Sentry Profile indicator log			RR	
Reset a triggered Sentry Profile icon within an indicator collection			RR	
Create a proxy endpoint		RR		

Tasks	super	senior	admin	user
Set properties of a proxy endpoint		RR		
Set monitor filters for proxy endpoints		RR		
Add and generate TME 10 Distributed Monitoring Inspector reports				RR

A.6 Tivoli Inventory

Table 40 shows the administrative tasks and relates to the required administrative role to perform the task for Tivoli Inventory.

Table 40. Tivoli Inventory

Tasks	super	senior	admin	user	Inventory_end_user	Inventory_view	Inventory_query	Inventory_scan	Inventory_edit	Query_view	Query_edit	Query_execute	Rim_view	Rim_update
Create an Inventory Profile	RR	RR												
Edit an Inventory Profile	RR	RR	RR						RR					
Clone an Inventory Profile	RR	RR												
View an Inventory Profile	RR	RR	RR	RR		RR								
Delete an Inventory Profile	RR	RR												
Set subscribers of an Inventory Profile[1]	RR	RR	RR											

Tasks	super	senior	admin	user	Inventory_end_user	Inventory_view	Inventory_query	Inventory_scan	Inventory_edit	Query_view	Query_edit	Query_execute	Rim_view	Rim_update
Distribute an Inventory Profile [2]	RR	RR						RR						
Distribute an Inventory Profile through the User Link[3]					RR									
Retrieve Inventory information from the Configuration Repository	RR	RR									RR	RR		
Use Inventory administrator web pages[4]													RR	RR
Add, edit or delete Software Signatures[5]													RR	RR
Create a Query Library	RR	RR												
Create a Query	TR	TR	TR											
Edit a Query	RR	RR	RR								RR			
Execute a Query	RR	RR	RR								RR			
Run a Query from a single client	RR	RR	RR								RR			

Tasks	super	senior	admin	user	Inventory_end_user	Inventory_view	Inventory_query	Inventory_scan	Inventory_edit	Query_view	Query_edit	Query_execute	Rim_view	Rim_update

[1,2]The subscribing administrator must have these roles over the policy regions containing the inventory profile and its subscribers.
[3]This task is initiated from the subscriber to the Inventory profile. User must enter the administrator's login account name and password to initiate a scan or to enter user information through the Web interface.
[4,5]This task requires both Rim_view and Rim_updates roles.

A.7 Tivoli Security Management

Table 41 shows the administrative tasks and relates to the required administrative role to perform the task for Tivoli Security Management.

Table 41. Tivoli Security Management

Tasks	super	senior	admin	user	security_admin	security_auditor	security_operator
Add security profiles as managed resources for a policy region		RR					
Set or change resource authorization roles		RR					
Create, delete, or clone a security profile		RR					
Access a security record							RR
Edit user default policies	RR	RR			RR		
Edit user validation policies	RR	RR			RR		
Set or change an administrator's notice group subscriptions		RR					
Populate a security profile			RR		RR		
Set distribution defaults			RR		RR		
Distribute security profiles			RR		RR		

Tasks	super	senior	admin	user	security_admin	security_auditor	security_operator
Create a system policy record			RR		RR		
Create a group record			RR		RR		
Create a resource record			RR		RR		
Create a role record			RR		RR		
Edit, delete, move, or copy security record			RR		RR		
Lock or unlock a user account record			RR		RR		
Validate records against profile policy			RR		RR		
Retrieve security profile copies from another profile manager			RR		RR		
Sort and display record attributes				RR			RR

A.8 Tivoli User Administration

Table 42 shows the administrative tasks and relates to the required administrative role to perform the task for Tivoli User Administration.

Table 42. Tivoli User Administration

Tasks	super	senior	admin	user	none
Add user profiles as managed resources for a policy region		RR			
Create, clone, or delete a user profile		RR			
Edit user default policies		RR			
Disable default policy for a platform					RR
Edit user validation policies		RR			

Tasks	super	senior	admin	user	none
Populate a user profile			RR		
Set distribution defaults			RR		
Add group profiles as managed resources for a policy region		RR			
Create, clone, or delete a group profile		RR			
Edit group default policies		RR			
Edit group validation policies		RR			
Populate a group profile			RR		
Set distribution defaults			RR		
Create or delete a user account record			RR		
Create a group account record			RR		
View a user account record				RR	
Edit a user account record			RR		
Merge user records			RR		
Distribute user profiles			RR		
Copy user records between user profiles			RR		
Move a user account record			RR		
Lock or unlock a user account record			RR		
Synchronize the profile database with system files			RR		
Validate records against profile policy			RR		
Sort and display record attributes				RR	
Delete or edit a group account record			RR		
Distribute group profiles to subscribers			RR		
Signal a process on a host			RR		

Tasks	super	senior	admin	user	none
Create, copy, edit, and delete a mail alias		RR			
View recipient for mail aliases information				RR	
Create, copy, edit, or delete a recipient for mail aliases		RR			
Update configuration files on the local host		RR			
Update configuration files on the remote host			RR		

Appendix B. Desktop design files

This appendix contains the desktop dialog's files used in Chapter 5, "Administrators' considerations" on page 67, and 5.3.2, "Administrators' visibility" on page 92.

B.1 Original desktop dialog file

The following represents an original, non-compiled copy of the Administrator desktop dialog. This file is named Adm.desktop.source.dsl and has been created be using the following command:

```
wgetdialog -r Administrator desktop | rdsl > /tmp/Adm.desktop.source.dsl
```

This file has been edited to remove the required menu items and customize the Tivoli administrator desktop.

```
Command Dialog
{
    Variables
    {
        String current_admin_name;
        CMsg desktop_name;
        String IR_object;
        String Install_object;
        String Backup_object;
        String Regions_object;
        SingleObject EvtSrvrOid = resolve_server@();
    }

    Attributes
    {
        BitmapTitle = desktop_icon;
        Iconic = NO;
        Name = desktop;
        Purpose = ICONIFY;
        DialogStyle = MODELESS;
        Title = $desktop_name;
        HelpMenu = help;
    }

    Gadgets
    {
        Menu
        {
            Attributes
            {
                TearOff = YES;
                Mnemonic = Msg(AdminCatalog,D,38);
                Name = system_menu;
                Title = Msg(AdminCatalog,Desktop,37);
            }

            Contents
            {
                Button
```

```
                {
                    Commands =
                        open%"1619823708.1.439#navigator#"();
                    HelpMessage = Msg(navigator_I18N_navigator,"Open the Desktop
Navigator",11);
                    Name = shortcut_menu;
                    Title = Msg(navigator_I18N_navigator,Navigator...,10);
                }

                Button
                {
                    Commands =
                        gui_backup%$Backup_object();
                    HelpMessage = Msg(AdminCatalog,"Create a backup of the Tivoli
installation",41);
                    Mnemonic = Msg(AdminCatalog,B,40);
                    Name = backup_tivoli;
                    Title = Msg(AdminCatalog,Backup...,39);
                }

                Menu
                {
                    Attributes
                    {
                        TearOff = YES;
                        Mnemonic = Msg(AdminCatalog,T,43);
                        Name = connect_tmrs;
                        Title = Msg(AdminCatalog,"TMR Connections",42);
                    }

                    Contents
                    {
                        Button
                        {
                            Commands =
                                ui_get_connections%$IR_object();
                            HelpMessage = Msg(AdminCatalog,"Get a list of remote TMR
connections",47);
                            Mnemonic = Msg(AdminCatalog,L,46);
                            Name = get_connections;
                            Title = Msg(AdminCatalog,"List Connections...",45);
                        }

                        Button
                        {
                            Commands =
                                ui_update_resources%$IR_object();
                          HelpMessage = Msg(AdminCatalog,"Update Resources from a Remote
TMR ",206);
                            Mnemonic = Msg(AdminCatalog,U,205);
                            Name = update_resources;
                            Title = Msg(AdminCatalog,"Update Resources...",204);
                        }

                        Button
                        {
                            Commands =
                                ui_remote_connect%$IR_object();
                           HelpMessage = Msg(AdminCatalog,"Connect to a remote TMR",50);
                            Mnemonic = Msg(AdminCatalog,C,49);
                            Name = normal_connect;
                            Title = Msg(AdminCatalog,Connect...,48);
                        }
```

```
                    Button
                    {
                        Commands =
                            ui_secure_connect%$IR_object();
                        HelpMessage = Msg(AdminCatalog,"Connect to a remote TMR using
the secure connection procedure",53);
                        Mnemonic = Msg(AdminCatalog,S,52);
                        Name = secure_connect;
                        Title = Msg(AdminCatalog,"Secure Connect...",51);
                    }

                    Button
                    {
                        Commands =
                            ui_disconnect%$IR_object();
                        HelpMessage = Msg(AdminCatalog,"Disconnect a remote TMR",56);
                        Mnemonic = Msg(AdminCatalog,D,55);
                        Name = disconnect;
                        Title = Msg(AdminCatalog,Disconnect...,54);
                    }

                    Button
                    {
                        Commands =
                            ui_policy_regions%$Regions_object();
                        HelpMessage = Msg(AdminCatalog,"Show Top Level Policy
Regions",203);
                        Mnemonic = Msg(AdminCatalog,T,202);
                        Name = policy_regions;
                        Title = Msg(AdminCatalog,"Top Level Policy Regions...",201);
                    }

                }
            }

            Menu
            {
                Attributes
                {
                    TearOff = YES;
                    Mnemonic = Msg(AdminCatalog,I,138);
                    Name = install;
                    Title = Msg(AdminCatalog,Install,137);
                }

                Contents
                {
                    Button
                    {
                        Commands =
                            product_install_current_license_dialog%$Install_object();
                        HelpMessage = Msg(AdminCatalog,"View current license and
licensed products",141);
                        Mnemonic = Msg(AdminCatalog,L,140);
                        Name = license;
                        Sensitive = NO;
                        Title = Msg(AdminCatalog,"View License...",139);
                    }

                    Button
                    {
                        Commands =
```

```
                        product_install_main_dialog%$Install_object();
                    HelpMessage = Msg(AdminCatalog,"Install a TME product",144);
                    Mnemonic = Msg(AdminCatalog,I,143);
                    Name = product;
                    Title = Msg(AdminCatalog,"Install Product...",142);
                }

                Button
                {
                    Commands =
                        patch_install_main_dialog%$Install_object();
                    HelpMessage = Msg(AdminCatalog,"Install a TME patch",258);
                    Mnemonic = Msg(AdminCatalog,P,257);
                    Name = patch;
                    Title = Msg(AdminCatalog,"Install Patch...",256);
                }

            }
        }

        Button
        {
            Commands =
                maintenance&.:();
            HelpMessage = Msg(AdminCatalog,"Enter TMR maintenance mode",195);
            Mnemonic = Msg(AdminCatalog,M,194);
            Name = maintenance_mode;
            Title = Msg(AdminCatalog,Maintenance...,193);
        }

        Button
        {
            Commands =
                create&.:(
about,
about);
            HelpMessage = Msg(AdminCatalog,"Display information about this
product",62);
            Mnemonic = Msg(AdminCatalog,A,61);
            Name = about_tivoli;
            Title = Msg(AdminCatalog,About...,60);
        }

        Button
        {
            Commands =
                quit_desktop&.:();
            HelpMessage = Msg(AdminCatalog,"Quit the Tivoli desktop",65);
            Mnemonic = Msg(AdminCatalog,Q,64);
            Name = quit;
            Title = Msg(AdminCatalog,Quit,63);
        }

    }
}

Menu
{
    Attributes
    {
        TearOff = YES;
        Mnemonic = Msg(AdminCatalog,E,67);
        Name = edit_menu;
```

```
                Title = Msg(AdminCatalog,Edit,66);
            }

            Contents
            {
                Button
                {
                    Commands =
                        select_all_icons&/.../icon_view();
                    HelpMessage = Msg(GenericCollectCat,"Select all icons",20);
                    Mnemonic = Msg(GenericCollectCat,S,31);
                    Name = select_all;
                    Title = Msg(GenericCollectCat,"Select All",6);
                }

                Button
                {
                    Commands =
                        deselect_all_icons&/.../icon_view();
                  HelpMessage = Msg(GenericCollectCat,"De-select all selected icons",21);
                    Mnemonic = Msg(GenericCollectCat,e,32);
                    Name = clear_all;
                    Title = Msg(GenericCollectCat,"Deselect All",7);
                }

                Button
                {
                    Commands =
                        remove_objects&/.../icon_view();
                    HelpMessage = Msg(GenericCollectCat,"Remove selected icons from
view",26);
                    Mnemonic = Msg(GenericCollectCat,R,33);
                    Name = remove;
                    Title = Msg(GenericCollectCat,Remove,25);
                }

                Button
                {
                    Commands =
                        delete_objects&/.../icon_view();
                    HelpMessage = Msg(GenericCollectCat,"Delete selected objects
(DANGEROUS!)",28);
                    Mnemonic = Msg(GenericCollectCat,D,34);
                    Name = delete;
                    Title = Msg(GenericCollectCat,Delete,27);
                }

            }
        }

        Menu
        {
            Attributes
            {
                TearOff = YES;
                Mnemonic = Msg(AdminCatalog,V,69);
                Name = view_menu;
                Title = Msg(AdminCatalog,View,68);
            }

            Contents
            {
                Button
```

```
                {
                    Commands =
                        view_by&/.../icon_view(TITLE);
                    HelpMessage = Msg(GenericCollectCat,"Display icons in abbreviated
form",18);
                    Mnemonic = Msg(GenericCollectCat,N,36);
                    Name = by_name;
                    Title = Msg(GenericCollectCat,"By Name",4);
                }

                Button
                {
                    Commands =
                        view_by&/.../icon_view(ICON);
                    HelpMessage = Msg(GenericCollectCat,"Display icons in full",17);
                    Mnemonic = Msg(GenericCollectCat,I,35);
                    Name = by_icon;
                    Title = Msg(GenericCollectCat,"By Icon",3);
                }

                Button
                {
                    Commands =
                        refresh_collection&/.../icon_view($owner);
                    HelpMessage = Msg(GenericCollectCat,"Rebuild and update icons",19);
                    Mnemonic = Msg(GenericCollectCat,R,37);
                    Name = refresh;
                    Title = Msg(GenericCollectCat,Refresh,5);
                }

            }
        }

        Menu
        {
            Attributes
            {
                TearOff = YES;
                Mnemonic = Msg(AdminCatalog,C,71);
                Name = create_menu;
                Title = Msg(AdminCatalog,Create,70);
            }

            Contents
            {
                Button
                {
                    Commands =
                        load&(
create_policy_region,
create_policy_region),
                        present&create_policy_region:();
                    HelpMessage = Msg(AdminCatalog,"Create a new Policy Region",74);
                    Mnemonic = Msg(AdminCatalog,R,73);
                    Name = policy_region;
                    Title = Msg(AdminCatalog,Region...,72);
                }

                Button
                {
                    Commands =
                        load&(
create_collection,
```

```
create_collection),
                        present&create_collection:();
                    HelpMessage = Msg(GenericCollectCat,"Create a new generic
collection",30);
                    Mnemonic = Msg(GenericCollectCat,o,38);
                    Name = collection;
                    Title = Msg(GenericCollectCat,Collection...,8);
                }

                Button
                {
                    Commands =
                        popup_create_console%$EvtSrvrOid();
                    HelpMessage = Msg(client_I18N_console,"Create an Event Console",2);
                    Name = event_console;
                    Title = Msg(client_I18N_console,"Event Console... ",1);
                }

            }
        }

        Menu
        {
            Attributes
            {
                Mnemonic = Msg(AdminCatalog,H,151);
                Name = help;
                Title = Msg(AdminCatalog,Help,150);
            }

            Contents
            {
                Button
                {
                    Commands =
                        display_help%$owner(
AdminCatalog,
"Message catalog not found. Consult your system administrator for assistance. If the
message catalog cannot be found in the NLSPATH, contact your Tivoli support provider.",
210);
                    HelpMessage = Msg(AdminCatalog,"Display help about the desktop",209);
                    Mnemonic = Msg(AdminCatalog,D,208);
                    Name = unnamed-GADGET-0;
                    Title = Msg(AdminCatalog,Desktop...,207);
                }

            }
        }

        Collection
        {
            Border = YES;
            CopyIn =
                {} [ copy_in&() ] Msg(AdminCatalog,"Copy managed object(s) into the
administrator's desktop",92);
            Name = icon_view;
        }

        Page
        {
            Border = YES;
            Name = status_view;
            Rows = 8;
```

```
            ReadOnly = YES;
            Title = Msg(AdminCatalog,"Operation Status:",93);
            TitlePos = TOP;
        }

        Group
        {
            Attributes
            {
                Alignment = STRETCH;
                Border = YES;
                Layout = HORIZONTAL;
                Name = logo;
                ChildColumnAlignment = STRETCH;
            }

            Gadgets
            {
                Message
                {
                    BitmapTitle = logo;
                    Name = logo0;
                    ChildColumnAlignment = LEFT;
                }

                Message
                {
                    Name = logo1;
                    Value =
                        " ";
                    ChildColumnAlignment = CENTER;
                }

                Message
                {
                    BitmapTitle = logo;
                    Name = logo2;
                    ChildColumnAlignment = RIGHT;
                }

            }
        }

    }
}
```

B.2 Modified desktop dialog file

The following represents the modified, non-compiled copy of the Administrator desktop dialog. This file has been modified in order to achieve the desired result in the Tivoli desktop of the helpdesk administrator. After editing the file, it must be compiled by using the following command:

```
dsl /tmp/Adm.desktop.source.dsl > /tmp/Adm.desktop.compiled.dsl
```

The next step is to assign the compiled dialog to the appropriate administrators by using the following command. In our example, the Tivoli administrator label is `helpdesk`.

```
wputdialog -l @Administrator:helpdesk desktop < \
/tmp/Adm.desktop.compiled.dsl
```

The following is the modified dialog file:

```
Command Dialog
{
    Variables
    {
        String current_admin_name;
        CMsg desktop_name;
        String IR_object;
        String Install_object;
        String Backup_object;
        String Regions_object;
        SingleObject EvtSrvrOid = resolve_server@();
    }

    Attributes
    {
        BitmapTitle = desktop_icon;
        Iconic = NO;
        Name = desktop;
        Purpose = ICONIFY;
        DialogStyle = MODELESS;
        Title = $desktop_name;
        HelpMenu = help;
    }

    Gadgets
    {
        Menu
        {
            Attributes
            {
                TearOff = YES;
                Mnemonic = Msg(AdminCatalog,D,38);
                Name = system_menu;
                Title = Msg(AdminCatalog,Desktop,37);
            }

            Contents
            {

                Button
                {
                    Commands =
                        quit_desktop&.:();
                    HelpMessage = Msg(AdminCatalog,"Quit the Tivoli desktop",65);
                    Mnemonic = Msg(AdminCatalog,Q,64);
                    Name = quit;
                    Title = Msg(AdminCatalog,Quit,63);
                }

            }
        }
```

```
        Collection
        {
            Border = YES;
            CopyIn =
                {} [ copy_in&() ] Msg(AdminCatalog,"Copy managed object(s) into the
administrator's desktop",92);
            Name = icon_view;
        }

        Page
        {
            Border = YES;
            Name = status_view;
            Rows = 8;
            ReadOnly = YES;
            Title = Msg(AdminCatalog,"Operation Status:",93);
            TitlePos = TOP;
        }

        Group
        {
            Attributes
            {
                Alignment = STRETCH;
                Border = YES;
                Layout = HORIZONTAL;
                Name = logo;
                ChildColumnAlignment = STRETCH;
            }

            Gadgets
            {
                Message
                {
                    BitmapTitle = logo;
                    Name = logo0;
                    ChildColumnAlignment = LEFT;
                }

                Message
                {
                    Name = logo1;
                    Value =
                        " ";
                    ChildColumnAlignment = CENTER;
                }

                Message
                {
                    BitmapTitle = logo;
                    Name = logo2;
                    ChildColumnAlignment = RIGHT;
                }

            }
        }

    }
}
```

Appendix C. Special notices

This publication is intended to help IT Architects, IT Specialists, IS managers, system administrators, pre-sales technical specialists with information on the logical design of a Tivoli solution. The information in this publication is not intended as the specification of any programming interfaces that are provided by Tivoli Management Framework, Tivoli Inventory, Tivoli Software Distribution, Tivoli Distributed Monitoring, Tivoli Enterprise Console, Tivoli Remote Control, Tivoli User Administration, Tivoli Security Management, or any other product mentioned in this redbook. See the PUBLICATIONS section of the IBM Programming Announcement for Tivoli Management Framework, Tivoli Inventory, Tivoli Software Distribution, Tivoli Distributed Monitoring, Tivoli Enterprise Console, Tivoli Remote Control, Tivoli User Administration, Tivoli Security Management for more information about what publications are considered to be product documentation.

References in this publication to IBM products, programs or services do not imply that IBM intends to make these available in all countries in which IBM operates. Any reference to an IBM product, program, or service is not intended to state or imply that only IBM's product, program, or service may be used. Any functionally equivalent program that does not infringe any of IBM's intellectual property rights may be used instead of the IBM product, program or service.

Information in this book was developed in conjunction with use of the equipment specified, and is limited in application to those specific hardware and software products and levels.

IBM may have patents or pending patent applications covering subject matter in this document. The furnishing of this document does not give you any license to these patents. You can send license inquiries, in writing, to the IBM Director of Licensing, IBM Corporation, North Castle Drive, Armonk, NY 10504-1785.

Licensees of this program who wish to have information about it for the purpose of enabling: (i) the exchange of information between independently created programs and other programs (including this one) and (ii) the mutual use of the information which has been exchanged, should contact IBM Corporation, Dept. 600A, Mail Drop 1329, Somers, NY 10589 USA.

Such information may be available, subject to appropriate terms and conditions, including in some cases, payment of a fee.

The information contained in this document has not been submitted to any formal IBM test and is distributed AS IS. The information about non-IBM ("vendor") products in this manual has been supplied by the vendor and IBM assumes no responsibility for its accuracy or completeness. The use of this information or the implementation of any of these techniques is a customer responsibility and depends on the customer's ability to evaluate and integrate them into the customer's operational environment. While each item may have been reviewed by IBM for accuracy in a specific situation, there is no guarantee that the same or similar results will be obtained elsewhere. Customers attempting to adapt these techniques to their own environments do so at their own risk.

Any pointers in this publication to external Web sites are provided for convenience only and do not in any manner serve as an endorsement of these Web sites.

Any performance data contained in this document was determined in a controlled environment, and therefore, the results that may be obtained in other operating environments may vary significantly. Users of this document should verify the applicable data for their specific environment.

This document contains examples of data and reports used in daily business operations. To illustrate them as completely as possible, the examples contain the names of individuals, companies, brands, and products. All of these names are fictitious and any similarity to the names and addresses used by an actual business enterprise is entirely coincidental.

Reference to PTF numbers that have not been released through the normal distribution process does not imply general availability. The purpose of including these reference numbers is to alert IBM customers to specific information relative to the implementation of the PTF when it becomes available to each customer according to the normal IBM PTF distribution process.

The following terms are trademarks of other companies:

Tivoli, Manage. Anything. Anywhere.,The Power To Manage., Anything. Anywhere.,TME, NetView, Cross-Site, Tivoli Ready, Tivoli Certified, Planet Tivoli, and Tivoli Enterprise are trademarks or registered trademarks of Tivoli Systems Inc., an IBM company, in the United States, other countries, or both. In Denmark, Tivoli is a trademark licensed from Kjøbenhavns Sommer - Tivoli A/S.

C-bus is a trademark of Corollary, Inc. in the United States and/or other countries.

Java and all Java-based trademarks and logos are trademarks or registered trademarks of Sun Microsystems, Inc. in the United States and/or other countries.

Microsoft, Windows, Windows NT, and the Windows logo are trademarks of Microsoft Corporation in the United States and/or other countries.

PC Direct is a trademark of Ziff Communications Company in the United States and/or other countries and is used by IBM Corporation under license.

ActionMedia, LANDesk, MMX, Pentium and ProShare are trademarks of Intel Corporation in the United States and/or other countries.

UNIX is a registered trademark in the United States and/or other countries licensed exclusively through The Open Company Limited.

SET, SET Secure Electronic Transaction, and the SET Logo are trademarks owned by SET Secure Electronic Transaction LLC.

Other company, product, and service names may be trademarks or service marks of others.

Appendix D. Related publications

The publications listed in this section are considered particularly suitable for a more detailed discussion of the topics covered in this redbook.

D.1 IBM Redbooks

For information on ordering these publications see "How to get IBM Redbooks" on page 277.

- *All about Tivoli Management Agents*, SG24-5134
- *Deploying a Tivoli Infrastructure in Large-Scale Environments*, SG24-5210
- *New Features in Tivoli Software Distribution 3.6*, SG24-2045
- *Creating Custom Monitors for Tivoli Distributed Monitoring*, SG24-5211
- *TEC Implementation Examples*, SG24-5216
- *Problem Management Using Tivoli Service Desk and the TEC*, SG24-5301
- *Implementing Remote Control in Large Enterprises*, SG24-5125
- *Problem Management Using Tivoli Service Desk and the TEC*, SG24-5301
- *Tivoli User Administration Design Guide*, SG24-5108
- *Getting Started With TME 10 User Administration*, SG24-2015
- *TME 10 Internal and Problem Determination*, SG24-2034
- *Tivoli Security Management Design Guide*, SG24-5101

D.2 IBM Redbooks collections

Redbooks are also available on the following CD-ROMs. Click the CD-ROMs button at `http://www.redbooks.ibm.com/` for information about all the CD-ROMs offered, updates and formats.

CD-ROM Title	Collection Kit Number
System/390 Redbooks Collection	SK2T-2177
Networking and Systems Management Redbooks Collection	SK2T-6022
Transaction Processing and Data Management Redbooks Collection	SK2T-8038
Lotus Redbooks Collection	SK2T-8039
Tivoli Redbooks Collection	SK2T-8044
AS/400 Redbooks Collection	SK2T-2849
Netfinity Hardware and Software Redbooks Collection	SK2T-8046

CD-ROM Title	Collection Kit Number
RS/6000 Redbooks Collection (BkMgr)	SK2T-8040
RS/6000 Redbooks Collection (PDF Format)	SK2T-8043
Application Development Redbooks Collection	SK2T-8037
IBM Enterprise Storage and Systems Management Solutions	SK3T-3694

D.3 Other resources

These publications are also relevant as further information sources:

- *TME 10 Framework 3.6 Planning & Installation Guide*, SC31-8432
- *Framework 3.6 User's Guide*, GC31-8433
- *TME 10 Framework 3.6 Reference Manual*, SC31-8434
- *TME 10 Framework Release Notes Version 3.6*, GI10-3028
- *TME 10 Inventory 3.6 Release Notes*, GI10-3011
- *TME 10 Software Distribution 3.6 AutoPack Guide*, GC32-0294
- *TME 10 Software Distribution 3.6 User's Guide*, GC31-8330
- *TME 10 Software Distribution 3.6 Reference Manual*, SC31-8331
- *Tivoli Software Distribution 3.6 Release Notes*, GI10-3014
- *Distributed Monitoring User's Guide 3.6*, GC31-8382
- *Distributed Monitoring 3.6 Collection Reference*, SC31-5118
- *Distributed Monitoring 3.6 Release Notes*, GI10-3023
- *TME 10 Enterprise Console User's Guide Version 3.6*, GC31-8506
- *TME 10 Enterprise Console Adapters Guide Version 3.6*, SC31-8507
- *TME 10 Enterprise Console Rule Builder's Guide Version 3.6*, SC31-8508
- *Tivoli Remote Control User's Guide 3.6.5*, GC31-8437
- *TME 10 Remote Control Release Notes Version 3.6*, GI10-3021
- *Tivoli Remote Control 3.6.1 Release Notes*, GI10-8022
- *TME 10 User Administration 3.6 User's Guide*, GC32-0291
- *TME 10 User Administration 3.6 One Password User's Guide*, GC32-0292
- *TME 10 User Administration 3.6 LDAP User's Guide*, GC32-0293
- *Security Management User's Guide 3.6*, GC31-8475
- *Security Management Releases Notes 3.6*, GI10-3049

- *Security Management Reference Manual 3.6*, SC31-5106

The following are product documentation and can only be acquired through purchase of the product:

- *Tivoli Framework 3.6.1 Release Notes*, GI10-8014
- *Tivoli User Administration 3.6.1 Release Notes*, GI10-8017
- *Tivoli Inventory 3.6.1 Release Notes*, GI10-8018
- *Tivoli Software Distribution 3.6.1 Release Notes*, GI10-8019
- *TME 10 Enterprise Console 3.6.1 Release Notes*, GI10-8020
- *Tivoli Distributed Monitoring 3.6.1 Release Notes*, GI10-8021

D.4 Referenced Web sites

These Web sites are also relevant as further information sources:

- `http://www.orb-data.co.uk/` Orb Data is a company specialized in the service delivery of Enterprise Management solutions based on the Tivoli product.

How to get IBM Redbooks

This section explains how both customers and IBM employees can find out about IBM Redbooks, redpieces, and CD-ROMs. A form for ordering books and CD-ROMs by fax or e-mail is also provided.

- **Redbooks Web Site** `http://www.redbooks.ibm.com/`

  Search for, view, download, or order hardcopy/CD-ROM Redbooks from the Redbooks Web site. Also read redpieces and download additional materials (code samples or diskette/CD-ROM images) from this Redbooks site.

  Redpieces are Redbooks in progress; not all Redbooks become redpieces and sometimes just a few chapters will be published this way. The intent is to get the information out much quicker than the formal publishing process allows.

- **E-mail Orders**

  Send orders by e-mail including information from the IBM Redbooks fax order form to:

	e-mail address
In United States	usib6fpl@ibmmail.com
Outside North America	Contact information is in the "How to Order" section at this site: `http://www.elink.ibmlink.ibm.com/pbl/pbl`

- **Telephone Orders**

United States (toll free)	1-800-879-2755
Canada (toll free)	1-800-IBM-4YOU
Outside North America	Country coordinator phone number is in the "How to Order" section at this site: `http://www.elink.ibmlink.ibm.com/pbl/pbl`

- **Fax Orders**

United States (toll free)	1-800-445-9269
Canada	1-403-267-4455
Outside North America	Fax phone number is in the "How to Order" section at this site: `http://www.elink.ibmlink.ibm.com/pbl/pbl`

This information was current at the time of publication, but is continually subject to change. The latest information may be found at the Redbooks Web site.

IBM Intranet for Employees

IBM employees may register for information on workshops, residencies, and Redbooks by accessing the IBM Intranet Web site at `http://w3.itso.ibm.com/` and clicking the ITSO Mailing List button. Look in the Materials repository for workshops, presentations, papers, and Web pages developed and written by the ITSO technical professionals; click the Additional Materials button. Employees may access `MyNews` at `http://w3.ibm.com/` for redbook, residency, and workshop announcements.

IBM Redbooks fax order form

Please send me the following:

Title	**Order Number**	**Quantity**

First name | Last name

Company

Address

City | Postal code | Country

Telephone number | Telefax number | VAT number

☐ Invoice to customer number ________________

☐ Credit card number ________________

Credit card expiration date | Card issued to | Signature

We accept American Express, Diners, Eurocard, Master Card, and Visa. Payment by credit card not available in all countries. Signature mandatory for credit card payment.

Glossary

ACL. Access Control List.

AEF. Application Extension Facility.

API. Application Programming Interface.

AS/400. Application S/400.

CLI. Command Line Interface.

DBA. Database Administrator.

DLL. Dynamically Linked Library.

DM. Tivoli Distributed Monitoring.

DNS. Domain Name Server.

ESM. Enterprise Systems Management.

FQHN. Fully Qualified Host Name.

GEM. Global Enterprise Manager.

GUI. Graphical User Interface.

IBM. International Business Machines.

INV. Tivoli Inventory.

IOM. Inter-Object Messaging.

ITSO. International Technical Support Organization.

LCF. Lightweight Client Framework.

LDAP. Lightweight Directory Access Protocol.

MDist. Multiplexed Distribution.

MIF. Management Information File.

NIS. Network Information Services.

NLS. National Language Support.

NT. Windows NT Operating Systems.

NTFS. NT File System.

OID. Object ID.

OMG. Object Management Group.

PDC. Primary Domain Controller.

RACF. Resource Access Control Facility.

RDBMS. Relational DataBase Management System/Server.

RIM. RDBMS Interface Module.

RPC. Remote Procedure Call.

SAM. Security Account Manager.

SD. Tivoli Software Distribution.

SIS. Software Installation Service.

SM. Tivoli Security Management.

TACF. Tivoli Access Control Facility.

TCP/IP. Transmission Control Protocol/Internet Protocol.

TEC. Tivoli Enterprise Console.

TIM. Tivoli Implementation Methodology.

TLL. Task Library Language.

TMA. Tivoli Management Agent.

TMF. Tivoli Management Framework.

TME. Tivoli Management Environment.

TMR. Tivoli Management Region.

TNR. Tivoli Name Registry.

TRAA. Tivoli Remote Access Account.

TRIP. Used to refer to the Tivoli Remote Execution Service.

UA. Tivoli User Administration.

UID. User Identifier.

VPO. Validation Policy Object.

VPN. Virtual Private Network.

WAN. Wide Area Network.

WINS. Windows Internet Naming Service.

Index

A

access control list 101
accountability 67, 86, 89, 147
ACL 101
Actions Restrictions 122
adapt the policy 147
Adapter Configuration Profile 20
administration mode 146
administrative notices 72
administrative roles 38
administrative tasks 75
Administrator 19
  Administrator list 73
  Administrator Name/Icon Label 73
  Group Name 74
  Physical design 73
  Set Administrator roles 74
  Set Logins 71, 76
  Set Notice Groups 72, 76
  Set Resource Roles 70, 75
  TMR Roles 70
  User Login Name 73
administrator design 90
Administrator desktop dialog 96, 259
administrator groups 144
administrator on demand 30
administrator structure 67
Administrator visibility 92
administrators collection 89
administrators desktops 27
Administrators group list 74
Administrators list 73
Administrators privilege 76
administrators responsibilities 149
administrators schema 160
administrators strategy 67
AEF 96
Anonymity 38
Application Management 150
Application profiles 43
application specific subregions 33
application usage 150
applications policy region 33, 36, 109, 174
applications profile manager 60
  Tivoli Distributed Monitoring 63
  Tivoli Inventory 62
  Tivoli Security Management 65
  Tivoli Software Distribution 62
  Tivoli User Administration 65
asset control 56
Attribute Default policies 29
Attribute Value Validation policy 29
auditing logins 84
auditing of users 89
auditing team 56
Australia 186
authorities 67
Authorization Roles 113
automation 20
AutoPack profile 20

B

best practices 5, 7, 21, 31, 51, 131
best practices definition 18
best practices initiative 18
blitz inventory scan 152
block distribution 57
Brazil 185
business application servers 80
business applications 36, 74
BWET Corporation 165

C

capability of authority delegation 68
case study 169
categorize 57
central point of operations 109
centralized administration 140
centralized management 106
centralized management paradigm 106
checking a policy 29
checking policies 130
Checking Security 100
checking the result 161
choosing an architecture 5
CLI 48, 91
close-fitting security 154
Collections 33, 75
command line interface 48
common denominator 81
common policies 27
complexity of administrator design 73

compromising security 31
conduct interviews 78
configuration management 41
considerations for administrators 67
Consistency 22
consolidate requirements 143
consolidating information 148
control and security 41
control subscription 48
controlling administration 137
corner stone 131
CPU 10
creating a logical design 143
creating an administrator 68
creating architectural alternatives 4
creating policy methods 126
Creation of a region hierarchy 29
critical considerations 77
cross subscription 110
cross TMR subscriptions 111
current procedures 146

D

Database profile manager 43, 44
Dataless profile manager 43, 45
DB2 44
decision analysis 6
decision support 56
default policies 117
default policy for profile manager 119
default user 82
defining policies 128
delimiter 21
demand scans 57
demands 35
design flow 154
design for Tivoli administrators 67
design fundamentals 3
design on paper 6
design process 143, 158
designing administrators 67
designing process 154
designing steps 156
designing the policy regions 29
desktop dialog file 259
Desktop Navigator 37
Desktops icons 90
destructive operations 95
destructive tasks 91
developing a logical design 12
dialog-select method 246
disabling policies 128
distributed administration 140
Distributed Monitoring 48
distributed object database 43
distributing administration 137
distributing profiles 134
distribution mechanisms 48
distribution methods 137
distribution of services 39
distribution path 50, 63
distribution performance 45
distribution process 52
distribution purposes 35
distribution times 111
distribution to all subscribers 47
distribution to multiple levels 49
DNS 167
domains 14
drag and drop 139
drivers 3

E

editing policy methods 127
Editing the IDMAP 99
Effective assignment 83
elementary pre requisites 3
enabling policies 128
Endpoint gateways 108
endpoints 19, 33, 179
endpoints icons 27
enterprise system management 91
enumerating all targets 152
evaluating the solutions 4
Event Classes 19
Event Group 19
Event Server 115
Event Source 19
exchanged resources between TMRs 112
exchanging resources 91, 111
execution of Tivoli tasks 84

F

fictitious company 185
file packages 20, 136
file transfers 244

fine grained design 154
firewalls 9
flexibility 63
formal procedures 148
foundation for the solution 4
framework maintenance 112
full access 82
functional building block 9
functionality 6

G
gather requirements 143
Gathering requirements 5
GEM 9
GEM servers 9
generic collection 19, 89
global policies 120
go back and redevelop 4
granting access to administrators 136
granularity of the resources grouping 154
group name 102
group of characters 21
Group Profile 20
grouping resources 141
GUI 43

H
Headquarter 185
help desk 35
heterogeneous system resources 67
hierarchical breakdown 173
hierarchical structure 89
hierarchy 46
hierarchy of policy regions 108
high availability 81
high-level design 5
high-level view 3
home grown applications 151
Hub TMR 105
Hub-Spoke architecture 105, 159
Hub-Spoke model 105
hub-wide activities 106

I
ID mapping profiles 70
identical names 20
IDMAP 97
implementation plan 7
Indicator 19
Indicator Collection 19
informal procedures 148
in-house applications 170
initial design 143
initial listing of responsibilities 149
initial policy region design 155
input requirements 77
insufficient authorization 95
interconnected TMRs 73, 91, 105
intermediate level of the hierarchy 111
internally developed packages 174
Inter-region administration 91
Interview the workers 78
Interviews 146
Inventory 48
Inventory distribution 152
Inventory scan
  On demand 56
  Scheduled 56
inventory strategy 152
IOM settings 22
issues on the physical level 8
IT architect 5

J
Job 19
job responsibilities 71
job title 78
junior administrator 47

K
key challenges 3
kind of resources to be managed 30
knowledge acquired 204
knowledge of customers requirements 5

L
length of names 21
lessons learned 7
Light Client Framework 91
local copies 49
logical design 111
logical design elements 11
Logical grouping of resource 29
logical layer 108

logical structure 41
logical Tivoli structure 42
Lotus Notes 57

M

major design options 140
Managed nodes 19, 33, 44
managed resources 28
Managed Resources policy 28
management disciplines 169
  Availability Management 10
  Deployment Management 10
  Operations/Administration Management 10
  Security Management 10
management object 27
management purposes 33
Managing Entries 99
Managing Maps 99
match resources 52
maximizing administrators 141
menu items 95
merge mechanism in Tivoli User Administration 59
methodology 143
methods 92
Mexico 185
Microsoft-style domain names 21
Modified desktop dialog file 266
monitor 49
multiple TMR scenario 20
multiple users 85
multiple-TMR solution 185
multi-tier TMR structure 14

N

name registry 20
name structure 24
naming conflict 21
naming convention 15, 19, 37, 73, 122, 154, 172
naming convention scalability 22
naming tivoli objects 19
Netware managed sites 33, 44
Netware sites 34
Network Information Services 44
Network Limitations 106
Network Management 150
network topology 105
Network topology structure 8
network traffic 9
NIS 44
NIS domains 44
Nodes policy region 33, 34, 108
nodes policy region 173
non profile based application 150
notice board 88
notice group 72, 76, 87, 88
notices 72, 76, 86
NT domain 83
number of administrator groups 154
Number of Clients 106
number of Tivoli administrators 79

O

object designator 21, 22
object designators indicator 22
object identifier 20
object name 73
Objects 92
one-way connection 105
operator friendly 37
optimal Tivoli architecture 7
organization 170
Organization's security policy 74
organizational procedure 148
Original desktop dialog file 259
oserv deamon 86
out-of-the-box solution 3
owner of a process 86

P

parent policy 126
partition groups 44
patches 160
PC managed node 33, 44
peers 5
performance impact 111
performance problems 57
Perl script
  add TMR role and change navigator 95
  change built-in navigator role 94
physical architecture 108
physical design 9, 73, 145
physical locations 145
physical sites 146
platform-specific naming convention 22
policies 12, 28, 153
policies commands 125

policies performance impact 120
Policy 117
  Attribute Defaults 28
  Attribute Value Validation 28
  Checking 130
  Default 117
  Defining 129
  Disabling 130
  Enabling 130
  Managed Resources 28
  Method 117
  Objects 117
  Profile based 118
  User Access 28
  Validation 118
policy arguments 127
policy based applications 28
policy driven object 117
Policy Method name 127
policy methods 117
policy methods values 123
  Binary File 123
  Constant values 123
  Empty 123
  Script 123
Policy Object name 127
policy objects 117
policy region best practices 32
Policy Region definition 27
policy region design 75, 172
Policy region grouping
  Application 32
  Geography 32
  Job Function 31
  Location 32
  Operating System 31
  Platform Type 31
  Sub Networks 32
  TME Roles 32
policy region hierarchy 29, 30
policy region schema 31, 153, 156, 158
policy regions 12, 19, 131
policy regions starting point 33
Policy regions usage 28
policy specialization 29
PolicyRegion desktop dialog 97
potential architecture solutions 4
potential targets 139
predictability 22
privilege 76
processing loads 111
profile based application 150
profile based applications 42
profile class 42
profile default record 118
profile distribution 42, 48
Profile endpoint 44
profile manager 19, 43, 44, 131
  default policy 66
  validation policy 66
profile manager best practices 51
profile manager default policies 119
profile manager design 50, 178
profile manager design goals 50
profile manager hierarchy 46, 132
profile manager logical structure 52
Profile manager policies 66
profile manager policies 119
profile manager schema 41, 159
profile manager validation policy 119
profile object 42
profile policies 118
profile records 45
profile type 42
profile validation records 118
ProfileManager main dialog 97
profiles 41
  Adapter Configuration Profile 42
  Autopack 42
  FilePackage 42
  GroupProfile 42
  InventoryProfile 42
  SentryProfile 42
  UserProfile 42
progressive refinement 155
Proxy endpoints 44

Q

QOPER 99
qualified name 81
queries 56
Query Library 254
questionnaires 145
questions for requirements gathering phase 14

R

rapid deployment 20

real world value 18
registry's check method 112
requirements gathering phase 4
requirements report 145
resource roles 70, 79, 90, 134, 153
Resource Type name 127
resources 61
resources management 41
resources types 19
responsibility matrix 149
restricted visibility 31
restricting users access 34
restriction control 92
RIM 114
RIM Considerations 114
RIM daemon 114
RIM host 114
RIM object 114
RIM servers 9
risk analysis 6
Roles 47
  Tivoli Distributed Monitoring 251
  Tivoli Enterprise Console 248
  Tivoli Framework 240
  Tivoli Inventory 253
  Tivoli Remote Control 244
  Tivoli Security Management 255
  Tivoli Software Distribution 245
  Tivoli User Administration 256
roles distribution 136
roles subscription 136

S

scalability 107
scheduled scanning 57
screen loads 27
security breaches 87
security constraints 31
security control requirements 41
security enforcement 122
security of the applications 157
security policies 147
security policy 35, 74, 145, 147
security policy requirements 147
security problems 136
Security Profile 20
security requirements 134
security to Tivoli built-in navigator 93
select-dialog-method 247
senior administrator 47
Sentry Profile 19
Server Loading 106
Service Pack maintenance 38
shortcuts 90
skills and experience 5
slow links 146
Software Distribution 48
software distribution operations 151
software distribution packets 135
solution design fundamentals 3
solution designer 144
sources of information 144
Specialization of policies 29
Spoke TMR 105
stand alone TMR 108
static user ID 99
subject matter experts 5
subregions 19, 28, 29
Subscriber Restrictions 122
Subscribers 38, 44
Subscribers policy region 33, 37
subscribers policy region 109, 135, 177
subscribers profile manager 38, 53
  Distributed Monitoring 57
  Inventory 56
  Software Distribution 55
Subscription hierarchy 111
subscription queries 56
Sydney 186
System Architecture and Design document 5
systems management 4
systems management project 8
systems management solutions 5

T

target endpoint 110
Task 19
Task Library 19
Task library 141
TaskLibrary view_dialog 97
TCP/IP names 21
TEC console 85
TEC servers 9, 107
testing the design 161
Texas 185
time-tested methodologies 7

Tivoli administrative structure 147
Tivoli administrator object. 28
Tivoli Administrators 21
Tivoli AEF 96
Tivoli architecture 41
Tivoli best practices definition 18
Tivoli built-in navigator 91, 93
Tivoli commands
  dsl 96, 266
  idlcall 95
  objcall 94
  wauthadmin 82, 83
  wchkdb 111, 112
  wchkpol 125
  wcrtpol 125, 126
  wdelpol 125
  wdistfp 138
  wdistrib 138
  wexpnotif 72, 76
  wgetdialog 96, 259
  wgetpolm 125
  widmap 69, 70, 74, 85, 99
  wln 32
  wlookup 122
  wls 95
  wlspol 125
  wlspolm 125, 126
  wputdialog 96, 267
  wputpolm 125
  wsetpr 125, 129
  wsndnotif 77
Tivoli community 18
Tivoli concepts 3
Tivoli consultant 14
Tivoli desktop 55
Tivoli desktop limit 86
Tivoli Distributed Monitoring 57
Tivoli generic collections 89
Tivoli logical design 10, 131, 143
Tivoli logical design activities
  consolidate requirements 12, 13
  construct a Policy Region schema 12, 15
  construct a Profile Manager schema 12, 16
  decide on a naming convention 12, 15
  evaluate the design 12, 17
  gather requirements 12, 13
  set the Tivoli administrators 12, 16
Tivoli logical design components
  Administrators Schema 11
  Naming Convention 11
  Policies 11
  Policy Region Schema 11
  Profile Manager Schema 11
  Resources 11
Tivoli logical design concept 11
Tivoli logical design developement 12
Tivoli logical design elements 11
Tivoli Management Agents 28
Tivoli Management Environment 28, 105
Tivoli Management Framework 41
Tivoli Management Region 105
Tivoli Name Registry 20
Tivoli navigator 233
Tivoli notice group 87
Tivoli object database 73
Tivoli object designator 24
Tivoli physical design 9, 171
Tivoli Plus Modules 57
Tivoli products 10
Tivoli Remote Control 35
Tivoli resource type 20
Tivoli resources 92
Tivoli Software Distribution 36, 38
Tivoli solution 41
Tivoli specialists 147
Tivoli tasks 84
Tivoli User Administration 36
  merge mechanism 59
Tivoli-based solution 165
TMA 28
TMA endpoints 41, 179
TME 28, 105
TME hierarchy 108
TME performance 145
TME wide operations 108
TMR 9, 19, 105
TMR Administrator 87
TMR boundaries 109
TMR roles 70, 79, 92, 113
TMR server name 21
TMR specific region 30
TNR 20
two way connection 116

U

understandable design 12
understanding the drivers 4

understanding the requirements 4, 144
unhindered control 35
uniformity 21
Unique login 81
Uniqueness of naming 20
UNIX 57
usage of a Hub-Spoke 107
User Access policy 29
user account 69
user account name 102
User Profile 20
using default policies 122
using policies 120
using validation policies 122

V
validated design 6
validating the basic architecture 5
validating the design 143
validation policies 118
validation policies for profile manager 119
validation process 143
variation over the basic design 159
violating the security policy 147
violation of policies 118
visualize subregions 31

W
WAN 146
What is a Logical Design 11
What-if analysis 6
Windows NT 38, 57
working with policies 120, 123

X
xterm session 69

IBM Redbooks review

Your feedback is valued by the Redbook authors. In particular we are interested in situations where a Redbook "made the difference" in a task or problem you encountered. Using one of the following methods, **please review the Redbook, addressing value, subject matter, structure, depth and quality as appropriate.**

- Use the online **Contact us** review redbook form found at `http://www.redbooks.ibm.com/`
- Fax this form to: USA International Access Code + 1 914 432 8264
- Send your comments in an Internet note to `redbook@us.ibm.com`

Document Number **Redbook Title**	SG24-5518-00 Best Practices for Tivoli Logical Design
Review	
What other subjects would you like to see IBM Redbooks address?	
Please rate your overall satisfaction:	O Very Good O Good O Average O Poor
Please identify yourself as belonging to one of the following groups:	O Customer O Business Partner O Solution Developer O IBM, Lotus or Tivoli Employee O None of the above
Your email address: The data you provide here may be used to provide you with information from IBM or our business partners about our products, services or activities.	O Please do not use the information collected here for future marketing or promotional contacts or other communications beyond the scope of this transaction.
Questions about IBM's privacy policy?	The following link explains how we protect your personal information. `http://www.ibm.com/privacy/yourprivacy/`

